Longman Social Policy in Britain Series
CRIME AND CRIMINAL JUSTICE POLICY

LONGMAN SOCIAL POLICY IN BRITAIN SERIES

Series Editor:
Jo Campling

Published Titles:

Health Policy and the NHS: Towards 2000, 2E
Judith Allsop

Foundations of the Welfare State
Pat Thane

Elderly People in Modern Society 3E
Anthea Tinker

*Social Work, Social Care and Social Planning:
the Personal Social Services since Seebohm*
Adrian Webb and Gerald Wistow

Forthcoming Titles:

Responding to Poverty
Saul Becker

Disabled People
Brian Oliver

Reshaping Personal Social Services
Robert Adams

Foundations of the Welfare State 2E
Pat Thane

LONGMAN SOCIAL POLICY IN BRITAIN SERIES

Crime and Criminal Justice Policy

Tim Newburn

LONGMAN
London and New York

Longman Group Limited,
Longman House, Burnt Mill,
Harlow, Essex CM20 2JE, England
and Associated Companies throughout the world.

Published in the United States of America
by Longman Publishing, New York

First published 1995

ISBN 0 582 234336 PPR

British Library Cataloguing-in-Publication Data

A catalogue record for this book is
available from the British Library

Library of Congress Cataloging-in-Publication Data

Produced through Longman Malaysia, GPS

CONTENTS

ACKNOWLEDGEMENTS

A number of colleagues took time out of their own extremely busy schedules, often at very short notice, to read, comment upon and improve my initial drafts of sections of this book. I am particularly grateful to Trevor Jones, George Mair, Rod Morgan, and Betsy Stanko for their advice and support. Sue Johnson and Peter Hall in PSI's library spent a great deal of time helping me gather together many of the materials that form the basis for this book, and then treated me with great patience when I failed to return any of them by their due dates. To Jo Campling my thanks for encouraging me to do this in the first place, and for knowing when to avoid asking how it was going.

As ever my thanks to Mary, Gavin, Robin, Lewis Huw and Owen Tomos for making it all worthwhile.

The publishers would like to thank the following for permission to reproduce copyright material:

Basil Blackwell Ltd. for 'Probation, pragmatism and policy', W. McWilliams, *The Howard Journal*, 26 (1987); 'Visions of Social Control', Professor Stanley Cohen, pp. 40–3; and 'Hooligans or Rebels?', Mr. S. Humphries, pp. 209–11.
Croom Helm for 'Imprisonment in England and Wales', C. Harding, B. Hines et al.
HMSO for extracts from 'National Standards for the Supervision of Offenders in the Community'; 'Digest 2 Home Office Research and Statistics Department'; 'Victims Charter'; 'The 1992 British Crime Survey'; 'CMND 7673'; 'CM 1456'; 'CM 2434'; 'CMND 8427 The Scarman Report'. Crown copyright is reproduced with the permission of the Controller of HMSO.
Penguin Group for 'Discipline and Punish', M. Foucault, 1979.
Victimology Inc. for 'Victim Support Schemes: The United Kingdom Model, H. Reeves, *Victimology* : An International Journal, Volume 10, 1–4, c 1985. All rights reserved.

Though every effort has been made to trace the owners of copyright material, in a few cases this has proved impossible and we take this opportunity to apologise to any copyright holders whose rights may have been unwittingly infringed.

LIST OF FIGURES AND TABLES

INTRODUCTION

This book, as the title indicates, is about criminal justice policy. The criminal justice system is that conglomeration of institutions and agencies which respond to – and on occasion attempt to prevent – crime. It is wider than the penal system, which is that part of the criminal justice system concerned with punishment or other types of response to criminal offences. Thus, the focus of this book is not only on the courts, probation and prison services but also, for example, on the work of the police and the treatment of victims in the criminal justice system. In taking such a broad focus as criminal justice policy, there are inevitably areas that receive somewhat less attention than others.

The text is designed as an introduction to the recent history of criminal justice policy, though with quite a lot of attention paid to longer-term historical transformations. It opens with an overview of the emergence of the modern penal system. The introductory chapter, together with the first sections in chapters three and four – which cover the growth of the new police and the development of the probation service – chart the birth of the modern criminal justice system. With chapter one focusing on punishment in the eighteenth, nineteenth and early twentieth centuries, chapter two then looks at developments in post-war Britain, focusing specifically on the growing prison 'crisis' of the last 20 years. The chapter concludes by examining the Woolf Report on the major prison disturbances in the early 1990s, the response to Woolf, and the emerging issue of privatisation.

After looking at the nineteenth-century origins of the modern police, chapter three examines the recent history of British policing beginning with the Royal Commission on the Police in the early 1960s. Although recent years have seen renewed calls for another Royal Commission, these have been staunchly resisted by successive Home Secretaries. However, the early 1990s saw a number of inquiries into policing, including the appointment of a Royal Commission on Criminal Justice (which examined areas of police powers and procedures), the Sheehy Inquiry (which considered rank structure, remuneration and conditions of service in the police) and an internal Home Office inquiry established by the Home Secretary (which resulted in a White Paper followed by new legislation affecting police powers and the structure of police committees amongst other things). All of these inquiries reported during 1993 and the chapter concludes by examining their various recommendations, together with the prospects for change that they herald.

Chapter four focuses on the changing role and functions of the probation service. It begins by looking at the emergence of probation around the turn of the century, and its development into a fully professional service. Following on from this discussion, chapter five examines the enormous expansion of 'alternatives to custody' that has taken place since the Second World War. Though the fine has been with us for a century, and a statutory probation service for 85 years, the vast majority of non-custodial penalties have developed largely in response to the growth in the prison population in the past 30 years. This chapter examines the use of fines (including 'unit fines'), the probation order, community service and the suspended sentence of imprisonment, and ends by considering the 1991 Criminal Justice Act, and subsequent amending legislation.

Juvenile courts only came into being after the Children Act 1908, and chapter six examines the developments leading up to the Act and the operation of the 'juvenile justice system' since that period. The key points in this history include the Children and Young Persons Act 1933, which required magistrates to have regard to the welfare of the child when sentencing; the Criminal Justice Act 1948 which introduced detention and attendance centres; the rising post-war juvenile crime rate which led to two White Papers and the now famous Children and Young Persons Act 1969; the 1982 Criminal Justice Act introduced several new disposals (youth custody, care orders with charge and control conditions, and community service); intermediate treatment; 'short, sharp, shock' detention centres; the development of the policy of diversion in the 1980s; the introduction of the Youth Court, and the introduction of new custodial measures to deal with 'persistent juvenile offenders'.

The final chapter looks at the position of victims of crime. It has become somewhat of a cliché in writing about victims of crime to say that they were once the forgotten party in the criminal justice process. However, in relation to victims of crime, great changes have taken place in criminal justice policy over the past 25 years, though not necessarily as a result of the development of a coherent policy for the treatment of victims. The UK was at the forefront of change with the setting up of the Criminal Injuries Compensation Scheme in the mid-1960s, and that together with the increasing use of court-based compensation orders by the criminal courts, and the emergence and growth of a voluntary Victim Support movement mean that victims have become a central facet of the avowed policies of both the major political parties. Though they are still marginalised by the adversarial system of justice (despite experiments with reparation schemes in the 1980s), victims can no longer be ignored by policy makers.

The emergence of the modern penal system

Generally speaking, historical studies of punishment tend to focus on the emergence of the prison and on the changes that took place in the nineteenth century and that have taken place since (for an exception see Beattie, 1986). As a consequence relatively little attention has been paid to the medieval prison which, although primarily a means of containment of those awaiting trial rather than a source of punishment itself, can nevertheless be seen as the precursor to the modern prison (Sharpe, 1988). The death penalty was the focus of the penal system in medieval times, and though it appears that levels of capital punishment were high – say by Victorian standards – from about the mid-sixteenth century, they had actually been significantly lower in the two centuries before that (Bellamy, 1973). The rate of imprisonment declined significantly towards the end of the seventeenth century, as did the use of public shaming rituals such as the use of the ducking stool and the parading of prostitutes.

In the century or so after 1688 approximately 200 new capital offences were placed on the statute books, many of which were property crimes, and this body of legislation has since been referred to as the 'bloody code'. Indeed, given that the major burden of law enforcement fell upon the shoulders of the voluntary constable, 'the wide range of capital sanctions served. . .to enforce the law through terror' (Harding et al., 1985:57). Nevertheless, the numbers of public executions appear to have fallen fairly consistently throughout the eighteenth century (Beattie, 1986; Sharpe, 1990). There was a developing debate during the course of the 1700s about crime and punishment in general and about capital punishment in particular. The bloody code came under increasing attack and one historian suggests that 'what is really remarkable about the century's penal policy is the almost constant search for viable secondary punishments' (Sharpe, 1990:40). Transportation was one of the other major forms of judicial punishment in the latter half of the seventeenth century, but by the turn of the century a number of colonies were beginning to refuse to receive any further convicts. However, the Transportation Act 1718 once again increased the numbers, and between that date and the suspension of transportation to America in 1775, 30,000 convicts were transported from England.

Prior to 1775, then, prison was used sparingly as a punishment. When it was used, sentences were generally short and generally confined to those found guilty of offences such as manslaughter,

Table 1.1   Distribution of punishments, Old Bailey, 1760–94

Year	Death sentence %	Transported/ hulks %	Whip/brand/ fine %	Imprisoned %
1760–4	12.7	74.1	12.3	1.2
1765–9	15.8	70.2	13.4	0.8
1770–4	17.0	66.5	14.2	2.3
1775–9	20.7	33.4	17.6	28.6
1780–4	25.8	24.1	15.5	34.6
1785–9	18.5	50.1	13.2	13.3
1790–4	15.9	43.9	11.7	28.3

Source: Ignatieff (1978:81).

commercial fraud and rioting. By contrast, for other major felonies like murder, highway robbery and arson the most usual penalty was the death penalty. That said, although in theory the criminal law was intended to be rigidly applied, in practice a significant element of judicial discretion was present. Thus, for example, Ignatieff (1978) notes that Judges in the Home Circuit in the 1750s commuted a third of the death sentences they had imposed and sentenced the offenders concerned to transportation instead. The use of such judicial discretion together with the introduction of new legislation during the eighteenth century meant that the use of transportation grew quickly. By the 1760s, transportation to the American colonies accounted for at least 70% of all sentences at the Old Bailey (see Table 1.1).

Hanging at this time was, like whipping, a public ritual carried out by a local official, generally with a sense of ceremony or theatre designed to maximise what was believed to be the deterrent potential of the spectacle [doc 1]. However, during the course of the century, the celebratory elements of the spectacle grew and it lost some its earlier solemnity, leading some to question its deterrent effects.

Imprisonment was, as noted above, used sparingly as a punishment before 1775. It was used by local justices to punish summary offences such as vagrancy, bastardy, embezzlement, and various forms of theft. The fact that relatively few offenders were in prison at this time was, it is suggested, not a function of an absence of sentencing powers on behalf of the local justices, and more a reflection of the relative absence of police to enforce such summary powers (Ignatieff, 1978). The emergence of the 'new police' in the early nineteenth century is covered in chapter 3.

There were three basic types of prison in use at this time: debtor's prisons such as the Dickensian Marshalsea; the county or borough gaol, of which there were more than fifty in existence in the middle of the century; and houses of correction or bridewells where the poor were supposed to be put to work. The system was under strain, however, and in 1750 a crisis of numbers and an outbreak of typhus focused attention on the prisons and began the process of reform. John Howard, a wealthy Bedfordshire businessman, is the person most closely associated with reform, though commentators have also pointed to the role played by such figures as Henry Fielding and Thomas Gibson (Gatrell, 1980; Sharpe, 1990).

Howard was, among many things, a sheriff, one of whose functions was to visit the local prison. Appalled at many of the practices and conditions he witnessed at Bedford gaol, in 1774 he began visiting all the prisons in England and Wales. At each institution he recorded its size, the nature of its population, the quality of the food served, the weight of the chains used and many details of the day-to-day life of the incarcerated. Whilst he was by no means alone at this time in condemning the conditions in the prisons, the 'originality of Howard's indictment [lay] in its "scientific", not in its moral character' (Ignatieff, 1978:52). His report, *The State of the Prisons*, contained many proposals for reform and had a significant effect on the public. Crucially, there was an emerging belief among the reformers that punishment had lost much of its authority because of the degree of discretion that had been allowed those who imposed it. In prison, not only was there an incredible level of squalor, but corruption flourished.

Pressure on the system increased markedly with the outbreak of the American War of Independence and the suspension of transportation to the colonies in 1775. The suspension was only ever intended to be temporary, and the first practical alternative that was put into practice was the employment of two floating prisons or 'hulks' – the *Justitia* and the *Censor* – which were moored on the Thames. Within two years the hulks contained over 2,000 convicts. The consequence of the war was far more fundamental, however, than merely forcing the state to use adapted warships as temporary prisons in place of the colonies. In fact, 'almost overnight, imprisonment was transformed from an occasional punishment for felony into the sentence of first resort for all minor property crime' (Ignatieff, 1978:81, and see Table 1.1 above).

Although at first many of the prison sentences that were handed out for these minor offences were relatively severe, the conditions in many of the prisons meant that many did not survive the sentence. Within a few years the average length of sentence had been reduced significantly. For seven years or so the system held up, but with the widespread outbreak of fever in 1783, together with the end of the war and a major increase in crime, there was a vast increase in the number of offenders being committed for trial. It was estimated by Howard that the prison population increased by almost three-quarters in the decade from 1776. The increases were accompanied not only by a deterioration in general conditions, but also by sporadic rioting in a number of gaols.

Contemporaneously with the changing balance of punishment from transportation to imprisonment, there occurred a decline in confidence in public rituals surrounding the punishment of the body. Branding had been abolished in 1779, whipping was declining markedly, Howard was campaigning vigorously against corporal punishment in prison and the frequency and nature of public executions was changing. The Tyburn processional, for example, in which offenders were taken by cart from Newgate prison to be publicly hanged at the Tyburn gallows had become particularly rowdy, and was officially stopped in 1783. Executions thereafter took place by the walls of the prison itself. Moreover, the level of pardons was increasing and only a relatively small proportion of those sentenced to death were actually hanged (Radzinowicz, 1948). This whole movement Ignatieff (1978:90) argues:

. . . indicates a loss of confidence in the morality and efficacy of ritual punishments, a growing resistance to the idea that the state should share the infliction of the punishment with the community assembled at the foot of the gallows or around the whipping post. Withdrawing the gallows under the shadow of Newgate and increasing the use of imprisonment denied the offender the opportunity for public defiance and the crowd the chance to turn the ritual to its own purposes. Compared to ritual punishment, imprisonment offered the state unparalleled control over the offender, enabling it to regulate the amount of suffering involved in any sentence, free of the jeers of the populace.

The one other alternative was once again to use transportation as a means of responding to the rise in crime. The Americas were no longer a possibility and Africa proved unworkable. By the mid-1780s, Australia was the preferred option. There was, however, a significant amount of resistance at home to the full-scale resumption of transportation and although it once again took its place as a major method of dealing with the most serious crimes (though it was used less frequently than before), minor property offences were no longer dealt with in this way. By the end of the decade imprisonment was taking the place of transportation as the punishment of 'first resort'.

In 1779, the Penitentiary Act was passed, which would have provided for the building of two penitentiaries to house those who would otherwise have been sentenced to transportation. The intention was that such convicts should be made to undertake hard and servile labour during the day and to be kept in solitary confinement at night. A reasonable diet was specified and clothes were to be provided. In this way, 'the imperatives of deterrence were harmonised with those of humanity' (Ignatieff, 1978:94). Though the original plan for two penitentiaries was never acted upon the idea of a national or central penitentiary finally got underway in 1816. By that time the deterrent value of transportation and of public hanging were being seriously questioned (though they had been subject to criticism for at least a century by this point), and some reformers wished to explore the idea of long-term imprisonment. Sited by the Thames at Millbank, the penitentiary, with its harsh regime, presaged a new austere period in British penal history.

In addition to the penitentiary, the other highly influential attempt to create a new model on which imprisonment could be organised was Bentham's 'Panopticon': a circular building in which cells were organised around, and visible from, a central observation or inspection tower. It was to be organised in such a way as to prevent communication between the incarcerated, but to facilitate their constant supervision. Bentham went to great lengths to persuade the authorities of the efficacy of his plans for a penitentiary, but by 1810 it had been rejected, in part, because of the very significant emphasis Bentham placed on the importance of labour as the basis of punishment, and his plans to run such institutions on a similar basis to the way in which factories themselves were run (Melossi and Pavarini, 1981).

In the late eighteenth and early nineteenth century the penitentiary system came under attack from a number of sources. First, the fact that they had been used to house political prisoners such as John Wilkes resulted in the growth of a popular campaign against the regimes in the penitentiaries, and especially against solitary confinement. Second, in the wake of the largely evangelical prison reform movement in the late 1800s there came a new philanthropic movement associated with Quakers such as Elizabeth Fry. By 1820, the prison system was desperately overcrowded and with too few staff to attempt to enforce discipline (Ignatieff, 1978). Outside the penitentiaries the 'hulks' were still operating – almost fifty years after their introduction as a temporary measure – and were the scene of widespread disorder and great danger.

The third source of pressure was a campaign for reform led by the Prison Discipline Society. One of the consequences of this campaign was the Gaols Act 1823. Although the legislation had little effect on either the nature of regimes or on general conditions, by requiring magistrates to submit annual reports on their prisons to the Home Secretary it set in motion the process that eventually led to centralised control of the prison system.

Crime was rising quickly at this point, as were the numbers sent to prison (Emsley, 1987). It was relatively petty offenders, however, that were filling up the gaols and there was widespread concern about the perceived rise of indiscipline among the agricultural classes and the metropolitan poor that provided the majority of these new inmates. New measures in prison were felt to be necessary and as the regime at the main convict prison, Millbank, became increasingly austere so local prisons began to tighten the nature of the regimes. One of the most significant developments first occurred at Coldbath Fields House of Correction in London where complete silence amongst inmates was introduced in the 1830s. The banning of all communication, the use of the treadmill (which had started some time earlier) and the introduction of a much more austere diet for inmates were the hallmarks of the new system of discipline which was in place around the country from the 1830s onwards. It was not only the penal system that was affected by the widespread concern about crime and disorder. This was also the point at which the 'New Police' emerged in an attempt to provide a more effective method of enforcing the summary powers that were available (see chapter 3) [doc 2].

In the penal sphere, 'the opening of Pentonville in 1842 represents a point of culmination in the tightening up of social controls underway since 1820' (Ignatieff, 1978:193). Whitworth Russell and William Crawford, the prison inspectors, began lobbying in the mid-1830s for the construction of a new model prison. Crawford had been to America to look at two models there: one organised around solitary confinement based in the Western Penitentiary in Philadelphia, the other a silent regime used in Auburn and Sing Sing. It was a prison along the lines of the Philadelphia model that the two inspectors pressed for, though they wished to modify the regime in a number of ways. Its essence nevertheless remained solitary confinement. What the nature of the regime was to be was the focus of one of the major debates of penology at the time. There were two basic schools of thought: one which believed in permitting association between inmates (though not necessarily allowing them to speak) and one which believed that association of any kind would lead to the development of an inmate subculture and moral harm. It was believed that separation was 'not only morally beneficial, by preventing contamination and providing an opportunity for reflection and self examination, but greatly facilitated the task of security and control' (Home Office, 1979, para 2.6). It was such beliefs which underpinned the development of the new convict prison, Pentonville.

In 1850, central control was formalised with the establishment of the Convict Service. This included the convict prisons, Millbank and Pentonville, two public works prisons (Portland and Dartmoor) one prison for juveniles (Parkhurst), the hulks and cells for separate confinement that were rented in certain local prisons. Transportation was finally ceased in 1853 and this gave further impetus to the increasing use of imprisonment for serious crimes, and not merely the summary offences and petty felonies which had been its primary focus in the previous period. The consequence was an increasing emphasis on long sentences of imprisonment. Those who would otherwise have been transported spent a period in solitary confinement in either Pentonville or Millbank and were then transferred to one of a number of centrally run public works or 'invalid' prisons where they engaged in 'hard labour' – usually quarrying. At the end of this period, the convicts were released on parole – what was then known as 'a ticket of leave' – though public confidence in the system was extremely low, and those on ticket of leave were often harassed (Tobias, 1972). The eventual consequence was the introduction of photographing those paroled in such a manner, in order to make their identification easier should their ticket need to be revoked, and indeed specific officers in the Metropolitan police were given the task of supervising such ticket of leave men in the capital. Though the probation service has its roots largely elsewhere (see chapter 4) the use of police officers in this manner marked the beginning of community-based oversight of offenders.

By the mid-nineteenth century, then, incarceration had become the major sanction for dealing with adult offenders. In essence, it took two forms: 'imprisonment' where sentences of up to two years were served in a local prison; and 'penal servitude' where sentences were five years or more and were served in a convict prison such as Millbank or Pentonville [doc 3]. The Penal Servitude Act 1865 restricted the use of remission with the intention that the general level of severity should be increased once more. Although the new measures 'were intended to increase the deterrence value of penal servitude, their ironic effect was to curtail the use of penal servitude and to make imprisonment in local prisons the mainstay of the whole system' (Garland, 1985:7).

Despite the new measures there was concern at this time that penal servitude remained insufficiently severe. From the 1860s the convict system came under the control of Sir Edward Du Cane, who during his working life was to have a profound effect on the whole of the prison system. The Prisons Act 1877 transferred justices' penal powers to the Home Office, and created the Prison Commission which was to be responsible for the organisation and administration of the new service, though assisted by the inspectorate which had been set up by the Gaol Act 1835. In addition to his control of the convict system, from 1877, Du Cane also became Chairman of the Prison Commissioners. Radzinowicz and Hood (1990) describe his philosophy as being based on the belief that the aim of punishment was both to deter and to reform, but that deterrence should always come before reformation. Under Du Cane the regimes at Millbank and Pentonville became significantly more austere. In addition, the use of flogging which had happened infrequently under his predecessor, Joshua Jebb, increased in frequency and severity.

During the period of Du Cane's Chairmanship, 1869–95, the numbers sentenced to penal servitude more than halved, as did the number confined in both convict and local prisons. By the end of the period, anyway, it was no longer possible to sustain a system based on large-scale public works. In 1893 a major public debate about the prison system began in the press. The system, it was suggested, was failing in its objective of deterring criminals whilst simultaneously being too harsh, and the focus of the attack was Du Cane himself who was criticised for being autocratic and secretive. As a response to the campaign a Departmental Committee under the Chairmanship of Herbert Gladstone was set up in 1894. The Gladstone Report, which reported within a year, is widely considered to be a landmark in British penal history, and it contained a number of far-reaching proposals.

The Report was critical of the failure to pay sufficient attention to 'the moral as well as the legal responsibility of the prison authorities'.

Crucially, it placed the reform or rehabilitation of prisoners, with deterrence, as the 'primary and concurrent objects' of the system. For the first time deterrence did not take priority over reform. The Committee's desire to reinforce the rehabilitative role of regimes led to the recognition of individual inmates' needs. As a result the Committee stated:

We think that the system should be made more elastic, more capable of being adopted (sic) to the special cases of individual prisoners; that prison discipline should be more effectually designed to maintain, stimulate, or awaken the higher susceptibilities of prisoners, to develop their moral instincts, to train them in orderly and industrial habits, and whenever possible to turn them out of prison better men and women, both physically and morally, than when they came in. (Quoted in Radzinowicz and Hood, 1990:577–8)

In addition, they recommended the introduction of a new form of classification of prisoners, of a measure of associated labour and of a new system of penal reformatories for young offenders. Although the Report paid credit to the efficiency with which Du Cane had reorganised the prison system since the 1877 Prison Act, the legitimacy of his administration had been fatally wounded and he resigned three days after its publication. He was replaced by Sir Evelyn Ruggles-Brise.

The Gladstone Report is viewed by many as ushering in an age of penal optimism (Sharpe, 1990) and, in part, this was underpinned by a fall in the prison population (see Table 1.2). The report did not, however, prompt quick action and it was 1898 before new legislation was passed. Even then the Prison Act had an extremely stormy passage, and the government was forced to state that there was no intention of 'revolutionising the present code; the alterations. . . will be few' (quoted in Radzinowicz and Hood, 1990:581). As Garland (1985) points out, it was only the issues that were the source of immediate concern that were acted upon at this stage and more than a decade passed before the more fundamental restructuring took place. Nevertheless, the next two decades saw a major transformation in the penal system; one which has been described as resulting in the construction of a new system of 'penality' (Garland, 1985).

The emergence of a new penal system?

England and Wales entered the twentieth century with a system of judicial punishments which showed, in embryo at least, a number of differing trends. At the centre of the system, practically and symbolically, stood the prison. Hardly thought of as a dominant form of punishment for the serious offender in 1800, by 1900 the prison was firmly established in both the popular consciousness and the practice of the courts as the most potent means by which the generality of offenders might be punished. (Sharpe, 1990:88)

Table 1.2   Prison population size, England and Wales, 1877–1900

Year	Average daily population
1877	30,962
1878	30,026
1879	30,134
1880	28,324
1881	28,043
1882	28,068
1883	27,140
1884	25,866
1885	23,714
1886	22,539
1887	21,799
1888	21,250
1889	19,748
1890	18,365
1891	17,425
1892	17,010
1893	17,524
1894	17,127
1895	17,614
1896	17,076
1897	17,051
1898	17,687
1899	17,210
1900	17,435

Source: Rutherford (1986b).

One of the changes made after the passage of the 1898 Act was the introduction of a new system of classification. This separated younger convicts from older, and first offenders from recidivists. Crucially, it was not merely a system of administrative classification, but a method of distinguishing the needs of individual prisoners. Whilst from a present-day perspective this may not seem a revolutionary alteration, it signalled a significant shift from Victorian penal practice in which uniformity was seen as the key. This is illustrated in the views of Du Cane written in 1885:

A sentence of penal servitude is, in its main features, and so far as it concerns the punishment, applied on exactly the same system to every person subjected to it. The previous career and character of the prisoner makes no difference in the punishment to which he is subjected. (quoted in Garland, 1985:14)

In addition to a growing emphasis on individualisation under Ruggles-Brise, regimes began to change. Privileges for the well-behaved were introduced after the turn of the century; there were increases in the number and frequency of letters and visits, a broader selection of books became available, and occasional entertainments were allowed.

Privileges can be withdrawn, of course, as well as given, and as the old controls of separation and silence were gradually eroded, new micro-forms of control, which sought conformity through the use of privilege were extended. In addition, the imposition of corporal punishment declined markedly, though demands that the penalty be abolished altogether were not acted upon. Significantly, however, the 1899 Prison Rules stated that it was the duty of all prison officers 'to treat prisoners with kindness and humanity. . .the great object of reclaiming the criminal should always be kept in view by all officers, and they should strive to acquire a moral influence over the prisoners by performing their duties conscientiously, but without harshness.'

In the aftermath of the resignation of Du Cane, when the implications of the Gladstone Report were still being digested, two well known literary figures had, in very different ways, a major impact on the penal debates of the period. The first, Oscar Wilde, was imprisoned for gross indecency in 1895. His sentence of two years was spent in Pentonville, Wandsworth and Reading. The harsh conditions in prison quickly took a heavy toll on Wilde and, as a result of some campaigning on his behalf, a number of improvements were made to his conditions. Although on release Wilde made some largely unsuccessful attempts to become involved in prison reform, the impact that incarceration had had upon him kept the question of prison conditions in the minds of some of the key actors.

The second literary figure was the author John Galsworthy. A visit to Dartmoor Prison prompted him to begin campaigning to bring an end to solitary confinement. As we have already seen, the resistance to permitting association among convicts was strong and the new Commissioner of Prisons, Ruggles-Brise, was only willing to reduce the period of separate confinement rather than abandon it altogether. This in itself was quite a significant victory for Galsworthy. By 1910, however, Galsworthy had written a play about penal servitude, *Justice*, and both Ruggles-Brise and Churchill, the Home Secretary, attended the opening night. At least partly as a result, the period of separate confinement was further reduced to one month for the less serious offenders and to three months for 'recidivists'. As Radzinowicz and Hood (1990:593) argue, to have conceded to the demands that were being made to end separate confinement 'would be to admit to unjustified practices in the past'. It was 1922 before separate confinement was abolished altogether.

On what basis then does Garland argue that the period between the Gladstone Report and the Great War saw the emergence of a new system of penality? In fact it is on the basis of a broad series of changes, the vast majority of which occurred outside the prison system. First of all the range of sanctions available to the criminal courts increased enormously at this time. There was, for example, the formalisation of probation and the introduction of probation orders as a result of the Probation of Offenders Act 1907 (see chapter 4).

Borstal training was introduced by the Prevention of Crime Act 1908 (see chapter 6). This sentence, which was available for offenders aged between 16 and 21, was semi-determinate and was to be followed by a period of licensed supervision. The same Act introduced a sentence of 'preventive detention' with a maximum of ten years for 'habitual criminals', again followed by supervision. In addition, new measures were also introduced – in 1898 and 1913 – to provide detention in an inebriate reformatory or in an institution for the mentally defective. Finally, new restrictions were introduced. The Children Act 1908, for example, abolished penal servitude for children and young offenders, and imposed restrictions on the use of imprisonment of 14–16 year olds.

Second, in addition to the increased range of sanctions available, Garland (1985) points to the increased range of agencies working in the penal field. Thus, as has already been suggested, the first decade of the century saw the emergence of the basis for a formal, national probation service, though it was some years before this was fully realised. A few years later, an association was established to organise and regulate the supervision of convicts on release.

Thirdly, there was the establishment of a number of new institutions in this period. From 1908, for example, the juvenile court had jurisdiction over all cases involving people under the age of sixteen. Other new institutions which were introduced included the Borstals – with a regime based on reformation and training – and preventive detention institutions such as that at Camp Hill, which were 'secure, but less rigorous than those of regular prisons' (Garland, 1985:22). The common feature of these agencies was the fact that they were targeted at specific populations of offenders; this was the beginnings of a system based on 'specialisation' and 'classification'. Garland sums up the developments thus:

Although most. . .took place outside the prison system, involving extraneous agencies and institutions, these changes clearly had a large impact upon the prison and its functioning. Many of these new sanctions. . .were conceived as direct alternatives to imprisonment, while others functioned to remove certain classes of offender out of the domain of the prison and into specialist institutions. The consequence was that the prison was decentred – shifted from its position as the central and predominant sanction to become one institution among many in an extended grid of penal sanctions. Of course it continued to be a sanction of major importance, but it was now deployed in a different manner, for a narrower section of the criminal population, and often as a back-up sanction for other institutions, rather than the place of first resort. (Garland, 1985:23)

Within this new penal complex, reform occupied a primary place. Whereas in the Victorian penal system it had clearly been placed behind deterrence as an aim of penal practice, in the period in which Ruggles-Brise was in charge of the prison system, the emphasis shifted towards reformation. Probation supervision, after-care, borstal training, even the prison itself, all were reoriented towards a new emphasis upon the possibilities of 'saving' rather than 'hating' criminals. As Garland describes in great detail, it would be inaccurate to suggest that there was a radical rupture between previous practices and those in evidence by 1914. As with many major historical transformations there were many visible elements of continuity as well as change. Nevertheless, he argues, there was an overriding element of discontinuity; one resulting in increasing diversity of penal practice. 'There has been a move from a calibrated, hierarchical structure (of fines, prison terms, death), into which offenders were inserted according to the severity of their offence, to an extended grid of non-equivalent and diverse dispositions, into which the offender is inscribed according to the diagnosis of his or her condition and the treatment appropriate to it' (Garland, 1985:28).

The inter-war years

In addition to Ruggles-Brise, the other major figure of the period was Sir Alexander Paterson. Early in life he was involved in voluntary social work and, in particular, with the care of borstal boys and discharged prisoners. In 1922 he became a member of the prison commission and spent the next two decades working for the reform of the prison system. There was significant optimism in penal circles at this time, and it was by no means unrelated to the decline in the prison population that had taken place since 1908. Although the prison commissioners anticipated a rise after the war, it did not materialise, and the prison population remained at around 12,000 up until the Second World War (see Table 1.3).

A mood of scepticism about the efficacy of prison, which is often felt to originate with Churchill's tenure at the Home Office before the First World War (Rutherford, 1986b) was carried over into the inter-war period. Two books published in the 1920s gave expression to this mood and reinforced the sense of scepticism. Sidney and Beatrice Webb's *English Prisons Under Local Government* viewed prison as 'demoralising and dangerous', and Hobhouse and Brockway's *English Prisons Today* argued strongly for greater use of existing alternatives to prison. The end-point of this optimism was perhaps the Criminal Justice Bill which was introduced to Parliament in 1938. The Bill included new restrictions on the use of custody, and would have introduced residential hostels – to be known as 'Howard Houses' – had the war not interrupted its progress in the House.

The increased variety of penal institutions and the emphasis on reform combined in this period to bring about the establishment of the first open prison. An experimental open prison had been established as early as the 1890s in Switzerland, and a number of open institutions were in operation in the United States in the early 1930s. The first open prison in Britain was at New Hall Camp near Wakefield Prison

Table 1.3   *Prison population size, England and Wales, 1901–45*

Year	Average daily population
1901	18,962
1905	21,423
1910	20,291
1915	11,266
1920	11,000
1925	10,509
1930	11,346
1935	11,306
1940	9,377
1945	14,708

Source: Rutherford (1986b).

in 1933. The fact that such an experiment could even be mounted in the 1930s illustrates how much change had taken place since the Gladstone Report less than forty years previously.

Perhaps the other major change – and one that had its origins in the Gladstone Report – was the already mentioned borstal system that was closely associated with Ruggles-Brise and later Paterson. Once again it was a foreign example that was crucial in bringing about change – this time the reformatory at Elmira in New York State. The aim was to provide a strict regime based on discipline, hard work and physical exercise. Indeed, the borstal regimes in many respects sought to emulate and recreate an ethos similar to that found at the time in the public schools, and the house system was introduced in the 1920s. There was, however, some opposition to the introduction of the borstal system and it was actually fairly slow to get off the ground. It was only by the late 1920s/early 1930s that it was seen as a core method of dealing with young offenders.

All this change did not take place, however, without significant grievances being felt and expressed. As the May Report noted, looking back on twentieth-century penal policy, although many commentators have suggested that the Gladstone Report represents a new, liberal trend in English penal policy, one saw it as 'the source of many of the problems which have affected the prison system and its staff ever since.' This is a reference to J.E. Thomas who argued (1972) that the reformulation of the central aims of the prison service to put reformation on a par with deterrence, caused confusion of purpose for prison officers. Staff became uncertain whether their control and discipline function was really central to the objectives of the prison system. Furthermore, he argued that the increased association between inmates actually made the control function more difficult.

Perhaps not surprisingly many prison officers felt that the increased demands being made upon them were not being met with better pay and conditions. From the turn of the century onwards, prison officers began to develop a collective outlook. The establishment of the *Prison Officer's Magazine* in 1910 provided an outlet for discontent within the service. A union – the National Union of Police and Prison Officers (NUPPO) was formed in 1913 and a Prison Officers' Federation in 1915. The Federation and NUPPO amalgamated in 1918, after the latter had apparently established the right to strike. As a consequence a number of prison officers became involved in the police strike of 1919. All of those who participated lost their jobs, and though the *Magazine* was resurrected in the 1920s (it had been suspended in 1918), it was not until 1938 that the Prison Officers' Association was established.

The substantial increases in police pay which had been recommended by the Desborough Committee in 1919 after the police strike, led to further claims by prison officers. The claim was rejected by a Committee of Inquiry, under the Chairmanship of Earl Stanhope, on the grounds that the tasks and responsibilities of prison staff were less than those of the police and that the actual incidence of serious injury was markedly lower. Indeed, certainly as far as the latter was concerned, this did appear to be the case. Although there were a small number of relatively minor disturbances, the majority of the prison system appears to have been relatively calm for the majority of this period. As the prison population rose after the Second World War, and even outstripped the increased capacity provided by the largest ever prison-building programme, so the frequency and violence of prison disturbances increased. So severe did things become in the 1980s and 1990s that numerous authors have described the modern penal system as being in 'crisis' (see for example, Cavadino and Dignan, 1992). The changes in the prison system since 1945 are covered in chapter 2.

CHAPTER 2

Prisons and imprisonment in post-war Britain

There is a major 'geological fault' in the prison landscape . . . the 'fault' is
the unpredictable and volatile size of the prison population.
Sir Brian Cubbon, former permanent secretary, Home Office (quoted in
Morgan, 1992a:236)

As we saw in chapter 1, the prison population in England and Wales
dropped from a high of over 30,000 in 1877 – when the Prison Act
was passed – to a low point of a little over 9,000 at the end of the
First World War. Thereafter, the population rose slightly, but generally
hovered between 10,000 and 12,000 in the years up to the Second
World War (see Table 1.3). It is the period since then that is the focus
for this chapter.

The expectation after the war was that crime levels would at
worst remain stable and, given the anticipated improvements in living
standards and the development of the welfare state, might even drop
(Bottoms, 1987). This, we know of course, is quite the reverse of what
happened. Indeed, so significant have the changes been, that it is hard
to credit that it was only half a century ago that only half a million
indictable crimes were recorded each year, and the prison population
remained under 15,000.

The story since has been one of expansion. The trend has not been
unilinear and there are important lessons to be learnt from the falls as
well as the rises. Nevertheless, it is the growth in the prison population,
indeed what has been referred elsewhere to as the 'crisis in prison
numbers' (Cavadino and Dignan, 1992), that has set the tone for much
that has happened in criminal justice policy-making since 1945.

By 1953 the average daily prison population exceeded the 1908
level for the first time (see Table 2.1). Substantial increases in
recorded crime after the war led to a fairly conservative response
by the government, somewhat in contrast to the relatively radical
overhaul that was going on in other areas of social life. The reformist
tradition that held sway in the decades leading up to the Second World
War, and that was associated with Paterson, did not survive for long.
Paterson died in 1947, and the Criminal Justice Act passed in 1948,
which contained many reforms that had been close to the statute books
a decade earlier, was by no means a uniformly liberalising piece of
legislation.

Although the 1948 Act restricted the use of imprisonment in several
ways, the pre-war idea of 'Howard Houses' for juvenile offenders was

Table 2.1   Prison population size, England and Wales, 1945–70

Year	Average daily population
1945	14,708
1950	20,474
1955	21,134
1960	27,099
1965	30,421
1970	39,028

Source: Rutherford (1986b).

dropped, whereas pressure from the Magistrates' Association for a new short-term, military style, custodial sentence was successful. The 1948 Act thus included a new detention centre order which was intended to be a short but firm sentence that would 'deter' certain hard-core young offenders. That said, arcane ideas of hard labour and penal servitude were done away with by the Act and this led the May Report thirty years later (Home Office, 1979) to describe the legislation as being 'firmly in the liberalising tradition' (para. 2.22).

The period from the Second World War until the early 1970s represents the time in which the 'rehabilitative ideal' (Allen, 1981) was at its height. In 1949, the English Prison Rules introduced for the first time the formula of 'a good and useful life' as being the primary aim of the 'treatment and training' to be provided in prison. The Chairman of the Prison Commissioners at the time, Sir Lionel Fox, explained the official purpose in greater detail:

[We seek] to provide a background of conditions favourable to reform, and where necessary and possible to foster this delicate and very personal growth by personal influences . . . Then, leaving deterrence to speak for itself, [training] concentrates on the social rehabilitation of the prisoner, so as to remove as many obstacles as possible to the maintenance, after discharge from prison, of such will to do right as may have become established or incipient therein . . . The protection of society is not well served if [the prisoner] comes back to it unfitted rather than fitted to lead a normal life and earn an honest living, or as an embittered man with a score against society that he means to pay off' (Fox, 1952, quoted in Bottoms, 1990b:4)

In the early years after the War, however, the numbers being imprisoned were already putting the system under immense strain. Although placing more than one prisoner in a cell designed for one happened extremely rarely up until this point, its frequency started to increase in the late 1940s, at one stage reaching its height of 6,000 prisoners incarcerated three to a cell, though this was down to 3,000 by 1955 (Ryan, 1983).

It was, as has already been suggested, the significant and sustained rise in recorded crime that was the primary motor behind the rise in the average size of the prison population in this period. Crime rose relatively consistently throughout the late 1940s, levelled off slightly in the early 1950s and then doubled between 1955 and 1964 (Maguire, 1994). It was to be some time before continued increases on this scale laid seige to positivistic assumptions that individuals could and would be reformed by the identification and application of a variety of forms of treatment. Nevertheless, the increasing numbers incarcerated in gaols in England and Wales put considerable pressure on the system.

Such pressure was increased within the system by the escalation of long-standing industrial relations problems. Decreasing numbers of staff during the war years increased the burdens on officers, and this was exacerbated by the increasing expectations that were placed on staff as a result of the emerging emphasis on rehabilitation and the sheer weight of numbers entering prison. The feeling amongst staff was that the increased responsibilities were not being matched by increased pay levels, and disputes over pay went to arbitration in 1950, 1952, 1954, 1956, 1957 and 1959. Indeed, in late 1957 the Wynn-Parry Committee was set up to look into remuneration and conditions of service; a Committee which made few changes of lasting consequence to officers' conditions of service, but did eventually settle on a pay formula – linked to civil service salaries – which allowed agreements to be reached for very nearly the next twenty years.

In response to mounting public concern about levels of crime, especially among young people, a White Paper – *Penal Practice in a Changing Society* – was published in 1959. Though much of it concerned proposals about police operations and for 'tightening up' the criminal law, it also focused on penal policy. A great deal was said about the size of the prison population, and particularly about the degree of overcrowding in detention centres. Details of a prison building programme were outlined and, despite the increasing evidence that was available about the relative ineffectiveness of custodial sentences as a method of rehabilitating offenders, the White Paper affirmed the government's commitment to the use of prison. As we will see in chapter 4, this was the point at which the diagnosticians held sway within the probation service, and a similar medical model underpinned official faith in the prison system. The White Paper included, for example, the announcement that work was to begin on the first purpose-built psychiatric prison at Grendon Underwood. Thus, at the end of the 1950s, tough talking on crime and penality was combined with a faith in rehabilitation that was largely undiminished.

As Lord Windlesham (1993) describes in some detail in his analysis of penal policy in this period, although there was considerable public concern about rising crime, and much government attention devoted to responding to the difficulties associated with rising crime and increasing prison numbers, there was one other issue which commanded the bulk of public attention: capital punishment. There was an attempt to include a clause abolishing capital punishment in the 1947 Criminal Justice Bill. The Labour Home Secretary, Chuter Ede, was against including such an amendment but, largely through backbench pressure, he was forced to accept a debate over a motion that the death penalty be suspended for five years. The vote was won in the Commons, but lost in the Lords and eventually, under pressure of time, the clause was dropped from the Bill.

Significant elements of the government were unenthusiastic about abolition and this was reflected in the terms of reference of the Royal Commission set up in 1948 to 'consider and report whether liability under the criminal law in Great Britain to suffer capital punishment for murder should be limited or modified.' Reporting in 1953, it recommended that juries should have the power to assess the appropriateness of the death penalty as against life imprisonment in individual cases. If anything changed the parliamentary mood during the course of the 1950s it was a series of cases in which either the guilt of the offender or the appropriateness of the death penalty was called in to question. The cases of Derek Bentley, Timothy Evans, James Hanratty and Ruth Ellis reinforced the abolitionists' case, though the Conservative government remained resistant to the idea of changing the law during most of the 1950s. Further pressure enabled a Private Members Bill to be introduced, and once again passed in the Commons in 1956 but, predictably, the House of Lords once again voted against the Bill by a huge majority. Public opinion was, however, changing, and there was widespread support for the Homicide Act, passed in the following year, which limited the death sentence to certain types of murder, such as killing a police or prison officer, and killing with a firearm. Nevertheless, it was not until the election of a Labour government in 1964 that abolition appeared a realistic possibility.

The 1960s were the scene of one of the periodic, yet very significant crises that grip the prison system from time to time. On this occasion it was a 'security crisis' (Rutherford, 1986b) or 'crisis of containment' (Cavadino and Dignan, 1992) and the response to that crisis has had a profound impact upon the prison system ever since. Up until the early 1960s issues of security had not been considered to be especially important, though the increasing numbers of prisoners convicted of the most serious crimes and sentenced to very long terms of imprisonment was beginning to put the issue of security on the agenda.

As can be seen from Table 2.2 there was a significant increase in both the absolute number of escapes and attempts and in the proportion of the prison population involved in escapes or attempts. Moreover, there were a number of highly publicised escapes by notorious criminals in the mid-1960s. Public attention had been focused on crime by such cases as the Great Train Robbery in 1963 and the imprisonment of the spy, George Blake, in 1964. In August 1964, however, accomplices of one of the mail train robbers, Charles Wilson, broke into Birmingham prison and helped him escape. He had served only four months of his thirty-year sentence. In July 1965, another of the gang, Ronald Biggs, also serving thirty years, escaped from

Table 2.2   Escapes and attempted escapes from penal establishments (male)

Year	Daily ave. population	Escapes and attempts	Escapes and attempts per 1,000 of the prison population
1895	14,954	9	0.6
1928	10,305	73	7.3
1938	10,388	211	21.1
1946	14,566	864	57.6
1956	19,941	932	46.6
1964	28,718	2,090	72.0

Source: Thomas and Pooley (1980).

the exercise yard at Wandsworth prison. Perhaps most embarrassingly of all, and certainly the final straw as far as the government was concerned (Stern, 1989) was the escape one year later of George Blake from Wormwood Scrubs.

The Home Secretary's response was to form a Committee under the chairmanship of Lord Mountbatten to examine why the escapes had taken place and to make recommendations for improvements to prison security. This immediate reaction was in stark contrast to the response to security problems in the 1930s where, on that occasion, the Prime Minister deemed it practicable merely to attempt to ride out the worst of the disquiet (Home Office, 1979; Thomas and Pooley, 1980).

The Mountbatten Committee's diagnosis was that the central problem lay in the insufficiently secure accommodation for the small number of very high risk prisoners, together with overly secure regimes for the rest. The major recommendations made by the Mountbatten Committee were that a system for categorising inmates should be introduced. The categories ranged from those requiring the highest possible degree of security, whose escape would pose a major threat to the safety of the public or the security of the realm, down to those in the fourth category who could reasonably be entrusted to serve their sentence in open conditions. The Committee also proposed that those in the top security category should be housed together in a new purpose-built top security prison, and this was given the name 'Vectis' and was to be located on the Isle of Wight, rather than in the currently existing maximum security blocks. 'Vectis' was to house approximately 120 prisoners and, if necessary, a second top-security prison would also be built. In 1967 the Prison Department compiled a list of all category A prisoners, which ran to a total of 138 (Cohen and Taylor, 1972). The intention behind the 'concentration' policy (Cavadino and Dignan, 1992) was that it would not only ensure that category A prisoners were kept in secure surroundings, but that security could be relaxed in other regimes.

The May Inquiry set up over a decade later reflected on the impact of the Mountbatten Committee's report and noted that it was 'hard to evaluate just how much of a change in ethos the Mountbatten report did initiate, but there is certainly a widespread belief that it ushered in an era in which concern with security became, and has remained, central to large parts of the system.' Sim (1991:110–11) has argued that Mountbatten's recommendations 'led directly to a major intensification in the levels of security and control experienced by prisoners as well as to a significant increase in the number of prison officers employed to manage the system'. The Committee's recommendation that prisoners should be categorised on reception was quickly accepted and acted upon, but the Vectis proposal was rejected. Instead, the Home Secretary asked a sub-committee of the Advisory Council on the Penal System to consider what type of regime would be appropriate for category A prisoners (those 'who in no circumstances must be allowed to get out').

The sub-committee, chaired by Professor Leon Radzinowicz, reported in 1968. It completely rejected the idea of concentrating high risk prisoners. It did so on the basis that providing adequate work and recreational facilities in an establishment catering for such a small number of category A prisoners would be problematic, and that those inmates who were unsettled or unsettling others could not be transferred. They concluded therefore that 'the chances of creating a tolerable and constructive regime in an establishment known to all involved as the end of the road, would be minimal' (Home Office, 1979, para.2.33) What they proposed was a policy that has since become associated with the term 'dispersal'.

By this is meant that category A prisoners are dispersed amongst a number of training prisons designed for that purpose, with up-graded security. The thinking behind this was that in such institutions a relaxed regime could be created as long as the perimeter walls were secure, and that it would then be possible to treat high risk prisoners very much like everyone else in the prison. As one member of the Committee put it, the aim was to disperse the category A prisoners 'into liberal prisons rather than concentrating them into an oppressive fortress that would cast a shadow over [the] whole prison system' (Leo Abse, quoted in Rutherford, 1986b:79).

At first there were three 'dispersal' prisons, by 1970 there were five and by 1980 seven. The degree to which such prisoners are actually dispersed, then, is more than somewhat limited and the policy is widely felt not to have been a success. As the May Report (Home Office, 1979) put it: 'The history of the seven "dispersal" prisons that . . . cater for this class of inmate within the system has not generally been a happy one.' Controversy has since raged over whether it is the dispersal policy itself which has led to inmate unrest, or factors connected more generally with the growth in the proportion of difficult offenders within the system; similarly it is alleged that the dispersal system entails the devotion of excessive amounts of security to categories of inmate who do not require it. Put crudely, the argument advanced by critics of this policy is that although dispersal largely solved the problem of perimeter security, it exacerbated the problems of internal control.

In essence, the consequence of adopting the policy of dispersal was to subject a very large number of prisoners to a degree of security deemed to be necessary in fact for very few. In terms of resources, it was the commitment of huge resources 'providing top security for thousands of people, for the benefits of hundreds (Stern, 1989:125). Thus, Stern (1989) estimated that in 1988, 390 convicted prisoners deemed to be Category A were housed in prisons with room for 2,968.

Downes and Morgan (1994:219) conclude that 'the unwanted side effects of these directives were to heighten security across the system, prioritise control and surveillance at the expense of other objectives (such as work, training, education, recreation, and better rights and conditions) and in combination with the impact of adverse research findings halt the spread of therapeutic regimes while leaving intact the differentiation between local and training prisons based upon that ideology.' Similarly, Sim (1991), in addition to noting the move towards the use of control units and segregation blocks as part of the dispersal policy, also identifies two other major sets of changes resulting from the Mountbatten and Radzinowicz Reports. First, he argues that the emphasis on blanket security and technological control was such that they increasingly dominated managerial thinking. Second, he suggests that the enforcement of the Prison Rules intensified, and even petty regulations began to be enforced more vigorously.

The control of Category A prisoners never really ceased to be a problem. At one of the dispersal prisons, Parkhurst, there was a high level of discontent at the level and methods of prison security used, and in 1969 over 150 prisoners barricaded themselves in association rooms together with a number of hostages. A petition signed by 120 prisoners was made public and the Home Secretary immediately ordered an inquiry. The report of the inquiry was, however, never made public and only a small number of staffing changes were made (for some details see Home Office, 1984b). Within a few months the worst prison riot for nearly forty years erupted at Parkhurst, in which 28 prisoners and 35 prison officers were injured (Ryan, 1983).

The response of the prison authorities to the control problems that arose at least partly because of the new emphasis given to security was oppressive. Three major approaches were employed: an increasing emphasis on physical force including the deployment of tactical intervention squads; the segregation of prisoners under 'Rule 43'; and the reallocation of prisoners considered to be disruptive. The recent history of prison disturbances illustrates the fact that none of these tactics alone or in combination were particularly effective.

Although officially, Prison Rule 1 still encapsulated the primary function of the prison service at this time, a White Paper, *People in Prison*, published in 1969, placed 'treatment and training' behind the aim of holding 'those committed to custody and to provide conditions for their detention which are currently acceptable to society' (quoted in King and McDermott, 1989). The White Paper included the term 'humane containment' for the first time in an official document, and the use of the term signalled the beginnings of a major shift in emphasis in penal policy.

Although numbers had been rising fairly steadily since the Second World War, the proportionate use of imprisonment had been decreasing. As Bottoms (1987) shows, however, it was not probation that was the main alternative, but the fine that was being used increasingly frequently. This trend toward declining proportionate use of custody came to an end in the mid-1970s (see chapter 5) – in 1974 the proportion of adult males given a custodial sentence had dropped as low as 15%. As Brake and Hale (1992:144) argue, 'since 1974 not only have the absolute numbers being sent to prison increased but the courts have become more punitive'.

The Criminal Justice Act 1967

By this stage, the relentless rise in prison numbers had been forcing the hand of policy-makers for some years. One method of attempting to influence the size of the population is through executive measures such as remission and parole. In theory, they may provide one possible safety valve when the pressure of numbers seems too great (Cavadino and Dignan, 1992). The practice of early release began with the 'ticket of leave' system in the nineteenth century, followed by unconditional remission at the turn of the twentieth. Although remission has most often been justified in terms of its effects on individual prisoners, there are a number of instances where it has been used by politicians to attempt to control overall numbers.

Perhaps the most clearly visible illustration of the impact of prison numbers on policy making lies in the introduction of parole in 1967. Although its introduction was defended on rehabilitative grounds (Home Office, 1965a; Morgan, 1983), the increasing size of the prison population also gave a strong political and pragmatic impetus to the change (Bottomley, 1984; Fitzmaurice and Pease, 1986; Maguire, 1992).

Parole was introduced during the period when the rehabilitative ideal was still relatively untarnished. The White Paper, for example, argued that 'a considerable number of long-term prisoners reach a recognisable peak in their training at which they may respond to generous treatment but after which if kept in prison they may go downhill' (para.5). However, if alleviating prison overcrowding was the central aim there was a fundamental problem with the way parole worked in practice. It is simply that crowding in the prison system has always been concentrated in the local prisons and remand centres, rather than in the training prisons where those most likely to be eligible for parole are accommodated.

The system of parole was subject to widespread criticism, the most far-reaching, and effective in the longer-term, came from Roger Hood. Maguire (1992:182) summarises his critique saying that Hood questioned 'the key premises underpinning its introduction and operation. He pointed out that there was simply no evidence of a "peak in training", or that, even if such a thing existed, it could be identified by the Board: indeed, it was questionable if any meaningful training at all took place in many prisons. The system encouraged manipulation and dissimulation by prisoners and was profoundly unfair. Above all it was wrong in principle for what were *de facto* sentencing decisions to be taken by a secret and unaccountable executive body, which gave no reasons for its decisions and which was not subject to appeal.'

The other major change brought about by the 1967 Act was the introduction of the suspended sentence of imprisonment. This was, as Bottoms (1977) has noted, the first completely new sentence since the introduction of statutory probation in 1908. By the mid-1970s it was the second most commonly used sentence for adult males in the Crown Court. Such a sentence had been proposed as early as 1950 but was rejected by the Advisory Council on the Treatment of Offenders in both 1952 and 1957. Two theories have been used to justify the suspended sentence: the first Bottoms calls the 'special deterrent theory' (offenders would be deterred from further offending by the knowledge that if caught prison would result), and the second the 'avoiding prison theory' (allowing courts to signal the gravity of the offence without having to resort to a custodial sentence). It has, however, only ever been the latter which has formed the basis for official justifications and defences of the sentence. The effect of the introduction of the suspended sentence is considered in greater detail in chapter 5; for now it is enough to note that although it was conceived of as an alternative to custody, the aim being to reduce the prison population, it only succeeded in that aim in a very temporary and very minor way.

Grievances among the incarcerated

Although as a result of the changes brought about by the Criminal Justice Act there was a reduction in the prison population in 1968, by 1970 it was beginning to rise quickly. Overcrowding was becoming a problem again (see Table 2.3) and it was the growing remand population that were bearing the brunt of the worst conditions.

With the increasing pressure within the system some form of disturbance was not unexpected and in 1972 that is what happened at Brixton prison, which was the main remand prison for London. It was at this time that the prisoners' rights movement took off.

Table 2.3   *Prison overcrowding in England and Wales, 1969–79*

Year	Three in a cell	Two in a cell
1969	7,653	2,886
1970	9,288	4,886
1971	8,238	6,212
1972	6,609	7,128
1973	4,221	8,388
1974	4,122	10,024
1975	5,298	10,342
1976	5,709	10,726
1977	4,950	11,040
1978	5,082	11,016
1979	4,833	11,752

Source: Fitzgerald and Sim, 1982:16.

PROP (Preservation of the Rights of Prisoners) was formed, mainly by ex-prisoners, but supported by academics, and a 'Prisoners' Charter' was drawn up. This made very broad demands including, among many others, the right to institute legal proceedings without the permission of the Home Office; the right to legal representation at disciplinary hearings; and the right to receive reasons from the Parole Board when applications were rejected. Later in the year a national demonstration was organised and it is estimated that between 5,000–10,000 prisoners took part in sit-down strikes in prisons around the country (Ryan, 1983; Rutherford, 1986b).

One of the responses to this was the threat of action by prison staff, including the possibility of a work to rule. The possibility of negotiations between PROP and the POA was rejected by the Home Office who said that further demonstrations would be dealt with severely. The importance of this is perhaps twofold. First, the demonstrations brought about further clampdowns in the prison system. Control units, for example, were introduced and the treatment meted out to some of the men segregated in such units together with the use of an increasingly paramilitary response to disorder, led to a new and bitter phase in the history of disturbances in British prisons. The regime in control units was informed by the idea of sensory deprivation. The cells were windowless and sound-proofed, lights were kept on at all times, association between prisoners was not permitted and prison officers were trained to minimise their communication with inmates and provided with footwear that muffled the sound of their approach (Coggan and Walker, 1982; Sim, 1991).

Secondly, and equally importantly, the prisoners' movement had quite a profound politicising effect on the prison officers themselves. The militant stance adopted by staff did not disappear in the early 1970s and Rutherford (1986b:82) has argued that by the end of the decade 'it was not prisoners but unionised custodial staff that posed the greatest challenge to the Home Office control of the prison system.'

The disturbance at Brixton in 1972 was followed later that year by further disturbances at Gartree and at Albany, though the most serious riot in the period happened four years later at Hull. Hull, originally a local prison, was reclassified as a training prison in 1966 and as a dispersal prison in 1969. The riot, which lasted for four days, resulted in damage to the prison estimated at £725,000 (Thomas and Pooley, 1980), a large number of injuries to prisoners as order was restored, and prosecutions of prison officers for assault. Similar brutality, it was claimed, was used in quelling another disturbance at Gartree in 1978, and the following year saw the introduction (their existence had never been officially mentioned) of the paramilitary Minimum Use of Force Tactical Intervention squad (MUFTI) to bring a disturbance at Wormwood Scrubs to an end. Rutherford (1986b) notes that the role of the POA was especially interesting after the end of the disturbance. He quotes the official inquiry as saying that in the particular wing of the prison involved in the disturbance: 'the local branch of the POA . . . sought to prevent a return to anything like the former regime in D Wing, and there were strong indications that the Governor came under pressure so severe that some of the policy decisions . . . he made at that time were against his own better judgement' (1986b:84). Indeed, Rutherford concludes that the POA, at both a local and national level, challenged 'the authority and administration of the prison system.' By 1978 over 60 branches of the POA were involved in over one hundred separate disputes (Ryan, 1983).

In the 1970s, then, the primary concerns within the prison system were concerns about control. Initially these concerns were focused on prisoners, on the largely peaceful demonstrations associated with the prisoners' rights movement, and on the more violent disturbances that occurred at a small number of prisons. Later on, however, the concerns became just as much, if not more about the control of staff. Although no officers were prosecuted for assaults on inmates in Wormwood Scrubs – despite a two-year police investigation – it was clear that something fairly urgent had to be done. By 1978 the prison service was in almost continual dispute with the Prison Officers' Association over staffing levels, over pay and conditions, and about overtime. As is almost always the solution in such cases, the response of the Home Office was to set up a Departmental Committee.

The May Report

The Committee, under the chairmanship of a High Court judge, Mr Justice May, was instructed by Merlyn Rees to inquire into the state of the prison services in the UK; and to have regard to the size of the prison population, the capacity of the prison service to accommodate it; the responsibility of the prison service for control, security and treatment of inmates; and the pay and conditions for staff. However, the Committee decided to interpret its terms of reference broadly because although 'it seemed inevitable to us that we should concentrate on the organisational, resources, pay and industrial relations issues, it was equally plain we could not ignore wider criminal justice matters . . . because we could not . . . make credible and worthwhile recommendations about the resources required for the prison system without an adequately informed view on the size and nature of the future prison population, including the possibility of reducing it' (Home Office, 1979, para.1.5).

The Home Secretary had impressed upon the Committee the urgency of the inquiry and, initially it was hoped that it would report within six months, but it eventually took a year. If anything, the delay probably heightened expectations of the Report at a time when concern was high anyway.

Lord Windlesham (1987:241) describes the Report as 'the most comprehensive account available on the state of British prisons – their populations, organisation, and staffing. Set up by a government of one complexion and reporting to that of another, it is free from political bias and is an invaluable repository of factual information.' On the other hand, for Fitzgerald and Sim (1980:84), it 'was an opportunity not simply to review but to change fundamentally the 100 year-old recipe of more prisoners and more prisons. In the event, it passed up that opportunity, preferring, like so many Inquiries before it, to represent the recipe for prison crisis as a recipe for prison salvation. It simply won't work.'

As part of its broad interpretation of its terms of reference, the Committee took evidence and made recommendations on the fundamental penal objectives and, in particular, on the future for Rule 1 [doc 4]. Two criminologists, Roy King and Rod Morgan, in their evidence to the Committee argued, successfully as it turned out, that the rhetoric of 'treatment and training' had had its day. They went on to argue that it should be replaced by a system based on the notion of 'humane containment', and underpinned by the principles of minimum use of custody, minimum use of security, and the 'normalisation' of the prison. Though accepting that 'treatment and training' was outmoded, the Committee rejected humane containment as a 'means without an end' resulting in prisons becoming human warehouses for inmates and staff. Consequently, they recommended that Rule 1 be rewritten and in rejecting 'treatment and training' introduced the idea of 'positive custody':

The purpose of the detention of convicted prisoners shall be to keep them in custody which is both secure and yet positive, and to that end the behaviour of all the responsible authorities and staff towards them shall be such as to:

(a)   create an environment which can assist them to respond and contribute to society as positively as possible;

(b)   preserve and promote their self-respect;
(c)   minimise, to the degree of security necessary in each particular case, the harmful effects of their removal from normal life;
(d)   prepare them for and assist them on discharge.

Some critics, however, were sceptical about the degree to which this represented anything much more than warehousing itself. Fitzgerald and Sim (1980:82) suggested that the proposed new Rule 1 simply represented a move from 'warehousing' to 'zookeeping' 'where some limited consideration is given to the state of the stored'.

Following its recognition that imprisonment should be used as little as possible, the May Committee backed policies to reduce the prison population but felt that there was little chance of their being successful. As a consequence it therefore recommended a massive building and refurbishment programme to end enforced cell-sharing and end slopping out, and this was acted upon without delay (King and McDermott, 1989). In 1982 the biggest prison building programme undertaken this century began, in which 25 new prisons were to be built at an estimated capital cost of over £1,300 million (Cavadino and Dignan, 1992).

The idea of 'positive custody' never garnered much support and during the 1980s considerable emphasis continued to be placed by campaigners on prisoners' rights and on timetables for the introduction of minimum standards and conditions (Morgan, 1994b). The committee's proposals to end cell-sharing and slopping out, for example, were linked to the European Standard Minimum Rules and, as King and McDermott (1989) argue, it looked for a while as though the government might respond to outside pressure by publishing a draft code of standards for the prison system. In 1982 the Home Office even undertook to do so but no such code ever appeared. The question of standards remains (see for example Casale, 1984, 1994; King and McDermott, 1989) but, as in other areas of criminal justice such as policing (see chapter 3) and probation (see chapter 4) government has actually placed much greater emphasis on financial management and on economy, efficiency and effectiveness; prisons had 'entered the Thatcher era' (Morris, 1989).

The prison crisis escalates

Whitelaw, the Home Secretary when the May Committee reported, was replaced by Leon Brittan who in 1983 announced new restrictions on the use of parole. This, together with the prison building programme that was by now underway, led Brittan at the party conference that year to say 'the measures that I have outlined . . . will put us on course for ending prison overcrowding by the end of the decade' (quoted in Morris, 1989:138).

Parole, as we have seen, was introduced in 1967 and, at the very least, there has always been an element of pragmatism underpinning its use. The element of pragmatism has become more evident as time has passed. After 1967 the first major change to parole was made in 1975 by the then Home Secretary, Roy Jenkins. Prompted by a desire to reduce the number of minor property offenders in prison, he encouraged the Parole Board to relax their policy in such cases, the assumption being that such offenders would be unlikely to commit serious offences on parole (Maguire, 1992). The effect was an almost 50 per cent rise in the proportion of licences granted between 1976 and 1980. '*De facto*, therefore parole began to shift from being an occasionally granted privilege towards, if not a right, at least a reasonable expectation, particularly on the part of prisoners sentenced to between 18 months and three years' (Maguire, 1992:183)

Prison numbers, however, were still a major problem and in 1981 the government seemed to be looking favourably on the proposals contained in the Home Office's Review of Parole in England and Wales (1981). This would have meant that prisoners serving between six months and three years would have been entitled to automatic release under the supervision of a probation officer after only one third of their sentence had elapsed (Cavadino and Dignan, 1992). There was considerable resistance in some quarters, and it has been argued that the judiciary threatened to undermine the policy by changing their sentencing practices (Ashworth, 1983) and as a consequence it was never introduced.

In 1983, however, using powers introduced by the Criminal Justice Act 1982 Leon Brittan announced a number of changes to sentencing and to the parole system. Maximum sentences for carrying firearms were increased, for example, and the power to refer 'over-lenient' sentences back to the Court of Appeal was introduced. It was the changes to the parole system, however, that were the most contentious. He announced that the threshold of eligibility for parole would be reduced from 12 months to six months – a largely liberal measure. However, he went on to say that in future Ministers (and not the joint committee of Parole Board and Home Office officials as it had been previously) would set a minimum tariff period to be served by life sentence prisoners, related to the circumstances of their offence, and that some categories of prisoner serving life (particularly those who had murdered prison or police officers, or children) would not be released until they had served a minimum period of 20 years. In addition drug traffickers sentenced to more than five years would 'be treated with regard to parole in exactly the same way as serious violent offenders – they should not get it' (quoted in Scraton *et al.*, 1991:137).

The Brittan rules were underpinned by a policy of 'bifurcation': the adoption of a relatively liberal approach in relation to those prisoners considered to be unlikely to commit particularly serious offences, whilst simultaneously adopting a tough approach to the treatment of more serious offenders, especially those convicted of crimes of violence. This policy of bifurcation has had a number of consequences. First, it has meant that there has been a considerable increase in the size of the long-term prison population. Second, it has been seen as unjust by prisoners who have suffered as a consequence of it. Both of these have contributed to the increasing problems within prisons over the past decade.

Changes in sentencing practice and in parole have had a marked impact not only on the size but also on the nature of the prison population. In the years after the Second World War life sentences were relatively rare. In 1945 approximately four fifths of offenders sentenced to custody were serving six months or less. Of the daily average prison population fewer than 20% of sentenced prisoners were serving 18 months or more (Morgan, 1994b). Now fewer than two fifths of offenders sentenced to custody serve sentences of six months or less, and whereas in 1957 there were a total of 140 lifers in the prison system, by 1987 250 a year were receiving such sentences (Scraton *et al.*, 1991). Furthermore, one of the consequences of the bifurcatory influences on sentencing and parole has been that although the proportions of sentences for property and violent offences has not changed all that markedly over the past three decades, the proportion of the prison population that is there because of a violent offence has increased significantly.

It was abundantly clear by the early 1980s that the dispersal policy in relation to the long-term prison population was not succeeding in terms of control. Disturbances continued and only two of the eight dispersal prisons had not been the site of a major disturbance by 1983 (see Home Office, 1984b, Annex D, and Bottoms and Light, 1987). In 1983, Leon Brittan announced the establishment of the Control Review Committee (CRC), an internal working party made up of civil servants and prison governors. The Committee, in its report, suggested that there was a 'disruptive population' of between 150–200 inmates who presented a major control problem and it recommended the introduction of five or six 'long term prisoner units' to relieve the problem. It also argued for the construction of two 'new generation' prisons in which the 300–400 top-security prisoners could be housed. A small number of special units have been established, but the idea of building 'new generation' prisons, though it also found favour with Woolf, has always proved too expensive an option. A powerful argument against the view that it is a small minority of 'dangerous' or 'disturbed' prisoners that are the root of the control problem has been made by King (1985:189)

Probably the most widely held view, both inside and outside the Prison Department, is that the worst control problems have been generated by comparatively few peculiarly difficult, recalcitrant and dangerous prisoners, some of whom may be psychologically disturbed. These prisoners are typically thought of as including terrorists, strong-arm men and leaders of criminal gangs, serving very long sentences of imprisonment; men who are as dangerous inside prison as they are outside . . . . It would be irresponsible and naive to deny that such men exist. Of course they do. But I do wish to argue that conceptualising the control problem as the product of 'difficult' or 'disturbed' individuals, and developing a reactive policy towards them, has been both partial and self-defeating. Partial in that it ignores all the structural, environmental and interactive circumstances that generate trouble, reducing it to some inherent notion of individual wilfulness or malfunction. Self-defeating in that the policy itself becomes part of those very circumstances that generate the trouble; it is likely that among those who get defined as troublemakers there are some who are made into troublemakers as a result of the way they are dealt with in prison. Just as there are some who come to prison as troublemakers. (quoted in Scraton *et al.*, 1991:143)

In the four years following the CRC's report, there were a number of disturbances of a quite serious nature in prisons in England. Among the dispersal prisons, Gartree and Parkhurst experienced protests in 1985 and then in the full range of institutions there were, from 1986 to 1988, 22 separate disturbances, 42 acts of concerted indiscipline, 25 roof-climbing incidents and 245 escapes (Scraton *et al.*, 1991).

   In addition to these disturbances there were, once again, a significant number of disputes involving prison staff. From the POA's position these disputes were about the conditions in which their members were working, the dangers they faced and the pay and general terms and conditions of employment experienced. From the Home Office's perspective, and the Home Office and the POA had now been locked in almost constant dispute for a decade, the key issue was overtime and how it might be reduced. In 1985 alone, prison officers took action at Wormwood Scrubs, Bedford and Parkhurst and the Home Secretary was booed at the POA conference (Sim, 1987).

   Officers were in dispute, disturbances by the incarcerated showed no signs of diminishing, even though the building programme was in full swing the prison population was continuing to rise and there appeared to be little evidence of the trend changing. The prospect of the government's vision of an 'end to overcrowding' becoming a reality seemed slim (Morgan and Jones, 1992). There remained considerable disagreement about the objectives of the service, and there was no commitment to enforceable standards. Indeed, evidence comparing conditions in the early 1970s and the mid-1980s showed that although there had been some improvement in sanitary facilities, 'on most measures, including access to those facilities, [the research] revealed consistently worse regimes . . . in spite of major improvements in staff:prisoner ratios' (King and McDermott, 1989:107). This represents a fairly comprehensive critique of the effectiveness of the May Inquiry.

   A study undertaken by the Prison Department and a team of management consultants in 1986 presented, according to the Home Secretary, Douglas Hurd, 'a telling indictment of the complementing and shift systems and the working practices that surround them' (McDermott and King, 1989:161). In a bid to resolve some of the problems related to staffing and working practices, the Home Office introduced what it called the 'Fresh Start' package, which sought to buy out overtime working albeit at the cost of still further increases in staffing. The basic idea was that the improved working practices that were proposed would produce cost savings, and a proportion of these savings would be reinvested to enhance regimes. Fresh Start abolished overtime, it reduced prison officers' working hours and, according to one observer, through its creation of a modern management structure, 'has moved the Prison Service from the 1950s to the 1980s organisationally' (Stern, 1989:158). Research conducted in five prisons in the immediate aftermath of the introduction of Fresh Start painted a rather more gloomy picture – certainly as far as the nature of the regimes was concerned (McDermott and King, 1989), and the Woolf Report records examples of officers continuing to work many extra hours per week. Thomas (1994:116) concludes that 'The results of Fresh Start were, to put it mildly, disappointing. To begin with it was not long before staff felt cheated. Woolf reports that staff felt "misled" and that "they do not believe that the Prison Service has delivered what it promised".' One consequence of this was that grievances among prison officers remained high, and therefore one source of tension within prisons remained largely unchecked.

One other source of tension was the conditions faced by remand prisoners. Historically, it has been the local prisons in which overcrowding has been at its most extreme, these also being the institutions in which remand prisoners are generally held. It was King and Morgan's (1976) study which first highlighted the particularly poor conditions faced by untried prisoners. Morgan (1994a) has argued that it is the 'treatment and training' philosophy which underpins the 'historical marginalisation' of prisoners on remand (at the time the philosophy was first employed there were relatively few prisoners on remand or awaiting sentence). His argument is that the adoption of that philosophy forced all prisoners into two categories: trainable or untrainable: 'Those deemed trainable – sentenced prisoners except those serving very short sentences (for whom there was held to be insufficient time) and the recalcitrant (for whom the time had apparently passed) – were to be classified and allocated to the 'training' prison whose regime was best fitted to meet their needs. Untrainable short-term sentenced prisoners (which included most fine defaulters) were to remain in the 'local' prisons where those prisoners morally and legally ineligible for training, the untried and the unsentenced, were also to be housed' (1994a:145).

As we have seen, during the course of the 1980s not only did the anticipated fall in the prison population not occur, but the numbers steadily increased. Facing the prospect of increased overcrowding rather than an end to overcrowding the government began to pursue alternative means of limiting the prison population. These included the introduction of bail information schemes, the Prosecution of Offenders Act introduced time limits for bringing cases to trial, guidelines for the committal of cases to the Crown Court were introduced, and advice was issued to sentencers to use remands in custody less frequently. There is some evidence that these measures had a levelling effect from about 1987 onwards (the overall prison population exceeded 50,000 in 1987) up until 1991 whereupon the level once again rose. Prior to 1987, the huge increase in the number of prisoners on remand or unsentenced accounted for a very significant proportion of the overall increase in the prison population. For example, Morgan and Jones (1992) show that whilst the increase in the overall prison population between 1975 and the early 1990s was 22 per cent, the number of untried prisoners increased by 142 per cent. Ironically, it was in the midst of the period when a degree of check appeared to have been placed on the level of remand and unsentenced prisoners inside that the major prison disturbances at Strangeways and elsewhere took place. In fact, as Morgan (1994a) points out, five of the six most serious disturbances at this time occurred either in remand establishments or in places where remand prisoners played a important part in the disturbances.

Strangeways and the Woolf Report

The disturbance that occurred at Strangeways in April 1990 was not only the most serious of all the disturbances that year, but was the longest and most serious riot in British penal history. It began on 1 April and continued until the 25 April. At the time Strangeways was the largest prison in England and Wales and, indeed, one of the largest in Europe. It was built in 1868 and 'was a fine Victorian building' (Woolf, 1991, para.1.19). The prison, not unusually for a local prison, was extremely overcrowded. Its certified normal accommodation was 970 and on 1 April 1990 it was holding 1,647 prisoners. Fewer than 700 of those prisoners were sentenced.

The Woolf Report (para. 1.22) noted that although improvements had been made to the living conditions in the prison in the three years prior to the riot, 'on 1 April 1990, the physical conditions, in addition to being grossly overcrowded, were still insanitary and degrading'. The disturbance began during a service in the prison chapel, the officers who were present quickly having to withdraw. During the ensuing disturbance and siege the inside of the prison was gutted, a total of 147 officers and 47 prisoners received injuries (including those affected by smoke or fumes) and one prisoner received injuries which it was thought may have contributed to his death. At the end of the disturbance the prison was entirely uninhabitable and the estimated cost of repair and refurbishment (though much of the refurbishment, it might be argued, was necessary anyway) was £60 million.

What happened in Manchester led, by one means or another, to protests and disturbances in other parts of the country including at Dartmoor prison, at Pucklechurch youth remand centre, at Glen Parva YOI, and at Bristol and Cardiff prisons. April 1990, Ryan (1992:51) has suggested, 'was perhaps the worst month in the history of the modern prison system'.

An immediate departmental inquiry was set up, and was to be conducted by Lord Justice Woolf. The eventual terms of reference[1] were: 'To inquire into the events leading up to the serious disturbance in Her Majesty's Prison Manchester which began on 1 April 1990 and the action taken to bring it to a conclusion, having regard also to the serious disturbances which occurred shortly thereafter in other prison establishments in England and Wales'. The Home Secretary in announcing the Inquiry made it clear that it would be up to Lord Justice Woolf to interpret the terms of reference as he saw fit and, with one notable exception, the interpretation was a broad one. Morgan (1992a:232), himself an assessor to the inquiry, noted that 'On one vital issue, however, Woolf refused to embark. He decided that sentencing policy lay outside his terms of reference.' The inquiry was carried out with considerable speed and the Report was published on 25 February 1991 to considerable acclaim.

In a number of respects the Report pulls no punches. It identifies a number of problems with the prison service in general [doc 5] and in relation to the riot at Strangeways Woolf concluded that 'The disturbance could have been avoided. When it occurred it should not have been allowed to engulf the whole prison. The disturbance should have been brought to an end earlier' (para.1.16). The Deputy Director of Prisons in London is severely criticised in the Report, as are the governors then in charge at Bristol and Dartmoor.

Central to Woolf's understanding of the disturbances is the recognition that 'there is no single cause of riots and no simple solution or action which will prevent rioting' (para.9.23) and the identification of three requirements which he suggests must be met if the prison system is to be stable. They are *security*, *control* and *justice*. Each, Morgan (1992a) suggests, are equally important and must be balanced. Security refers to the obligation of the Prison Service to prevent inmates escaping; control with the obligation to prevent prisoners being disruptive; and justice the obligation to treat them with humanity and 'to prepare them for their return to the community in a way which makes it less likely that they will reoffend' (para. 9.20). Woolf argues that sufficient attention must be paid to all three of the requirements and that the three must be kept in balance. A lack of balance is likely to lead to disruption and disturbance

---

[1]When the Inquiry was first set up on 5 April its terms of reference were limited, for obvious reasons, to the disturbance at Strangeways. Revised terms of reference were issued on 10 April.

and, as Morgan (1992a:233) notes, 'It is apparent that, in Woolf's view, the Prison Department has overemphasised security, given insufficient weight to justice and often adopted inappropriate control measures.' What then is Woolf's solution?

The Woolf Report, which runs to almost 600 pages of analysis and documentation, culminates in a dozen major proposals [doc 6]. The first recommendation is for closer co-operation between the different parts of the criminal justice system. To facilitate this, Woolf proposed the establishment of a central Criminal Justice Consultative Council supported by a series of regional committees. The second recommendation is for more visible leadership of the Prison Service by a Director General 'who is, and is seen to be, the operational head and in day to day charge of the Service'. This should be achieved through the establishment of a 'compact' or 'contract' between Ministers and the Director General of the Prison Service. The Director General should be responsible for the performance of the 'contract' and publicly answerable for the operations of the service.

The third and fourth recommendations are for increased delegation of responsibility to governors of establishments and an enhanced role for prison officers. 'Compacts' or 'contracts' appear once again in recommendation five. Woolf suggests that there should be a compact for each prisoner setting out the prisoner's expectations and responsibilities in the prison in which he or she is held.

Sixthly, Woolf recommended the setting up of a national system of accredited standards with which, in time, each establishment would be required to comply. The Report also encourages the increased use of alternatives to custody, particularly the use of probation and bail hostels. Seventhly, in a more concerted attempt to restrict future overcrowding, Woolf recommended a new Prison Rule which would prevent an establishment holding more prisoners than is provided for in its certified normal level of accommodation. Parliament would have to be informed if, under exceptional circumstances, the rule were to be departed from.

Woolf's eighth recommendation was for a public commitment by Ministers for a timetable to provide access to sanitation for all prisoners not later than February 1996. The ninth recommendation was for better prospects for prisoners to maintain their links with families and the community through more visits and home leaves and through being located in community prisons as near to their homes as possible. Recommendation ten, that prisons should be divided into small and more manageable and secure units, reinforces the thrust of the previous recommendation.

Woolf's eleventh recommendation was for a separate statement of purpose, separate conditions and generally a lower security categorisation for remand prisoners. The final recommendation was for improved standards of justice within prisons. These include the giving of reasons to prisoners for any decision which materially and adversely affects them, a grievance procedure and disciplinary proceedings which ensure that the governor deals with most matters under his present powers, relieving boards of visitors of their adjudicatory role (Shaw, 1992).

The response to Woolf

The genius of the Woolf Report lies in its ability to locate a grave breakdown in law and order in the context of the long-standing problems of the prison system – overcrowding, decrepitude, poor management, a lack of justice and humanity. The full history of the Woolf inquiry has yet to be written, but it was clear to observers that Waddington and his senior civil servants were appalled by the breadth of approach which Woolf immediately brought to his task. It would have been easy, safe even, for Woolf to have concentrated on the locks and bars aspects of security and control. It is to his very considerable credit that, with one or two exceptions, he avoided such an approach. (Shaw, 1992:164–5)

The expectations that awaited the publication of the Report were high. Nevertheless, 'to a considerable extent [Woolf] confounded the sceptics and produced a document which met with approval across the political spectrum and was acclaimed by penal pressure groups as the most important examination of the prison system this century' (Player and Jenkins, 1994:10). Some of the government's responses to the Woolf Report were announced by the Home Secretary in February 1991, though the major response came in a White Paper, *Custody, Care and Justice* (Home Office, 1991), in September 1991. The more immediate response by the Home Secretary was that provision would be made for more generous visiting allowances, an increase in the number of telephones available to prisoners, and an acceleration of the timetable for an end to slopping out, the revised plan being that no prisoner should be slopping out after the end of 1994.

The White Paper, it is fair to say, received a mixed reception. However, several important commentators have admitted that it was more faithful to the spirit of Woolf than they had expected (see for example King, 1994). On the positive side, for example, the White Paper accepted the recommendation that a Criminal Justice Consultative Council be created together with local area committees, though both the Woolf and White Paper proposals fall short of recreating a body along the lines of the previously influential Advisory Council on the Penal System, or the more recent suggestion of a Sentencing Council (Ashworth, 1992). The national Council came into operation in late 1991 and the area committees in 1992. Although the then Lord Chief Justice, Lord Lane, resisted having the judiciary chair the Council or be represented on area committees (Morgan, 1992a) his successor, Lord Justice Taylor, reversed this decision and whilst the new arrangements are not ideal, they are probably 'the best that can be achieved for the time being' (Roberts, 1994:241).

The references in Woolf to a 'structured stand-off' between ministers and the Director General of the prison service, together with the establishment of some form of contract between the parties to govern the running of the system was essentially in line with extant government policy anyway and the subsequent transfer of the prison service to agency status has underlined the general process that was already underway. The White Paper also accepted the need for standards, and committed the government to introducing a code of standards focused on the service to be provided for prisoners, though there was continuing resistance to introducing *legally enforceable* standards (Casale, 1994).

Where outright rejection came, however, was over the proposals to introduce a new prison rule to eliminate overcrowding. Woolf had even suggested that the Home Secretary might use his powers of executive release rather than allow serious overcrowding, and had recommended that a statutory limit be placed on the length of time that prisoners could be kept in police cells. The response in *Custody, Care and Justice* accepted that there was a need to reduce overcrowding (para. 1.34), but did not see this as the priority that Woolf had done and certainly seemed to sense no urgency in the matter. Part of the reason for this was a surrounding sense of optimism about population levels. Numbers had fallen from over 50,000 in 1988 to below 45,000 in 1990 and, given the large number of additional prison places resulting from the prison building programme, it seemed likely that an end to serious overcrowding was near.

Indeed, the White Paper commented that 'the prison system is in sight of providing sufficient places to match the average size of the prison population', though it recognised that this was dependent upon the sentencing trends of the courts and the impact of the Criminal Justice Act 1991. The prison population continued to fall, and sharply, during 1992, particularly after the introduction of the Criminal Justice Act in the October, but this was short-lived as indeed were many aspects of the Act (a brief history of the 1991 Act is contained in chapter 5). By the spring of 1993 the population once again started to rise and, with the Home Secretary making plain his faith in the deterrent effect of the prison system at the Conservative Party conference that year: 'Let us be clear. Prison works. It ensures that we are protected from murderers, muggers and rapists – and it makes many who are tempted to commit crime think twice', it has continued to rise. So steep has the rise been that a Home Office projection of future trends, which suggested that the population would rise to 51,600 by the year 2001 (Home Office Statistical Bulletin 6/93) has been shown to be far too conservative in its estimates. The prison population once again exceeded 50,000 in October 1994 and is in fact expected to reach over 55,000 by the turn of the century ('Jails "set to explode" with 50,000 prisoners', *Guardian*, 15 October 1994).

Woolf, as we have seen, placed considerable emphasis on the

role of overcrowding in the issue of control in prisons, yet he also made some very specific recommendations about discipline and grievance procedures within prison. Over 1,200 prisoners wrote to the Woolf Inquiry with complaints about the disciplinary system (Morgan and Jones, 1991). In many respects Woolf reiterated the view taken by the Prior Committee (Home Office, 1985) which had been strongly critical of the role of the Board of Visitors in disciplinary proceedings. In the event, Woolf concluded that it was not 'possible or reasonable to expect a Board of Visitors to act as both watch-dog and as an adjudicatory body' (para, 14.390) and recommended that they cease to have a disciplinary function. He rejected the idea of a specialist Prison Disciplinary Tribunal and, instead, proposed that disciplinary and criminal offences should be separated and that governors should hear the former and that the latter should be referred to the Crown Prosecution Service (CPS) (Livingston, 1994). In relation to complaints Woolf recommended the addition of an independent element in the form of Complaints Adjudicator. The majority of these recommendations were accepted by the government and although it took a significant length of time for the Prisons Ombudsman (as the Adjudicator is now called) to be appointed, the post became operational in 1994.

The final element of the Woolf Report that it is necessary to focus upon here is the emphasis upon community and, specifically, the recommendation in relation to community prisons. Stephen Shaw (1992) has suggested that Woolf's use of the term 'community prison' whilst perhaps the most significant phrase in the whole report, is also rather vague about what it might mean. The vagueness arises from the fact that two separate notions are actually employed: first, the notion of prison and community being integrated (something close to what King and Morgan (1980) referred to as 'normalisation'. Second, is an idea that has been characterised as 'comprehensive prisons' (Shaw, 1992) where prisoners of very varying types (different classifications, remand and sentenced, adult and young, perhaps even male and female) are held on one site but are housed in separate units. Woolf proposed that prisons should accommodate no more than 400 inmates, separated into units housing 50–70 prisoners each.

The White Paper, though recognising the length of time that such a policy might take to implement, nevertheless commented positively on the idea of multi-functional community prisons. In particular it stated that the government would: 'identify a number of existing and new local prisons which might be replanned as multi-functional community prisons; consider whether there are existing prisons which could be more directly linked to a local prison so that prisoner's sentence plan could provide for the prisoner to progress mainly through that cluster of establishments' (para 5.16). Observers have, however, pointed out that the White Paper appears to contain a very limited conception of the role and nature of the community prison. In particular, the Prison

Service 'appears wedded to single-purpose prisons and sees the shifts that have occurred in different sections of the population as an obstacle in the way of Woolf's ideas' (Roberts, 1994:237).

Privatisation and penal policy

From approximately 1982 onwards, the government began vigorously to pursue its 'Financial Management Initiative' (FMI), designed to encourage efficiency and cost savings by applying private sector management methods to the public sector, and imposing market disciplines on them. The 1980s also saw the emergence of an issue that had begun to threaten other public services: privatisation. Privatisation and the FMI were of course linked, for increasing restrictions on staff levels and resources in the public sector increase the opportunities for competitors from the private sector.

In fact there was relatively little interest shown in the idea of prison privatisation up until 1986/7. In 1984, the Adam Smith Institute, perhaps the most forceful proponents of privatisation, had advocated full-scale privatisation of the prison system (Adam Smith Institute, 1984), whereas milder proposals were offered in 1985 by two academic Social Democrats, and in 1987 by Lord Windelsham the then Chairman of the Parole Board (for details see Ryan and Ward, 1989; Rutherford, 1990). Crucially, however, in 1986 the Home Affairs Committee had recommended experimentation with private sector construction and management of custodial institutions, and that such experiments should be based in remand establishments.

Following the 1987 election, a Home Office junior minister visited the United States to examine private prisons there, and at approximately the same time a new consortium of two British firms and the Corrections Corporation of America – a leading player in private prisons there – was formed to actively campaign for prisons privatisation in the UK. Nevertheless, by the end of the decade little progress appeared to have been made and Rutherford (1990:62) concluded, for example, that 'in the immediate future, the private sector's role in prison management in Britain is likely to be marginal at most.'

Things have, however, changed quite quickly. The Criminal Justice Act 1991 contains a provision which allows the management of any prison, not just remand centres, to be contracted out to any agency the Home Secretary considers appropriate. In April 1992 Group 4 Security won the contract to manage a new purpose-built institution for remand prisoners, the Wolds, and a second prison, Blakenhurst, opened in 1993 under the management of UK Detention Services. It was feared that the transfer of the Prison Service to agency status was part of a process of wholesale privatisation, but this has been denied by the Home Office. Nevertheless, the private sector is playing an increasing role in providing services within prisons generally, together with what appear to be plans to extend significantly the private management of prisons. In 1993, tenders were invited for the running of existing as well as new prisons, including Strangeways and it has been suggested that up to half of the existing estate may be market tested.

It is too early to know what the consequences of privatisation will be. There are signs that high standards are being delivered at some of the privately run institutions (Morgan, 1994a) though it certainly cannot be assumed that extending the process will speed up the types of changes in regimes recommended by Woolf. On the contrary 'one obvious danger is that, as ministers distance themselves from the operational concerns of the new Prison Agency debates about resources will be increasingly defined in terms of internal good husbandry and relegated from the political agenda' (Player and Jenkins, 1994:27).

The aims of imprisonment?

It is clear from an examination of the history of imprisonment that differing theoretical answers to the fundamental question 'What is prison for?' can in fact have important consequences for daily life in prisons. Experience therefore suggests that, without an adequate statement of aims, we shall not develop the best practicable kind of daily regime in prisons. (Bottoms, 1990b:3)

As we have seen in this and the previous chapter, the prison has been viewed in different ways at different times and, accordingly has been perceived as performing a different function within the penal system. Crudely speaking, it moved from being merely a repository for those awaiting trial, sentence or death in the sixteenth and seventeenth centuries to a site where punishment was inflicted on an increasingly wide range of offenders during the course of the eighteenth and nineteenth centuries. As the end of the nineteenth century neared so the emphasis upon the reform and rehabilitation of offenders grew, and the primacy of this role was reinforced by the Report of the Gladstone Committee in 1895. From the mid-twentieth century for almost thirty years – perhaps the high point of penal optimism – the notion of 'treatment and training' became the explicit guiding principle of the prison system.

With the emergence of research which questioned the effectiveness of treatment (Brody, 1976; Lipton et al, 1975) the rehabilitative ideal began to collapse and faith in the efficacy of treatment and training diminished. In their evidence to the May Inquiry in 1979, King and Morgan were critical of Prison Rule 1 on grounds far broader than merely some form of penal pessimism. Morgan (1994b: 895) describes their position as rejecting Rule 1 because it was 'so vague that it had never been operationalised. Indeed, it was inspired by aspirations incapable of fulfilment, something the prison staff had always known. Moreover, it quite arbitrarily excluded remand and trial prisoners from view' (Morgan, 1994b:895). King and Morgan (1980:31–2) suggested that it would be better to attempt to turn the practical and prosaic concept of 'humane containment' into a reality:

Humane containment refers explicitly to the prison system, which forms only a part of the wider criminal justice system. We believe that what we regard as humane containment is most compatible with what has come to be called the 'justice' or 'due process' model for dealing with offenders generally. Taken together they best fit the state of current knowledge about law and order and the effectiveness of criminal sanctions. They therefore offer the best basis at this time for the development of a coherent policy for the future of the prison system.

Humane containment was to be underpinned by three principles: the minimum use of custody; the minimum use of security; and, the 'normalisation' of the prison. The May Committee, however, rejected the idea of 'humane containment', though it did accept that Rule 1 needed to be rewritten and in attempting to do so it introduced the notion of 'positive custody'. This in turn, however, has not been adopted. In Bottoms' (1990b) view, it is the humane containment formula that has been the more influential on debates about prison since 1980, particularly because of its 'congruence' with the demands for improved rights and standards for prisoners which dominated much of this period. Nevertheless, 'there has remained a persistent unease within the prison service about the starkness' of this simple phrase, leading Bottoms (1990b:9) to suggest that the central problem with the notion is that it is perceived to be ontologically insufficient.

At least for a period the question of the aims of imprisonment dropped off the agenda and, largely because of the increasing emphasis upon financial management, the penal debate became more and more influenced by questions of economy, efficiency and effectiveness. A statement of tasks of the prison service was set out by the Director General in 1983, and it began 'The task of the Prison Service is to use with maximum efficiency the resources of staff, money, building and plant made available to it by Parliament in order to fulfil' four functions which include keeping untried and unsentenced prisoners in custody until it is time to bring them to court; keeping sentenced prisoners in custody; to provide 'as full a life as is consistent with the facts of custody'; and to help prisoners keep in touch with the community. This lead Stern (1989:50) to comment:

It may seem a sad decline from the high ideals of changing human beings and sending them back out into the world crime-free to aspirations of giving prisoners a regular bath and ensuring they get their visits from their families. However, since we are still a long way from realizing even these modest ambitions for a good proportion of our prisoners, it at least has the advantage of being both measurable and achievable.

We have moved then from a position in which at least some emphasis was placed upon a moral mission, to one dominated by what Garland (1990) characterises as institutionally-defined managerial goals, and Rutherford (1993) calls 'expedient managerialism'. Expedient managerialism, he says, gives priority to narrowly-defined performance measures and to short-term trouble-shooting over any articulation of purposes and values. This, as we shall see in subsequent discussions of, for example, policing and probation, can just as well be applied to other parts of the criminal justice system.

Since the publication in 1983 of the statement of tasks, there has subsequently been the report of the Control Review Committee (Home Office, 1984b) which, like the statement of tasks adopted by the Scottish Prison Service in the same year, distanced itself in some important respects from the 1983 formulation. In 1985, the ex-Governor of Wormwood Scrubs published a report entitled *A Sense of Direction*, in which he stressed the principles of 'individualism, relationship and activity' (Dunbar, 1985:84). In 1988 and 1989 the English and Scottish Prison Services issued mission statements, the former characterised by Bottoms (1990b:15) as containing a 'humane containment plus' formula, the latter improving upon this somewhat by adding the aim of providing: 'prisoners with all possible opportunities to help them to lead law-abiding and useful lives'.

Where, then, does Woolf come into all this? As one of the assessors to the Inquiry has noted: 'At first glance the Woolf Report is disappointingly thin when it comes to a discussion of the purposes of imprisonment. No history of the debate is provided and there is no radical critique of the Prison Service's current statement of purpose. However, Woolf's brief criticism of existing formulations – the absence of any reference to justice and the failure to provide specifically for unconvicted prisoners – unlocked a process of logic with radical implications' (Morgan, 1994a:111).

Woolf's formulation, as we have seen, rested on the suggestion that a balance needed to be created between security, control and justice. Security and control had dominated the debate for some years, and it is the addition of 'justice' which has influenced the debate. Whilst the Woolf formula falls well short of a new statement of aims, it does at least recognise that even though the primary purpose of prison is not positive for those incarcerated, some form of moral duty must be placed upon the prison service to ensure that inmates and officers' sense of dignity is maximised and that their sense of injustice is minimised [see doc 7]. This, together with increasing the opportunities for prisoners to take responsibility for their behaviour, lie at the heart of Woolf's recommendations for reducing reoffending.

Nevertheless, and as has effectively been the case throughout the history of the modern prison, much is going to depend on how many people are actually incarcerated. If the prison population continues to rise, as it is predicted to do, then the chances of further major disturbances being avoided cannot be great. The sense of grievance and injustice which is documented at length in the Woolf Report will

CHAPTER 3

The police and policing policy

Until relatively recently the image of PC George Dixon (of Dock Green) was so all-pervasive, that it was easy to persuade ourselves that we had only just emerged from a 'golden age' of policing in which there had been general respect for, and consensus about, the role of the constabulary. Whilst this would certainly be a gross overstatement, it would also be wrong to characterise the history of British policing as one beset by conflict for, after a period of quite intense resistance to the introduction of the 'new' police, the period from perhaps the 1870s to the late 1950s was one of relative acceptance and general calm in relation to policing. This is not to suggest, of course, that conflict – sometimes of a quite serious nature – did not occur, simply that in relative terms there would appear to have been, in this period, broad acceptance of the legitimacy of the police. This situation has, quite clearly, changed, and it is a brief history of this process of change – particularly over the past twenty years – that is offered here. It is important to consider the history of the police in England and Wales and, accordingly, this chapter is divided into three main sections: first, policing in England and Wales prior to the establishment of the Royal Commission on the Police in 1960, second the period from 1960 to the election of the Thatcher government in 1979 and, third, police and policing policy since 1979.

The emergence of the modern police service

While the principal duty of the new police when they were first established in London in 1829 was declared to be the prevention of crime, as the nineteenth century wore on, English policemen found themselves carrying out a variety of tasks which fitted the older definitions: they regulated traffic, ensured that pavements were unimpeded, kept a watchful eye for unsafe buildings and burning chimneys, administered first aid at accidents and drove ambulances, administered aspects of the Poor Law, looked for missing persons, licensed street sellers and cabs, and supervised the prevention of disease among farm animals. Such tasks rarely figure prominently in police histories or police memoirs, and some of these tasks have subsequently been yielded to specialist agencies; yet the fact remains that since their creation the police have become more and more responsible for the smooth running of a variety of different aspects of society and not simply for the prevention and detection of crime and the maintenance of public order. (Emsley, 1991:3)

The term 'constable' originated in Norman times, and by the thirteenth and fourteenth centuries there were a variety of posts with this title, the majority of which were linked to manors or parishes. The medieval constable was responsible for making regular reports to the local court leet and with maintaining the King's peace. It is suggested by some police historians that the emergence of the office of justice of the peace in the fourteenth century usurped the position hitherto occupied by the constable and led to the decline of this office from this point to the emergence of the new police 400 years later (see Critchley, 1978). The extent of the declining importance of the office of constable is disputed by Emsley (1991) and others, though he accepts that it may have been in decline from the late seventeenth century onwards.

Eighteenth-century England was characterised by increasing concerns about crime. Though there is also dispute as to the extent to which there was any real basis for such fears (see Reith, 1938; Emsley, 1991), outbreaks of disorder such as the Gordon Riots certainly gave the impression of increasing lawlessness. By the mid to late eighteenth century crime and disorder were perceived to pose a threat to social stability. One consequence, at least in London, was the emergence of the 'trading justice' – the man who 'probably because he lacked sufficient estate, opted to profit from the fees paid for performing judicial tasks' (Emsley, 1991:18) – and professional thief-takers who profited from the existence of rewards for bringing offenders to justice. The most famous of these thief-takers were the Bow Street Runners, employed by Henry Fielding who, whilst probably not as corrupt as others working at the same time, were certainly not 'above suspicion' (Emsley, 1991:19). By the end of the eighteenth century Fielding's operation, which had begun with the runners, had expanded to include a variety of patrols, including armed patrols.

It was around this time that proposals started to emerge for a co-ordinated police service for London – the word 'police' being quite common currency by this point. It was not until 1829, however, that Robert Peel was successful in getting legislation through Parliament to introduce the Metropolitan Police. Though many of the more traditional histories of the police have presented this development as a logical and successful progression from earlier arrangements, Emsley (1991:23), for example, suggests that the new police constables were 'initially at least, probably less efficient than several of the old night watches'. Crime prevention was, as has been noted, the primary responsibility of this new force. Emsley (1983) in his historical study of the emergence of the modern service quotes from the Metropolitan Police's first instruction book which indicated that 'every effort of the police' was to be directed at the prevention of crime. It went on:

'The security of person and property, the preservation of the public tranquillity, and all other objects of a police establishment will thus be better effected than by the detection and punishment of the offender after he has succeeded in committing the crime. This should constantly be kept in mind by every member of the police force, as the guide for his own conduct. Officers and police constables should endeavour to distinguish themselves by such vigilance and activity as may render it impossible for any one to commit a crime within that portion of the town under their charge.'

Though such a short description implies a myriad of responsibilities (the prevention of crime, the maintenance of order, and the detection and punishment of the offender) the 'New Police' actually possessed relatively limited functions and powers. Crime prevention – the supposed core of the role – was actually fairly narrowly conceived at the time, largely as a 'scarecrow' foot patrol function. There has been a long and protracted academic debate about the reasons for the introduction of the Metropolitan Police in the 1820s, though the control of what was perceived to be a markedly rising crime rate and the maintenance of social order are accorded a central role in both the 'traditional' and the 'radical' histories (see Critchley, 1978, and Silver, 1967 for differing histories and Reiner, 1992 for an overview and synthesis).

Though the Metropolitan Police was the first, and remains the largest and best known of the constabularies, forces were set up in the provinces within a matter of years of the establishment of the new police in London. Though the Metropolitan Police was a major influence on the development of forces outside London, the Metropolitan model was experimented with in other areas and was by no means uncritically adopted [doc 2]. Although the central tasks of these forces were similar to those outlined by Rowan and Mayne, a wide variety of other duties were soon acquired by the police. Many of these – inspectors of nuisances, of weights and measures, inspectors under the Diseases of Animals Acts, the inspection of dairies and shops, contagious diseases, explosives, bridges, even in the case of some borough forces running both fire and ambulance services (Critchley, 1978), together with informal services such as 'knocking up' people for work (Emsley, 1983) – were what would most accurately be described as 'service' functions. Though never important enough to form the defining characteristic of the police, such functions were nevertheless one element in the process of legitimisation of the police during the course of the nineteenth century (Reiner, 1992). Nevertheless, it was in general the law enforcement and order maintenance functions that continued to be considered to be the core activities of police officers.

That this was the case is illustrated quite well in Reiner's (1992) discussion of the process of increasing legitimisation of the police in this period. He argues that one of the elements of police policy which contributed towards their legitimation was the appearance that the police were 'effective'. The criteria by which this effectiveness was judged are illuminating:

By the 1870s then, the police had come to be seen as offering an effective law enforcement service to the middle and upper classes, who complained when its quality seemed to decline. The working class too made use of it, but the less respectable sections of this class were predominantly at the receiving end of law and order campaigns. (Reiner, 1992: 72)

There were, by this point, three types of police authority in existence. Peel's Metropolitan Police Act 1829 established a new 'police office' at Westminster, and two justices, responsible to the Home Secretary, were to be responsible for control over the new force. The Act made the Home Secretary responsible for approving the size of the force and gave him the power to command the two justices (later Commissioners) to execute specific duties. Although the power of the Home Secretary over the police generally, and not just the Metropolitan Police, has come in for increasing criticism, Lustgarten (1986) argues that, given that in 1829 the electorate consisted of only a tiny fraction of the male population and that monolithic party government underpinned by the whip system did not exist, the arrangements for the governance of the capital's police were 'designed to ensure the maximum accountability that the political system was capable of constructing at the time'.

The broad parameters of the system of accountability for the Metropolitan Police have remained largely unchanged since its inception and the establishment, for example, of elected local representative government for London in 1888 did not prise control away from the Home Office. As has been suggested above, although the Metropolitan Police was the first of the forces to be established, the arrangements for its governance were not copied when other forces were set up and, indeed, the mechanisms of accountability for provincial forces continue to be organised on a different basis.

With the growth of provincial police forces there developed two alternative systems of local accountability. The Municipal Corporations Act 1835 established Watch Committees which possessed the power to appoint officers and establish regulations for the running of the town forces. Following this the County Police Act 1839 gave justices of the peace the power to appoint a chief officer of police who held statutory office and could only be dismissed at Quarter or General Sessions. The standing of the county force chief constable was much greater than that of the borough chief; at the same time the county forces were much more closely tied to the Home Office. The 1839 Act stated that all county forces were subject to rules concerning 'government, pay, clothing and accoutrements of constables' to be promulgated by the Home Secretary (Lustgarten, 1986).

The establishment of police forces did not become compulsory until the County and Borough Police Act 1856 which reinforced the power of the Watch Committee and of the justices. The Act did, however, introduce the first provision for central inspection of police forces, empowering the Crown to appoint three inspectors of constabulary to assess the efficiency of all forces. The power of the centre was at this point, and for some years to come, 'limited in both character and amount' (Critchley, 1978), but tended to grow thereafter. The Local Government Act 1888 established the administrative pattern for policing for almost the next century. It established County Councils and, under their aegis, standing joint committees consisting of two thirds elected councillors and one third local magistrates to be the police authority for county forces, an arrangement which was applied to all police authorities by the Police Act 1964.

There were a number of well-publicised disputes between chief constables and Watch Committees around the turn of century, each of which revolved around, though none resolved, the question of whether a chief is entitled to act independently in enforcing the law. At the turn of the century practices varied greatly from force to force with some chief constables being largely subservient to their Watch Committee and others acting quite independently on occasion (Brogden, 1982; Spencer, 1985).

By the time of the First World War over 50,000 men were employed in constabularies across England and Wales. The war, however, both depleted police numbers and added a layer of duties that had not been present in peacetime. Dissatisfaction over pay and conditions – which also affected the prison service at this time (see chapter 1) – led to the establishment of the police and prison officers' union in 1913. A dispute over the legitimacy of union membership resulted in a police strike for about a week in London in 1918 and spurred on unionisation outside the capital. Fears about unionisation grew apace and in 1919 the Home Secretary introduced a Bill which sought to implement the Desborough Committee's recommendations on police pay – which was to be substantially increased – and on unionisation – which was to be outlawed.

The First World War, and the police strikes that almost immediately followed its conclusion, were the source of the next important set of structural changes to policing and its governance. The Home Office had begun, via Her Majesty's Inspectorate of Constabulary (HMIC), to oversee the activities of all police forces, and growing central control and supervision was made possible through the Police (Expenses) Act 1874, which increased the Exchequer grant to local police forces from one quarter to cover one half of police expenditure. (It was not until the Local Government Act 1985 that it was increased, this time to the 'symbolic' figure of 51%.) During the war, the government began to assume the role of a co-ordinating body, setting up committees and issuing Circulars and instructions under the emergency regulations

(Critchley, 1978), thus forging the first links between senior officers and the Home Office.

The Police Act 1919 gave the Home Office increased powers over the regulation of pay, conditions and discipline in all police forces, and also set up an advisory body before which such regulations were to be laid (Critchley, 1978; Jefferson and Grimshaw, 1984). At the same time, a police department was set up in the Home Office which, similarly, had responsibility for provincial police forces as well as the Metropolitan Police.

From this point onwards, the history of police accountability is one dominated by increasing central control, generally at the expense of local police authorities (Jefferson and Grimshaw, 1984; Lustgarten, 1986). Lustgarten in fact suggests that from the 1920s two trends were visible. The first was increasing Home Office influence through legislation and through less formal means, and the second was increasing freedom of action on the part of chief constables, eventually enshrined in the 'principle of constabulary independence'. In both cases, local police authorities were the 'losers'. The next major piece of legislation was the Police Act 1946 which gave the Home Secretary power to compulsorily amalgamate police forces with populations below 100,000.

Within a decade and a half a Royal Commission was sitting and was about to propose some of the most far-reaching changes to British policing for a century and a half. What were the reasons for such a development? Interestingly, although the period 1955–64 has rightly been described by Stevenson and Bottoms (1989) as a 'decade of transition' as far as the politics of the police were concerned, they also show that in official documents at least, the Home Office actually painted quite a positive picture of policing in the latter half of the 1950s. However, there was increasing concern shown by the Home Office at increases in recorded crime at this time, and by chief constables about the more visible developments in youth culture which were held to be indicative of declining morals.

Behind the public presentation of official confidence in the police, by the mid to late 1950s there was increasing concern about the effectiveness of the police, and towards the end of the decade a number of well-publicised disputes between police authorities and their chief constables threw the issue of the accountability of the police into sharp relief. In 1958, for example, the Nottingham Watch Committee requested that the chief constable report on an investigation he had instituted in connection with corruption charges involving members of the City Council. The chief constable refused and the Watch Committee used their power to suspend him. The Home Secretary ruled that such an action interfered with the chief constable's duty to enforce the criminal law free from political control and reinstated him. In 1959 the House of Commons debated a motion censuring the Home Secretary for making £300 of public money available to settle an action brought against a Metropolitan Police constable as the result of an alleged assault. These, and a number of other *causes célèbres* put the issue of accountability high on the agenda – though the focus was on individual officers rather than on force policies – and led to the establishment of a Royal Commission on the Police.

The police and policing after the Royal Commission

The Royal Commission on the Police 1960

It was, then a number of very small-scale scandals in the late 1950s, together with a steadily rising crime rate, which prompted the instituting of a Royal Commission on the Police to examine a series of issues which continue to be high on the political agenda in the 1990s: police pay, police accountability and the possibility of a national police force. The latter was rejected, though a number of arguments in favour were advanced in a minority report, many of which are resonant of the effectiveness and efficiency arguments that continue to be deployed in support of such a move. Stevenson and Bottoms (1989:10–11) conclude that, 'Overall, one is left with the clear impression of a Commission impressed with some of the logic of the nationalisers' case, but regarding it as simply too radical in the context of the times'.

The recommendations made by the Royal Commission in its final report (1962) formed the basis for the Police Act 1964, which is the primary statute defining the responsibilities of the three main bodies responsible for the police: the police authority, chief constable and the Home Office. More particularly, the Royal Commission, set up in 1960, was given the central task of reviewing: 'the constitutional position of the police throughout Great Britain, the arrangements for their control and administration, the principles that should govern remuneration of police officers and, in particular, to consider:

(1) the constitution and functions of local police authorities;
(2) the status and accountability of members of police forces, including chief officers of police;
(3) the relationship of the police with the public and the means of ensuring that complaints against police are effectively dealt with' (Royal Commission on the Police, 1962).

Spencer (1985:23) makes the important observation that the Royal Commission, although tasked with examining the issue of accountability, did not have among its objectives 'ensuring that policing policies reflected the needs and priorities of the communities they served' and, as a consequence, their recommendations did not cover such ground. The recommendations that the Commission did make with regard to accountability were, in the main, implemented by the Police Act 1964 and they have formed the basis for practice ever since. Once again, the general trend brought about by the Royal Commission and the Act was to reinforce the powers of chief constables and the Home Office at the expense of local authorities (Marshall, 1978).

The Royal Commission began from the position that 'the problem of controlling the police can . . . be restated as the problem of controlling chief constables' – a statement which has been much contested since. It went on to note that chief constables were accountable to no one, nor subject to anyone's orders for the way in which they settled general policies in relation to law enforcement and that, therefore, with regard to establishing more effective supervision, 'the problem [was] to move towards this objective without compromising the chief constable's impartiality in enforcing the law in particular cases' (Royal Commission on the Police, 1962, para.92).

The Police Act 1964

This Act replaced the old system of Watch Committees and joint standing committees with a single system of police authorities. The Watch Committees had been composed entirely of councillors, whilst half of the members of the joint standing committees were magistrates. The new authorities were to consist of two thirds councillors and one third magistrates and, outside London, these authorities took two basic forms – though a third emerged more recently with the abolition of the Metropolitan authorities. The most common was the police authority which covered one county. This was a committee of the county council, usually referred to as the police committee, and was like other council committees except that none of its decisions, other than financial ones, could be overruled by the full council. The second type was the combined police authority which existed where police forces served more than one county. They consisted of councillors and magistrates from each county, and were wholly independent of each and all of the constituent councils.

All police authorities were under a duty to secure the maintenance of an 'adequate and efficient' force for their area, though these terms were undefined. In the event the Police Act 1964 empowered police authorities to:

(1) appoint a chief constable, his deputy and assistants, subject to the approval of the Home Secretary;
(2) determine the overall establishment, and number of each rank, of the force;
(3) provide vehicles, clothing and equipment;
(4) determine the overall budget of the force, subject however to the requirement that costs incurred under authority of central government Regulations, or any statute, must be met;
(5) require its chief constable to submit a report in writing on matters connected with the policing of the area.

Consequently, the only statutory duty owed by the chief constable to his police authority was the submission of an annual report, though the authority could 'require' that he also provide a written report on any matter related to policing of the area. This is, then, a form of what Marshall (1978) has termed 'explanatory' accountability, wherein the police are required *post hoc* to explain the policies they have followed or actions they have taken. Though potentially powerful, this provision in the 1964 Act provided little actual leverage, for a chief constable could refuse to make such a report if he believed it would contain information 'which in the public interest ought not to be disclosed, or is not needed for the discharge of the functions of the police authority'. Furthermore, police authorities had no powers to instruct chief constables to change any policies set out in the reports provided them. The 'unsatisfactory, indeed somewhat ludicrous result' according to Lustgarten (1986) was 'that police authorities are dependent on their chief constable for information, making their ability to offer effective criticism subject to the co-operation of its primary target. And the position of the Home Secretary as ultimate arbiter quietly emphasises the power of central government in policing matters.'

One of the major changes made by the Act was the enshrining in statute of the fact that supreme responsibility for local policing lay with chief constables, each force thenceforward being 'under the direction and control' of its chief officer. In order to do this he was empowered by the Act to appoint, promote and discipline all officers up to the rank of chief superintendent. The Act also required chief constables to investigate complaints against the police and to submit all complaints that reveal that a criminal offence has been committed to the Director of Public Prosecutions.

The third pillar of what has since become known as the 'tripartite structure' is the Home Secretary. Many of the powers conferred on the police authority were only exercisable with the approval of the Home Secretary. Thus, although the chief, deputy and assistant chief constables were appointed by the police authority, such decisions had not only to be approved by the Home Secretary, but they were subject to regulations promulgated by him. In addition, the Home Secretary could require a police authority to retire its chief constable 'in the interests of efficiency', though this provision has never been formally invoked.

Although a number of changes were made during the 1970s and 1980s, this was the basic structure that underpinned the process by which the police in England and Wales were made accountable for their general policies (the complaints procedure for dealing with allegations of individual misconduct is considered below) up until the passage of the Police and Magistrates' Courts Act 1994. Although there was an initial acceptance of the new arrangements brought about by the 1964 Police Act, together with continuing support for the police, this changed significantly, and perhaps irrevocably, during the following decade. A number of factors contributed to this change and two key elements are considered here: the move to Unit Beat Policing, and a series of corruption scandals which tarnished the image of the Metropolitan Police in particular, but perhaps policing in general.

The introduction of Unit Beat Policing

In August 1967 the Home Office issued a circular which encouraged police forces to adopt a new system of policing which reduced the number of officers on foot patrol, and put them into cars. This was felt to have the advantage of allowing much wider geographical areas to be covered on a 24 hour basis and, together with the personal radios that were to be issued, of enabling officers to respond much more juickly to calls from the public. According to its proponents UBP vas going to enable a better service to be offered to the public in ull the major areas of police work: in the maintenance of public order, in the detection of crime, and in the prevention of crime, whilst also improving relations with the public. This is now widely presented as oeing the polar opposite of what has happened in practice partly, it is suggested, because the whole idea was fundamentally misconceived, but also because it was undermined by a combination of insufficient resourcing and a police culture which played down the 'service' element of the system and exploited the opportunities it provided for 'action' (Holdaway, 1983). One of the unintended consequences of the reorganisation then, was to highlight the 'crime fighting' aspects of police work, and to devalue the service role. Reiner (1992:76) suggests that with the transformation of patrol into a 'fire brigade' service, the emphasis was placed on 'technology, specialisation and managerial professionalism as the keys to winning the fight against crime'.

The crucial change brought about by UBP, it is argued, was the move away from foot patrol and into panda cars. Although there was never any systematic evaluation of the impact of UBP (Weatheritt, 1986), a general consensus has nevertheless emerged, which blames many of the perceived modern ills at its door. On one level, the absence of evidence is irrelevant, for the fact is that the universal criticism of the new system reveals a great deal about where things are believed to have gone wrong irrespective of when and why they actually went wrong:

The pandas were, it is widely agreed, a disaster. They distanced the police from the public and, it has been suggested, encouraged policemen to see themselves in uncomplicated terms as knights-errant in the war against crime rather than as members of the community fully bound up in all aspects of its life and so lessening the likelihood of crime occurring in the first place. (Manwaring-White, 1983; quoted in Weatheritt, 1986:96)

The main charge laid at the door of UBP is that, albeit unintentionally, it was partly responsible for a sea-change in the style and image of British policing, a new style that not everyone was entirely comfortable with. As Chibnall (1977) described it: 'The "British bobby" was recast as the tough, dashing, formidable (but still brave and honest) "Crime-Buster"' (quoted in Reiner, 1992:76). However, just around the corner were a series of well-publicised cases that would challenge the reputation for honesty.

The uncovering of corruption in the 1970s

In the space of less than ten years at least four separate corruption scandals involving Metropolitan Police officers were uncovered. It all began with journalists from *The Times* tape-recording conversations between detectives and criminals in which the covering-up of serious crimes was being discussed. Equally as shocking as these revelations was the subsequent apparent inability of those tasked with investigating these abuses to secure co-operation within the force and to discipline those officers involved. This pattern continued with other allegations against officers from the Drug Squad and the Obscene Publications Squad (Cox *et al.*, 1977). There were even allegations towards the end of the decade that detectives had been involved in major armed robberies. Once again, even after the appointment of a new Commissioner – Sir Robert Mark – to tackle the problem, these scandals proved stubbornly resistant to successful investigation. The huge and heralded Operation Countryman (an inquiry into alleged Metropolitan Police corruption headed by the chief constable of Dorset), for example, set up by Mark's successor, Sir David McNee, also petered out in an unseemly exchange of allegations and counter-allegations of malpractice, incompetence and corruption. If the general public had ever accepted the image of George Dixon at something approximating face-value, they were unlikely to do so after this.

Although there was growing concern about police effectiveness and honesty during the 1960s and 1970s, there remained for most of this period a striking lack of political controversy about policing. Whilst the emergence of the 'new' police in the 1820s was the subject of considerable resistance and political debate, much of the history of British policing has been characterised by an absence of political controversy, and a deliberate avoidance of 'politicking' by police representatives. This situation began to change in the 1960s with campaigns for better pay. More recently, however, the Police Federation has become a vocal and influential pressure group, even going so far as to place an advertisement in the national newspapers in the run-up to the 1979 General Election, linking rising crime with the failure of the Labour administration's policies, and recommending a series of changes that were far from dissimilar to those being proposed by the then Conservative opposition. The crucial development which saw the police thrust into the centre of political controversy was the election of the radical Thatcher government. The Thatcher administration was preparing for a period of radical and controversial change which, it was anticipated, would lead to conflict, and in which the police would need to play, or be persuaded to play a central role.

A changing political context: policing since 1979

Soon after the 1979 General Election, the new Conservative government honoured its pledge to implement in full the Edmund Davies Committee's far-reaching recommendations on increasing police pay. Up until this point there had been a large measure of agreement between the two main political parties in relation to the police and policing. However, the increasing political profile of senior officers and other representatives, together with a series of significant public disagreements with Labour Party spokesmen (over the policing of the Grunwick dispute, rising crime rates in the late 1970s, and the policing of the riots in the early 1980s) led to the end of this bipartisan consensus. The policing of the miners' strike in 1984 brought the relationship between the police and the Labour Party to an all time low.

It would be wrong, however, to create the impression that some form of straightforward party political alignment has developed over the past decade. The reality has been that despite Mrs Thatcher's 1985 conference promise that 'the government will continue steadfastly to back the police. If they need more men, more equipment, they shall have them', police criticism of government policy has increased rather than decreased (Rawlings, 1991). There are a number of quite specific reasons for this. These are: the ending of the police's apparent immunity from the government's public expenditure cuts as the equation 'more money equals less crime' began to look increasingly untenable; the problems that are perceived to stem from the Police and Criminal Evidence Act (PACE) 1984 and the introduction of the Crown Prosecution Service; and the ever more visible spectre of privatisation. The relationship between the police and the incumbent government was also lastingly affected by the urban riots of early 1980s and the way in which the police were deployed during the miners' dispute later in the decade.

Urban unrest and policing the riots

During the 1980s the Conservative government introduced what has been described by one commentator as the 'single most significant landmark in the modern development of police powers': the Police and Criminal Evidence Act 1984. The following year it also removed the police's prosecutorial role with the introduction of the Crown Prosecution Service (CPS), and in 1986 passed legislation to alter significantly the public order laws (via the Public Order Act 1986).

All of these developments can, at least in part, be traced back to the urban unrest of 1981.

Although it is the Brixton disorders which are most often remembered, the first 'riot' in 1981 occurred in central London as violence broke out during a protest march organised by the New Cross Massacre Action Committee. Three months later, on 10 April 1981, an hour-long riot occurred in Brixton. This was the prelude to a full weekend of disorder in which over 400 police officers were reported injured, over 250 people arrested, and over 7000 police officers involved in attempting to restore order (Scarman Report, 1982, paras 3.79–3.94). Further serious disorder occurred in Liverpool, and later in the cities of Birmingham, Sheffield, Nottingham and Hull among others. Following a police raid on houses in Railton Road, rioting again broke out in Brixton in July, and then, briefly, again in Liverpool.

As has been suggested, in the aftermath of the 1981 riots Lord Scarman was appointed to inquire into the causes of the unrest in Brixton in April and to make recommendations. From the inception of the 'new' police onwards, there has been disagreement about the main or central functions of the police, and this was an issue that Scarman also tackled and which has continued to be the subject of vigorous debate since. For Sir Robert Peel, the main task for the police was 'crime prevention', though this was extended by Sir Richard Mayne in his 1829 instructions to the 'New Police of the Metropolis' in which he singled out 'the prevention of crime . . . the protection of life and property, the preservation of public tranquillity' as the core policing duties (Emsley, 1983). Scarman, too, was in favour of this formulation, though in the event of a conflict of aims, he felt that the maintenance of public tranquillity was the primary responsibility (doc 8) – i.e. he recognised that there would inevitably be situations in which the enforcement of the law would have to come second to the maintenance of the public peace.

Beginning from this position, Scarman was critical of the policing of Brixton and especially the heavy-handed 'Swamp 81' operation. In response to high levels of street crime, a saturation exercise had been planned in which large numbers of police officers patrolling the streets and using 'stop and search' powers, would attempt to 'detect and arrest burglars and robbers' (Scarman Report, 4.39). During the operation, the officers in the Brixton area made almost 950 'stops', which resulted in 118 arrests. More than half the people stopped were black. A total of 75 charges were brought, though only one was for robbery, one for attempted burglary, and 20 for theft or attempted theft. As a result of his inquiry, Scarman concluded that the lack of consultation with community representatives prior to 'Swamp 81' was 'an error of judgement' (Scarman Report, 4.73), that the whole operation 'was a serious mistake, given the tension which existed between the police and local community' (ibid., 4.76) and that 'had policing attitudes and methods been adjusted to deal fully with the problems of a multi-racial society, there would have been a review in depth of the public order implications of the operation, which would have included local consultation. And, had this taken place, I believe . . . that a street "saturation" operation would not have been launched when it was' (ibid., 4.77).

Scarman's recommendations as a result of the inquiry were wide-ranging and took in such diverse areas as recruitment of ethnic minorities to the police, increasing consultation through the introduction of statutory liaison committees, the introduction of lay visiting to police stations, the independent review of complaints against the police, and the tightening of regulations regarding racially prejudiced behaviour by officers. The Report emphasised the need for change and 'was the trigger for a reorientation of policing on a wide front. Indeed by the late 1980s, (Scarman's) ideas had become the predominant conception of policing philosophy amongst chief constables' (Reiner, 1992). Before this took place, however, there was one other major policing operation which was to have a major effect on the future of the service.

Policing the miners' strike

The tactics employed during this dispute had a profound effect not only on the nature and style of public order policing in this country (Waddington *et al.*, 1989), but also on public perceptions about the police more generally. With respect to the former, Jefferson (1990: 1–2), although using a degree of hyperbole, suggests that the new image of public order policing is 'not one of a line of bobbies defensively "pushing and shoving", but of "snatch squads": menacing teams of officers, unrecognizable in visored, "NATO-style" crash helmets and fireproof overalls, advancing behind transparent shields being banged by drawn truncheons, making "search" sorties into crowds of fleeing demonstrators for the purpose of arrest, or a spot of retributive "destruction".' Despite the rather colourful language, this picture of public order policing accords with what many people will have seen on television over the past ten years.

The turning point in the policing of the 1984–5 miners' strike is widely regarded as being what has since become known as the 'battle of Orgreave'. New training and tactics for public order policing had been instituted in the early 1980s, and the new style which was formulated in the then unpublished ACPO *Public Order Manual of Tactical Options and Related Matters* was first unveiled at Orgreave. Perhaps the most controversial of the manoeuvres adopted was that of using mounted officers to charge into the ranks of the pickets followed by sorties of officers with long shields, short shields and batons, all organised in a highly militaristic manner. The drift towards the type of paramilitarism first evident at Orgreave and later used at many other disputes and demonstrations (Northam, 1989) has led to an extended debate about the likely long-term impact of the use of such tactics. (See, for example, the continuing debate between Jefferson and Waddington which started with their articles in the *British Journal of Criminology*, vol.27, no.1, 1987, and has led to numerous other articles and to two books: Jefferson, 1990; Waddington, 1991.)

What is uncontestable though is that the public image of the police has changed, perhaps for ever. Although militaristic public order policing and 'individualistic' mainstream policing are diametrically opposed, equally they cannot be fully separated (Morgan and Smith, 1989). Waddington (1991) concluded in relation to the strike, that the 'television pictures of a police officer apparently hitting a prostrate picket repeatedly with his truncheon at the Orgreave coke works during the miners' strike did immense damage to the police reputation for restraint'. In addition, however, as Morgan and Smith (1989) suggest 'the change in public order policing has created conditions in which the legitimacy of the police is bound to be examined and questioned more closely than in the past'.

The Police and Criminal Evidence Act 1984

The changing climate within which the police were operating was also signalled by the proposals contained in the draft Police and Criminal Evidence Bill published in 1982, much of which arose out of a report by the Royal Commission on Criminal Procedure (RCCP) published during the previous year. The RCCP focused on the rights of suspects, an issue that had been debated vociferously for some time, but which had been brought to a head by the 'Confait case' in which, it was eventually found, three boys had been convicted of murder on the basis of false confessions. The Judges' Rules, which at that time formed the basis for suspect's rights, were identified by many commentators as being inadequate, and were examined closely by the Royal Commission. The RCCPs report had been controversial when it was published, receiving support from the police but being widely criticised by left and liberal spokespeople inside and outside parliament. The Police and Criminal Evidence Bill which was first introduced in late 1982 went through a number of phases before it reached the form that we now recognise as PACE, and was itself widely criticised by almost all groups that had an interest in it, though there now appears to be a measure of agreement as to its worth. The Act was enacted at the end of 1984, and not only extended police powers in a number of important ways but also introduced far-reaching procedural safeguards (some of which were revised in 1991) to guard against abuses of these powers. There is not the space here to go into great depth about the content of the legislation, but it is worth considering three areas of change in a little detail.

(i) Police investigation

PACE replaced a variety of statutory and common law rules which had previously regulated police investigative powers. Thus, one of the core aims of the Act was to attempt to balance police powers with protections for the arrested person. PACE, which extended police powers of arrest, detention and stop and search, was therefore accompanied by four codes of practice and these replaced the extant Judges' Rules that laid down procedures for the questioning of suspects. The four codes of practice were contained in s.66 of the Act and covered police statutory powers to stop and search; the search of premises and the seizure of property; the detention, treatment and questioning of persons by the police; and identification procedures. A fifth code covering tape-recording of interviews with suspects was introduced subsequently, and in 1991 revised codes of practice, directed primarily at reinforcing the suspect's right to legal advice, came into operation. It appears this may have had quite a significant impact for there is some evidence that the judiciary have adopted a stricter attitude towards infringements of the PACE codes of practice than they did towards the old Judges' Rules (Feldman, 1990). Research on the impact of PACE and the revised codes of practice has, however, been equivocal, with clear gains and continuing problems with regard, for example, both to suspects' rights and complaints against the police (see *inter alia* Brown, 1989; Brown *et al.*, 1992; Maguire and Corbett, 1991; McConville *et al.*, 1991). There can be little doubt, however, that the Act has had an impact on the behaviour of police officers, and on the culture of policing, and the worst fears of its critics should certainly have been allayed (Benyon and Bourn, 1986).

(ii) Police accountability

Lord Scarman's chief recommendation on accountability was that local community consultative committees should be set up. In Scarman's view, there had been insufficient formal liaison between the black community and the police in and around Brixton, and the absence of such communication was both a symptom and a cause of the 'withdrawal of consent' that underpinned the policing problems in the area (Morgan, 1992c). He concluded that 'a police force which does not consult locally will fail to be efficient'.

Scarman dashed the hopes of many critics of the existing arrangements by endorsing the 'tripartite' structure. He did, however, suggest that police authorities could act more effectively and vigorously if there were better arrangements for local consultation in areas considerably smaller than those covered by whole forces. He favoured the introduction of a statutory duty to make such arrangements 'at police divisional or sub-divisional levels'. This, as Morgan (1992c) concludes, 'was the participative mechanism on which he pinned his faith that policing would in future be more congruent with the wishes of people locally.'

Scarman's recommendation that local consultative committees should be established was quickly followed by a Home Office Circular (54/1982) supporting such arrangements and, as an illustration of the influence of Home Office Circulars in the area of policing generally, a large number of police authorities, in the main supported by their chief constables, established such committees in their regions. Statutory provision for the making of arrangements 'in each police area for obtaining the views of the people in that area about matters concerning the policing of the area and for obtaining their cooperation with the police in preventing crime in the area' were introduced under s.106 of the Police and Criminal Evidence Act 1984 (PACE).

On the basis of his analysis of the varied political and administrative statements, oral and textual, issued by ministers and civil servants since 1981, Morgan (1992c) suggests that police consultative committees (PCCs) have, at least in the minds of officials, four major objectives. The first is as a forum in which consumers of police services may articulate and communicate to the providers of the service what it is they want. This is related to Scarman's view that effective policing can only be maintained if the police are aware of public concerns and priorities. The second aim is the perceived need to educate the public. This arises from the simple observation that given that police resources are finite, they need to be rationed in some fashion. Consequently, one way of avoiding the widespread alienation that would follow from the police continually failing to meet public expectations, is to persuade the public, through education, to temper the demands they make on the police. The third function of PCCs, he suggests, is to resolve conflict. Given that policing involves coercive powers and, indeed, that the communities being policed may impose conflicting demands on the police (Smith, 1987), it is necessary to have forums in which disputes can be resolved. Finally, he suggests, the hope was that PCCs would form the basis for police–public co-operation for crime-preventive activities.

The Scarman Report was widely criticised for having recommended statutory consultation rather than control by some form of elected police authority, and whilst the latter might not have been the solution to the problem of accountability, the available evidence does not suggest that the consultative committees have been particularly successful either. Research by Morgan and colleagues (Morgan, 1987; Morgan, 1989; Morgan and Maggs, 1985) found that PCCs were, in the main, dominated by police and police authority members, and that they seldom contained people who were or were likely to be critical of the police. Consequently, police accounts tend to dominate proceedings and tend to be accepted by the committees. Morgan concludes that in terms of accountability PCCs have achieved little other than legitimising current practices and arrangements.

One further development which also arose out of recommendations made by Lord Scarman in his report on the Brixton disturbances also needs to be described here. He suggested that there 'should be random checks by persons other than police officers on the interrogation and detention of suspects in the police station' (Scarman Report, 1981:s.7.10). The Home Office issued a guideline document in 1983 and pilot schemes were established in six police authorities and one Metropolitan Police District. There was considerable delay before the Home Office subsequently issued a Circular (12/86) which commended the introduction of lay visiting schemes 'wherever local wishes and circumstances might make them appropriate'. Arrangements for schemes are left to individual police authorities, and their objectives are stated to be 'to enable members of the local community to observe, comment and report upon the conditions under which persons are detained at police stations and the operation in practice of the statutory and other rules governing their welfare, with a view to securing greater understanding of, and confidence in, these matters' (quoted in Kemp and Morgan, 1990).

Lay visitors were to be allowed access to areas of police stations where 'persons are detained pending interview, release or production in court, including the cells, charge areas, detention rooms and medical rooms . . . [but] not CID or other operational areas'. They were to be allowed to speak to detained persons, including remand prisoners, examine documents such as custody records which relate to their detention and treatment whilst in the station, but not records which relate to the investigation of any offences it is believed they may have committed. However, the police retain considerable control over access to prisoners. Thus, seeing detained persons or their custody records requires the written consent of the detainee, and it is the responsibility of the officer in charge of the station to obtain that consent. Permission can be withheld by the police in 'exceptional circumstances', and interviews in progress may not be interrupted.

The rights of suspects in police stations had been a central concern of PACE, though the arrangements for lay visiting were not, unlike police consultative committees (PCCs), made statutory under the Act. The creation of PCCs, the introduction of lay visiting and new rules governing the treatment of suspects in police stations were all, at least to an extent, part of a general process of increasing the visibility of police activities with a view, as Circular 12/86 outlining lay visiting suggested, to increasing public confidence in such work.

Finally under this section on accountability it is important to mention one further development although, strictly speaking, it does not relate to the Police and Criminal Evidence Act. As has been suggested, the early 1980s were a time in which policing in general and the tripartite structure in particular came under increased scrutiny (Reiner, 1993). In the local government elections in 1981 radical Labour councils were returned in all the Metropolitan areas, and the police authorities in those areas gradually began to attempt to exercise some of their powers. There were a number of major clashes between authorities and chief constables – several key exchanges are described later in the paper – and such conflict contributed to the overall disenchantment with which the government viewed these particular councils. The Local Government Act 1985 abolished these authorities, and replaced them with joint boards which, it has been argued, have proved more accommodating to police influence than their predecessors (Loveday, 1987; Reiner, 1993). Joint Boards were made up of nominees of constituent district councils and, as far as it was practicable, the membership reflected the local party political balance. In general this meant a move away from Labour domination or control in the metropolitan areas (Loveday, 1991) and, additionally, resulted in an increased profile for the magistrate members of police authorities.

(iii) Police complaints

Largely as a result of the pressures stemming from the corruption scandals of the 1970s the government set up a part-time lay body, the Police Complaints Board (PCB) in 1976 to monitor the investigation of complaints against the police. The PCB achieved remarkably little, however, and was replaced by the Police Complaints Authority (PCA) after PACE. The PCA is a full-time body with the power to supervise investigations of any serious complaint – those in which it is alleged that the actions of an officer led to the death of or serious injury to a member of the public, or any other case it deems to be in the public interest. Procedures for the informal resolution of minor complaints were also introduced. Research has contained both positive and negative conclusions about the operation of the new system in practice. On the one hand, it has been suggested that the system is staffed by committed and able police investigators; that police officers responsible for complaints and discipline were increasingly impressed by it; and that the 'informal resolution' procedure appeared promising. On the other hand, there still appears to be an overwhelming majority of 'dissatisfied customers' – be they officers or complainants (Maguire and Corbett, 1991). The subject of police complaints has always aroused considerable debate, and there would seem to be continuing suspicion by the public of any system that involves the police investigating themselves, and suspicion by officers themselves of bureaucracies which they feel are unsympathetic to the job they are faced with. Widely known by officers as the 'Prosecute Coppers Association', the PCA attracted a motion of no confidence at the Police Federation's Annual Conference in 1989 (Rawlings, 1991).

Financing the police

Not only did the Conservative Party use the issue of 'law and order' as one of the central planks of its platform in 1979, but, as has been suggested, the Thatcher administration moved quickly once elected to put some of its financial promises into practice. The recommendations of the Edmund-Davies Committee were implemented quickly, and, in addition, police manpower – as it is generally still referred to – increased by just over 6% in the period 1979–84. More remarkably, in the same period public expenditure on the police doubled from £1,644 million to £3,358 million. Recorded crime continued to rise, however, despite this increased financial commitment. The total number of notifiable offences stood at just over 2.5 million in 1979 but had risen by approximately 37% to almost 3.5 million by 1984 [doc 9]. In addition, the official clear-up rate for notifiable offences declined from 41% in 1979 to 35% in 1984. What is more these trends continued throughout the 1980s: expenditure on the police rose a further 20% by 1987 (see Fig. 3.1) whereas notifiable offences rose a further 6% to over 3.7 million (see Fig. 3.2) and clear-ups fell to 33% (*Social Trends* volumes 11–19).

Perhaps not surprisingly against this background, from approximately 1982/3 onwards, the government began vigorously to pursue its 'Financial Management Initiative' (FMI), designed to encourage efficiency and cost savings by applying private sector management methods to the public sector, and imposing market disciplines on them. Although initially it looked as if the police might be safe from such scrutiny, the publication of Home Office circular 114/1983 (and later the even tougher 106/1988), largely without consultation with police representative bodies, signalled that the financial climate had changed. The circular outlined potential new management strategies for the police – now generally referred to as 'Policing by Objectives' (PBO) – many of which had influential supporters within the police. Kenneth Newman, for example, had introduced very similar initiatives into the Metropolitan Police before the circular was published. Nevertheless, both ACPO and the Police Federation were, on occasion, very hostile to the new emphasis on 'value for money'. This core issue in this conflict has been summed up by Rawlings (1991:46) as the government's view that 'PBO will lead to a more efficient and effective use of resources and, almost as a by-product, will tend to hold down the numbers of police officers and so reduce costs, police organisations regard its primary objective as being the cutting of expenditure through a reduction in the number of police officers without any real concern about the effect this may have on policing'.

In addition to the problem that crime continued to rise inexorably despite the increase in resources, one of the key reasons that the conservative government felt able to adopt such a stringent financial policy, particularly in its second term of office, was that recorded levels of public satisfaction with the police had been declining for some years. Although public confidence remained high with 85% of the public who had an opinion rating the performance of the police

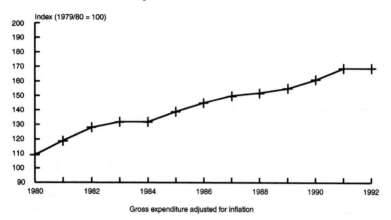

Fig. 3.1   Police expenditure

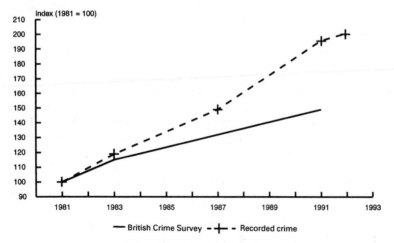

Fig. 3.2   Notifiable offences

as either 'good' or 'very good' in 1988, the trend was nevertheless
in a downwards direction. Thus, for example, 92% of the public had
rated the police in that manner in 1982, and other data from the
three British Crime Surveys conducted in the 1980s showed that the
proportion of the public who gave the police the highest possible rating
dropped from just over one third in 1982 to under a quarter in 1988

(Mayhew *et al.*, 1989). Furthermore, this decline in confidence was observed in most major social groups and communities including those non-Metropolitan areas traditionally supportive of the police (Skogan, 1990; Tuck, 1989).

The spectre of privatisation

The 1980s also saw the emergence of an issue that had begun to threaten other public services: privatisation. Privatisation and the FMI were of course linked, for as police representatives were quick to point out, restrictions on manpower and resources increase the opportunities for competitors to provide services hitherto the preserve of the police. Recent years have seen considerable increases in the size and significance of the private security sector, increasing civilianisation (and use of 'specials') within the police, plans to privatise the Police National Computer and to formalise a customer/contractor relationship between police forces and the Forensic Science Service, each of which gave some credence to police fears.

The impact of both financial constraint and the spectre of privatisation was to open up a debate about the future shape of policing in Britain. Throughout the 1980s, as the Conservative Party increasingly turned its attention to the police, so ACPO and the Federation became ever more visible in public debate, and the Labour Party belatedly entered the fray with a range of proposals for policing, many of which were very close to the opinions being expressed by senior officers (Reiner, 1992; Sheerman, 1991). The apolitical stance of senior officers, and the previously existing bipartisan consensus on policing have both disappeared, but they have not been replaced by an easily identifiable alignment between police representatives and one or both of the major political parties. The accord in the early 1980s between the police and the Thatcher government was undermined by the FMI and the threat of increasing privatisation, together with an attempt from the centre to gradually increase control of the police through Home Office circulars, the expansion of the Common Police Services budget and the National Criminal Intelligence Service. Indeed, Reiner (1991 and 1992) has suggested that we now have a *de facto* national police force.

It was, in part at least, the increased scrutiny of the police by the government pursuing its FMI, and the inability of the police to control local crime rates, together with declining public confidence in the police, that was the driving force behind a renewed evaluation of the police function, and a desire by some senior officers to reassess the role and function of the service. One consequence of this was increasing attention on the idea of the prevention of crime, and an growing emphasis on the role of the 'community' in the prevention and detection of crime.

Crime prevention and community policing

As one example, although crime prevention has since the inception of the new police been thought of as a key function of the service, there has generally been a lack of clarity about exactly what this is to mean in practice. Indeed, it was not until after the publication of the report of the Cornish Committee on the Prevention and Detection of Crime (Home Office, 1965b) that specialist crime prevention departments began to come into being in any number. The Committee recommended, *inter alia*, the need for specialist police officers who would be experts in crime prevention technology; that an officer of at least the rank of inspector take the role of force crime prevention officer, and that a more professional approach was needed in respect of the publicity material used by the police.

Perhaps anticipating one of the potential problems with this approach, the committee pointed out that the creation of the specialism should not be taken to imply that the responsibility of other officers with regard to crime prevention had lessened. Furthermore, in what has by now become a standard crime prevention argument, it emphasised the importance of building relationships with organisations outside the police, and as part of this process of eliciting such support it recommended the setting up of 'crime prevention panels'.

Such panels have no formal status and have generally been chaired by the police themselves (Home Office, 1971). Their purpose is to consider crime prevention proposals and to help in the process of publicising campaigns and initiatives aimed at improving (usually physical) security measures. Because of their lack of status and the fact that there has never been any requirement to set them up in local areas, crime prevention panels developed in a largely *ad hoc* way and, following the lead taken by the nascent crime prevention departments which exercised a strong influence over them (Home Office, 1971), tended to focus fairly narrowly on physical security (Gladstone, 1980).

Despite the apparent rise in the stock of crime prevention with central government, responsibility within police forces for crime prevention work remains the domain of specialist crime prevention units and crime prevention officers (CPOs). It is worth considering briefly what it is that these officers do. In the main, crime prevention is a small-scale police specialism, with crime prevention officers (CPOs) usually representing less than 1% of a force's establishment (Harvey *et al.*, 1989) and rarely occupying ranks higher than chief inspector. Crime prevention officers are usually located within departments with 'community' in their title (community liaison, community involvement and so on) or within CID. Whatever the location, crime prevention work tends to remain fairly marginal rarely permeating 'the force much beyond the designated officers, whatever the line of responsibility upwards' (Harvey *et al.*, 1989:88).

The relatively narrow focus of crime prevention panels has largely been replicated within police forces, and recent research tends to suggest that the tasks actually undertaken by CPOs have, in practice, been very limited. Harvey *et al.* (1989) found that although a broad range of officers within community liaison departments or their equivalents felt that they were engaged in crime prevention work, there was a tendency for force CPOs to demarcate very clearly between crime prevention work and 'community' work. Particular emphasis, for example, was placed on the need for technical or hardware expertise, and this 'bias' was reinforced in the training CPOs received at the Stafford Crime Prevention Centre.

In a similar vein, research on the work of CPOs in London (Johnston *et al.*, 1993), based on observation and worksheets, concluded that the majority of work undertaken by the officers fell into the following ten categories: residential surveys, commercial/industrial surveys, alarm problems, firearms, displays, talks, designing out crime, initiatives, crime panels, and training. Although, once again, this is quite a broad list, the research suggests that the vast majority of CPOs' time was devoted to surveys and to meetings about firearms and alarms. The bulk of the work was of a technical variety, largely concerned with target hardening, surveillance, entry/exit screening and access control – all standard techniques of 'situational prevention' (Clarke, 1992).

Johnston *et al.* (1993) also argued that because much of the work is of a fairly narrow technical kind that most police 'crime prevention activity (is) largely *reactive*, responding to the demands of the public to do surveys . . . or responding to the need of the service in general to try to reduce the time spent of false alarm calls' (Johnston *et al.*, 1993:5). The work of crime prevention design advisors was more proactive, but little connection was found between this work and local crime problems. They concluded that although the work was justifiable in that it was largely done in response to public demand, the delivery of the service 'was not co-ordinated with the rest of the policing service, nor was it necessarily planned to focus on the Division's main priorities for crime prevention'.

Where more socially-based or 'community' initiatives were undertaken, it was generally unclear on what basis they were being encouraged. Thus, Harvey *et al.* (1989:90) suggest: 'In the plethora of activities initiated and encouraged – soccer, netball, youth clubs, "Cops, Kids and Carols" concerts, shooting (sic), and schools liaison – the common good seems to be the encouragement of friendly relationships between police and juveniles. Work described as crime prevention sometimes appears, in fact, to be principally public relations with no clearly articulated connection between a good press and crime preventive effects'.

As crime continued to rise, despite the increase in resources devoted to policing in the early 1980s, one of the key messages emanating from the police was they could not be expected to carry responsibility for the prevention of crime unaided. As a result, increasing emphasis came to placed upon the 'community' both in relation to policing generally and, more specifically, in relation to crime prevention (cf Willmott, 1987). Indeed, the impetus for this began even earlier, crucial in this regard being a Home Office circular (211/1978, which became known as the Ditchley circular). This recommended improved co-ordination between criminal justice agencies, together with community-based initiatives as a solution to what was perceived at that time to be the piecemeal approach to dealing with juveniles.

The so-called 'community-policing' approach that developed is most closely associated with John Alderson, the one-time Chief Constable of Devon and Cornwall, who emphasised the importance of close relationships between police and public and, consequently, the broad service role of his constabulary (Alderson, 1979). The emphasis upon community and upon what has since become known as 'inter-agency co-operation' broadened the focus of crime prevention from its previous preoccupation with technology, 'target-hardening' and opportunity reduction, to the social conditions which provide the context of, and the social organisations which are involved in regulating that behaviour defined as criminal. Such an approach has been quite widely referred to as 'social crime prevention' (Clarke, 1981) to distinguish it from 'situational crime prevention' (Clarke and Mayhew, 1980; Clarke, 1992), and whilst this distinction is not necessarily always helpful (Bottoms, 1990a), it nevertheless retains considerable currency within criminology. The changing emphasis within crime prevention was also reflected, for example, in the curriculum at the Home Office Training Centre at Stafford which, according to Laycock and Heal (1989), moved away from 'the previous locks and bars emphasis towards community involvement, crime pattern analysis and inter-agency work'.

Community-focused policing initiatives were many and varied during the 1980s, and although little rigorously collected evidence is available, there is little to suggest that much success has been achieved. Thus, research on *inter alia* community constables (Brown and Iles, 1985), directed patrolling (Burrows and Lewis, 1988), focused patrolling (Chatterton and Rogers, 1989), neighbourhood policing (Irving *et al.*, 1989) and Neighbourhood Watch (Husain, 1988; Bennett, 1990; McConville and Shepherd, 1992) has illustrated the difficulties in planning, implementing and evaluating community-focused crime prevention measures. Implementation is perhaps the important word here for the majority of problems that have been identified have stemmed from programme failure (Hope, 1985) rather than, it is argued, fundamental flaws in the philosophy that underpins them.

Though initially treated as a peripheral specialism of low status and interest when placed alongside crime fighting (Graef, 1989), the 1980s saw an increasing emphasis placed on crime prevention, with a concomitant rise in the visibility of such work (or at least the publicity given to the work) within the police, to the point at which Reiner (1992:99) even felt able to assert that crime prevention departments became the 'belles of the ball'. Though this is a considerable overstatement, a number of very significant changes did take place during the 1980s, and in his review of these developments, Bottoms (1990a) highlights the setting up of the Crime Prevention Unit in the Home Office in 1983, the issuing of the 1984 interdepartmental circular on crime prevention (Home Office and others, 1984), the two seminars on crime prevention held at 10 Downing Street in 1986 – one chaired by the Prime Minister the other by the Home Secretary – the 'Five Towns Initiative' launched in 1986, followed by the Safer Cities Programme in 1988 and the launch of the charity Crime Concern. To this list one might add the reconstituting of the Home Office Standing Conference on Crime Prevention, the second Home Office circular which updated 8/84, and the formation of the ACPO sub-committee on crime prevention. Bottoms concluded that:

By any standards, this is a formidable list of developments. The 1980s, we can safely assert, has put crime prevention firmly on the map: a conclusion which is true not only in Britain, but also, at a minimum, in France, in the Netherlands and in the Council of Europe.

The current situation is, as has been argued, one in which there are mixed messages about crime prevention. Central government stresses the importance of crime prevention initiatives and programmes and, at least at a rhetorical level, argues that the prevention of crime should be considered to be a central part of the standard policing function. Similarly, the police themselves are quick to support the idea that this area of work remains fundamental. By contrast, however, the reality within the police is rather different. As the research of both Harvey *et al.* (1989) and Johnston *et al.* (1993) that was reported above shows, CPOs and the departments within which they work remain fairly marginal within most police forces, and crime prevention work remains a fairly narrowly defined specialism. More importantly perhaps even than this is the fact that despite the increasing emphasis upon community involvement and multi-agency work, the fundamental weakness in crime prevention policy is that it is generally unclear which agency has primary responsibility for crime prevention (see Jones *et al.*, 1994, ch.2)

Into the 1990s

The renewed scrutiny of the police which followed the period after the miners' strike and the introduction of PACE was, in this case, stimulated by the continuing increase in levels of crime, and the uncovering of a large number of miscarriages of justice. The release of the Guildford Four, the Birmingham Six, the Maguires, the acquittal on appeal of the 'Tottenham Three', and the widespread allegations concerning the West

Midlands Serious Crimes Squad led, directly or otherwise, to a situation in which public confidence in the police fell to an all-time low. Calls for a new Royal Commission on the Police have been staunchly resisted by successive Home Secretaries, but the seriousness of the Birmingham and Guildford cases made some form of review inevitable, and the Home Secretary responded by appointing a Royal Commission on Criminal Justice, to be chaired by Lord Runciman.

Successive Commissioners of Police have instituted major programmes of reform aimed at improving police–public relations, and a largely 'service-based, consumerist' view of policing is now espoused by police managers' (Reiner, 1992). It has looked for some time, however, that internal reorganisation and re-presentation was going to prove insufficient, and the possibility of even more significant change was signalled by the appointment of a reformist Home Secretary, Kenneth Clarke, after the 1992 General Election. Those who had followed the career of Mr Clarke through the Departments of Health and Education expected swift and far-reaching action, and they were not disappointed, for within six months of his taking office he had instituted two reviews of different aspects of policing. Three inquiries which were in whole or in part focusing on policing were therefore set in train. It is worth considering here both the remits of these inquiries and the broad recommendations coming from each.

The White Paper on Police Reform

The chances of there being radical reform increased with the announcement by Clarke to the Home Affairs Committee that he was considering the possibility of reforming the structure of policing and of the structure of accountability of the police. This review, which was conducted entirely within the Home Office, had no official terms of reference. Despite, or perhaps because of this lack of official profile, it managed to cause at least as much controversy as the other inquiries put together. The furore – in which it was reported that Mr Major had stepped in to chair a cabinet sub-committee meeting on the review in order to calm a row ironically between Clarke and the then Environment Secretary, but now Home Secretary, Michael Howard – was apparently caused by a proposal to remove some elected members from police authorities and to replace them with businessmen. The course of the inquiry was accompanied by a succession of leaks to the press, and the 'kites which were flown' included the possibility of reducing the number of police forces by up to half; the privatisation of a number of current policing functions; the removal of any local funding of the police; and the abolition of local police authorities and their replacement with government appointed boards.

When on 28 June 1993 the Home Secretary eventually made a statement in Parliament, the plans that he suggested would be contained in the Police Bill in the autumn did indeed contain many of the proposals that had been discussed in the press in the previous months. They included:

1   Altering the composition of elected police authorities so that the 16-person committees would comprise eight local councillors and three magistrates being joined by five members appointed by the Home Secretary 'for their management or financial experience and local knowledge'.
2   Introducing an advisory body for London to help the Home Secretary 'oversee the performance' of the Metropolitan Police.
3   Introducing national league performance tables utilising approximately six key performance indicators such as response times to emergency calls and clear-up rates.
4   Giving chief constables greater financial control over local budgets but also introducing strict cash limits.
5   Moving the focus of policing from force headquarters to local or basic command units.
6   Encouraging the recruitment of up to an extra 10,000 specials, and extending their role to include beat duties.
7   At some stage in the future an as yet unspecified number of forces may be amalgamated, but this is unlikely to happen until some of the other major reforms have been implemented.

Reactions from the police staff associations were varied. The Police Federation were critical of the proposal to redesign police authorities, their chairman, Alan Eastwood, suggesting that it was a blow for local democracy. The Superintendents' Association opposed the proposal for the introduction of national league tables on the grounds that there was a risk that they would simply measure quantity rather than quality, and might fail to take account of local differences. By contrast, John Barrow, the President of ACPO, welcomed elements of the Report – particularly the proposals for greater financial freedom for senior officers and for the new pay formula, though he too was critical of the plans for police authorities. We will return to the Police and Magistrates' Courts Act below.

The Sheehy Inquiry

Announced to general surprise at the Police Federation conference in May 1992, the terms of reference of the inquiry were 'To examine the rank structure, remuneration, and conditions of the police service in England and Wales, in Scotland and in Northern Ireland, and to recommend what changes, if any, would be sensible'. It was chaired by Sir Patrick Sheehy, the chairman of BAT industries, and its other members were: Mr John Bullock (Joint Senior Partner, Coopers

Lybrand), Professor Colin Campbell (Vice Chancellor, Nottingham University), Mr Eric Caines (Director of Personnel, NHS), and Sir Paul Fox (former Managing Director, BBC Television). It was intentional that none of the members of the Inquiry had any experience of policing.

The Inquiry eventually reported on 1 July 1993 (Inquiry into Police Responsibilities and Rewards, 1993) just two days after the publication of the White Paper and, once again given the level of discussion in the press prior to its publication, contained little in the way of surprises. It made 272 recommendations in all designed, it was suggested, to 'reward good performance and penalise bad'. Some of the major recommendations included:

1 New recruits to the police to be hired on ten-year fixed-term contracts which would be considered for renewal subsequently every five years.
2 Abolition of the ranks of deputy chief constable, chief super-intendent and chief inspector.
3 The introduction of a severance programme to enable the termination of the contracts of up to 5,000 middle-ranking and senior officers.
4 The introduction of performance-related pay, with up to 30% of the salaries of chief constables and their assistants being linked to performance-related bonuses.
5 The reduction of starting pay and the linking of pay rates to non-manual private sector earnings.
6 The ending of many forms of overtime payment and the freezing of housing allowances.

Reactions to the Sheehy Inquiry Report were varied. The Police Federation reacted negatively arguing that the recommendations would remove the vocational aspect of the work, turning it into a 'job like any other job' ('Police threaten "open conflict"', *Financial Times*, 1 July 1993). The Superintendents' Association echoed this sentiment suggesting that recruitment, retention and motivation would all be hit by the proposals, though there was cautious approval from some quarters for the financial and structural re-organisation heralded by the Report.

In the main the proposals contained in both the Sheehy Inquiry Report and the White Paper were discussed together by the national press, and one academic commentator suggested that 'though separate, these two initiatives must be regarded as a single centralising package' (Waddington, 1993). His argument was that the White Paper's proposal to reduce local authority representation on police authorities and the Sheehy Inquiry's support for the introduction of fixed-term contracts that would be reviewed by the Home Office was merely another element in a century-long process involving the 'gradual accretion of central control over the police'. This was certainly the implication drawn in relation to the White Paper by *Police Review* (2 July 1993) whose editorial comment concluded: 'This White Paper is committed to devolving command to basic units while it creates a strong central control system. It could be named the "Home Office Rules"'.

The Royal Commission on Criminal Justice

Set up in the aftermath of the release of the Birmingham Six in March 1991, the first Royal Commission to consider the police since that appointed in 1960 was given wide terms of reference, but not wide enough according to some critics. Sir John May had been appointed in October 1989 to lead an inquiry into the circumstances surrounding the convictions of the Guildford Four and the Maguires, and the eventual overturning of the convictions for Birmingham pub bombings prompted a broad review of criminal justice.

The Home Secretary, Kenneth Baker, announcing the appointment of the Royal Commission under Lord Runciman, said that the aim of the review would be to 'minimise so far as possible the likelihood of such (miscarriages of justice) happening again. The review was to cover all stages of the criminal justice process: the investigation and pre-trial stages (the management of the investigation by the police and the role of the prosecutor); the role of expert witnesses and, in particular, that of forensic scientists and the reliability of scientific evidence; the place of the right of silence in criminal proceedings; the possibility of a role for investigating magistrates; the conduct of criminal trials and the duties and powers of the courts. In addition, the review was to examine appeals procedures, the powers of the Court of Appeal, and the investigation of alleged miscarriages of justice once appeal rights have been exhausted – including the functions at present carried out by the Home Secretary' (Hansard, 14 March 1991, 1109–10).

The Commission reported on Tuesday 6 July 1993 and its report included a total of 352 recommendations (Royal Commission on Criminal Justice, 1993). Many of these focused upon court procedures – such as the right to trial by jury, the right of silence and the introduction of an element of formal plea bargaining – though some were directed at the police, though they were largely uncontroversial and were perhaps not as far-reaching as some commentators had expected. Thus, the Commission in deciding that it would not be necessary to have supporting evidence for confessions in order to secure a conviction, recommended that police investigations should not be closed down after a confession is made. Interviewing training should be given to all officers, it suggested, and training in the supervision of investigations is also necessary, the Commission argued, as is improved management and supervision of 'specialist squads'. Continuous videotaping of police custody suites should also be brought in, and the taping of witness statements should be increased. It also recommended that custody records should be computerised and that all forces should have a helpline that officers could use to report any concerns that they had about malpractice of fellow officers. The Commission defended the retention of the right of silence. Some commentators have suggested that this defence was rather 'half-hearted' (Sanders and Young, 1994: 374) and, as we shall see, legislation has recently been passed which significantly amends this 'right'. Finally, the Commission suggested that the acquittal of an officer in criminal proceedings should not be a bar to disciplinary proceedings with possible dismissal, and that the standard of proof should not be the same as that in a criminal court.

The Home Office Review of Core and Ancillary Tasks

This, however, was not the last of the reviews of policing set up at this time. In addition to the Royal Commission, the Sheehy Inquiry, and the internal Home Office review which led to the White Paper, a further inquiry – known as the Review of Core and Ancillary Tasks – was also set in train. The terms of reference of the review were: 'To examine the services provided by the police, to make recommendations about the most cost-effective way of delivering core police services and to assess the scope for relinquishing ancillary tasks.' The starting point for the review team was the observation that demands on the police continue to grow at a rate that outstrips increases in police resources and places a strain on the service. They suggest, therefore, that 'some of the resources needed to improve performance in core areas of work supporting key and national objectives will have to be found by releasing resources currently absorbed by peripheral non-essential tasks or by finding more cost-effective ways of delivering core tasks'. The Inquiry was, in essence, a further step along the road towards privatisation of certain police functions. Although the initial aims of the Inquiry appear to have been modified as work has progressed, the underlying rationale continues to be the desire to limit public expenditure in this area. An interim report from the Inquiry was published late in 1994 (Home Office, 1994b) and the Final Report will be published in 1995.

The Home Office Review of Core and Ancillary Tasks has explicitly looked for ways to extend one particular form of privatisation – contracting-out – to the police service. Although few would advocate a wholesale 'hiving off' of policing, there are organisations, such as private security firms, carrying out functions which overlap with police activities. When policing is seen in its broad symbolic sense, it is much easier to portray it as a public good which must be provided by the state. But when it is broken down into its constituent functions, it is possible to identify tasks which could be, and sometimes already are, undertaken by organisations other than the police. Hiving off these functions to private organisations would arguably allow the police to concentrate on their 'core' activities without undermining their position.

The Police and Magistrates' Courts Act 1994

As has been suggested above, the Police and Magistrates' Courts Bill caused considerable controversy both inside and outside Parliament. Much of the controversy surrounded differing interpretations of the likely implications of the Bill for the governance of the police. Thus, for example, Sir John Smith, then President of ACPO, took the view that 'we are witnessing a move, perhaps unintended, for national control of the police by central government'. Such an interpretation was stoutly resisted by government spokesmen, with Lord Mackay, who introduced the Bill in the House of Lords saying, 'This is not the centralisation of policing, as is often suggested. It is precisely the reverse. It is giving away to police authorities and to chief constables various powers which the Home Secretary presently has. It is making those local police authorities stronger, more independent and more influential. It is enabling policing to be done locally, to be the responsibility of local people, and for policing to be accountable to local people'.

The proposals for restructuring local police authorities were discussed at length in the Second Reading debate in the House of Lords in January 1994, and such was the strength of opposition across the benches that the Home Secretary immediately dropped the proposal that he have the power to appoint the chairman of the authorities, and also that all authorities be limited to 16 members. After a further debate in the Lords the proposal that the Home Secretary also appoint the five (or larger number in bigger authorities) new non-elected members was also withdrawn. It is now accepted that authorities will be able to choose their own chairmen, and in each police authority area there will be a local selection panel consisting of one person appointed by the Home Secretary, one by existing members of the police authority, and the third chosen by the other two. This panel will select a shortlist of 20 candidates, from which the Home Secretary will choose ten to go forward to the final round, when the councillor and magistrate members will select the final five appointees.

The newly constituted police authorities are required to determine objectives for the policing of the authority's area during the forthcoming financial year; to issue a plan setting out the proposed arrangements for the policing of the authority's area for the year ('the local policing plan'); to include in the local policing plan a statement of the authority's priorities for the year, of the resources expected to be available and of the intended allocation of those resources; and that a draft of the local policing plan 'shall be prepared by the chief constable for the area and submitted by him to the authority for it to consider'.

These proposals, together with a degree of financial devolution, formed the basis of the government's claim that the new police authorities will be independent strengthened bodies, with powers to hold local chiefs to account. With regard to finance, in the Lords debate, Lord Mackay said that the new police authorities would 'be free-standing with their own money and their own standard spending assessments. Decisions about policing will be taken by the police authority. They will not be taken by a committee of a local authority which can be over-ruled by the local authority.' The police authorities will therefore be independent of local councils, yet subject to significant oversight by the Home Office, a situation which prompted Vernon Bogdanor to claim that 'the Bill establishes a national police force under the control of the Home Secretary' (*The Times*, 19.1.94). What then are the controls that may be exercised by the Home Office?

The Act enables the Home Secretary to set objectives for policing and to require police authorities to set performance targets for measuring the achievement of those objectives. It also enables him to issue codes of practice relating to the exercise of police authority functions. Reinforcing the importance of national objectives, Lord Mackay said in opening the debate on the Bill in the Lords that 'the primary duty of each police authority will be to secure the maintenance of an efficient and effective police force . . . this small but important change will ensure that police authorities give priority not only to achieving value for money with the resources available, but also to ensure that the results are consistent with the objectives that have been set'.

What is contained in the Act goes beyond setting targets for the police. First of all, the Home Secretary will determine a set of objectives, and following that he may then direct individual police authorities to establish performance targets. A variety of individually tailored conditions may be added to these, depending on his view of the force and the authority. Police authorities will, therefore, have to follow a set of objectives established annually by the Home Secretary, they will have to establish targets and formulate a local policing plan, but they will not be allowed to do this independently. The local objectives will have to be consistent with national ones. Furthermore, the Home Secretary will be able to issue codes of practice for the new authorities, and local policing plans will be governed by these codes and by directions to be issued by the Home Secretary. Thus, as one commentator has argued, the context of the functions of police authorities is to be substantially different, for it may reasonably be inferred that part of HMIC's function in future will include reporting on the performance of the authority's duties as well as those of the force (Grenyer, *Police Review*, 24 December 1993).

The Act also gives the Home Secretary powers to order force amalgamations. Because the proposals over the constitution of local police authorities dominated the political debate at the time, the issue of force amalgamations – touted so strongly prior to Sheehy – was largely overlooked. The Home Secretary said that he had no immediate plans for amalgamating forces and yet the Police and Magistrates' Courts Act includes striking new powers. It gives the Home Secretary power to amalgamate forces without having any form of local inquiry as would be the case under the 1964 Police Act, and contains no requirement on him to justify his plans before an independent inspector, or even to do more than give reasons to those that have objections to his proposals. This certainly represents a remarkable concentration of power centrally over decisions about the structure of local forces.

Finally, the Act replaces the existing provisions on police grant under which the Home Secretary refunds 51 per cent of police expenditure. Under the terms of the Act each police authority will receive a cash limited amount of police grant, though there is still confusion over how grants are to be allocated in the future. The new police authorities will also receive funding through revenue support grant, non-domestic rates and the council tax. The Act establishes new police authorities as major precepting bodies for local government finance purposes. In terms of financial devolution, the Home Secretary no longer decides how many police officers a police force will have. That is to be decided by the chief constable and the police authority.

One crucial new power contained in the Act is that which enables the Home Secretary to direct police authorities to spend above a certain amount in total – that is to increase any precept that is made. It seems likely that such a measure has been introduced at least partially after the recent experience of Derbyshire Constabulary which has twice been refused a certificate of efficiency after local disagreements over a realistic budget for the force. The Home Office minister, Charles Wardle, described Derbyshire County Council as having made 'adverse spending choices'. The new powers will allow the Home Office to dictate, where it considers necessary, increased expenditure on policing against the will of the local police authority.

One of the issues that has not been resolved by the Act is the anomalous position of the Metropolitan Police. The Home Secretary is set to remain the police authority for the capital despite his predecessor's view that 'London needs a police authority, and the arrangement whereby the Home Secretary is in theory the police authority for London is not adequate if we are to hold the Metropolitan Police to account, and if we are to assist them by giving clearer guidance on priorities' (Kenneth Clarke, 1993, quoted in Hansard 18.1.94). A body is to be appointed to advise the Home Secretary on the running of the Metropolitan Police, but this falls some way short of a full-scale police authority for London.

There is little doubting the potential for centralisation under the new arrangements. A key factor in the degree of centralisation that emerges in practice will be the way in which the new police authorities and chief constables adapt to the new arrangements. One possible approach is for local government to campaign for a reversal of the changes and a restoration of the old arrangements, and some of the local authority associations appear to be adopting this type of line. A recent AMA discussion paper on quangos, for example, recommended that 'the changes of the Police and Magistrates Courts Act 1994 should be reversed and the pre-1994 situation restored' (Association of Metropolitan Authorities, 1994:17). The report stated that it was 'unlikely that these changes will stand the test of time'. However, successful reversal of the new arrangements seems unlikely, to say the least, in the foreseeable future and, given what we now know about the shortcomings of the extant arrangements, it would be a highly dubious exercise anyway.

In addition to encouraging further centralisation of control over local constabularies, the 1994 Act also carries potentially greater freedom within total budgets for police forces and police authorities to allocate spending. Even more important are the provisions under the new Act for local policing plans. In laying down that the local police authority (not the chief constable and not the Home Secretary) shall 'determine policing objectives' and to this end, publish an annual policing plan, the Act potentially encourages greater local influence over the development of policing policy. How meaningful this part of the Act will be in terms of local influence depends, of course, on what are the main influences on this plan and attention has tended to focus on the national objectives. But it is yet to become clear what forms these will take, or that these will dominate in practice. The national objectives laid down by the Home Secretary for 1994 were at a fairly general level and, for example, included maintaining, 'and if possible increas[ing], the number of detections for violent crimes' and targeting 'and prevent[ing] crimes which are a particular local problem in partnership with the public and local agencies'. It is not immediately apparent that objectives such as these will seriously undermine the ability to respond to local policing needs, although of course the nature of the national objectives may become more specific in future years.

The local policing plans are to be developed in close co-operation with the chief constable, and it remains to be seen who in practice, the chief or the local police authority, will have the greater influence. Although it has been suggested that chief constables on fixed-term contracts may be primarily influenced by the need to meet nationally-set performance criteria, this is not a *fait accompli*. The strong opposition that chief police officers have voiced towards further centralisation may make them more receptive to local influences and inputs than was previously the case.

It is even possible to find potential benefits even in that most contentious part of the new Act: the introduction of local appointees with relevant experience. It is quite possible, in principle, that the addition of non-elected 'experts' might help rather than hinder local police accountability. This, of course, would only be the case if it is implemented in the right way. It would require the elected members on the new police authorities to assert their authority and use the appointees as a resource, rather than be dominated by them. The problem is to find ways of defining what is to count as relevant expertise, and guaranteeing that such appointments are genuinely local in nature.

Although much of the debate over the Act has focused on the role of police authorities and chief constables, it is the more local level, the level of the Basic Command Unit, where local input is most important. A recent report from the Audit Commission (Audit Commission, 1994) examines the possibilities provided by the Act for an increase in the trend to financial delegation within police forces. An earlier paper by Morgan (1987: 40) noted that 'the principal determinants of the quantity and quality of police services locally – manpower allocation, the deployment of equipment, decisions about priorities and police tactics, etc. – though decided by police managers on the basis of indices of alleged consumer needs and demands are, for the most part, fixed centrally (within force headquarters and the Home Office) according to unstated criteria and unrevealed data'. Prior to 1994, Home Office controls over police establishment prevented forces from delegating to local commanders significant controls over staffing mix and levels. From April 1995, this will now be possible. The Audit Commission have noted that several forces are considering the possibility of such delegation, and recommend that 'other forces should at least explore the opportunities, identify the managerial problems and determine what safeguards would be needed to protect the force's overall interests'. Critics of the Act argue that any openings for delegation to the local level will be rendered meaningless by the imposition of national published performance indicators laid down by the Home Secretary. Once again, however, it is by no means certain that forces will follow national indicators slavishly. As the Audit Commission points out, it is important to see them as lessons learned rather than points scored.

The changes brought about by the Act are clearly far from ideal, and are intended to tip the balance further towards central control. It is important to recognise, however, the failings of the extant system of local governance and, second, that some of the failings were due to the inability or unwillingness of police authorities to exploit the powers they had. To what extent the new police authorities seek to exploit the new powers they have been given under the Police and Magistrates' Courts Act 1994 will determine whether policing policy in the last five years of the century does more than reflect the combined views of ACPO and central government.

Conclusion

The day-to-day practice and the public face of policing in Britain has changed significantly in the past 20 years. The continued escalation of official crime rates, the precipitous decline in public faith in the police, have coincided over the past decade with a reformist government determined to overhaul public services, particularly by applying private sector management strategies, and increasing competition through privatisation. It all came to a head in the early 1990s, and a process of fairly radical change has begun with the Police and Magistrates' Courts Act.

It is in the area of policing that what has been referred to as 'market-based criminal justice' (McLaughlin and Muncie, 1993) in England and Wales has perhaps been most visible over the past decade and a half (though prisons, as we have seen, are not far behind). The bipartisan consensus that existed certainly up to the mid-1970s and perhaps to the end of the decade, was abandoned by a 'law and order' espousing Conservative government that poured significant resources into policing in the hope that this would have a noticeable impact on crime rates. Not only were crime rates not lowered, however, but they continued to rise at an ever increasing rate. The party of law and order manifestly failed to increase the general populace's sense of safety and security and the 1979 manifesto promise to 'spend more on fighting crime whilst we economise elsewhere' started to look like a fairly unsound investment. They were quick to blame the police for failing to deliver, though other favourite folk devils were also invoked to explain why crime continued to increase. One of the enduringly popular scapegoats was always the 'permissive society' (Newburn, 1991); Norman Tebbit, for example, suggesting that the aetiology of crime could be found in: 'the post-war funk which gave birth to the permissive society, which in turn generates today's violent society' (quoted in Rawlings, 1991:43).

By the mid-1980s the police had lost their apparent immunity from the managerial imperatives that were being imposed on the rest of the public sector. From about 1982/3 the government began to pursue its Financial Management Initiative, using private sector management methods to impose market disciplines upon the police. During the 1980s Her Majesty's Inspectorate of Constabulary gradually increased its financial scrutiny of individual forces and by the late 1980s the Audit Commission began to investigate not only the financing of the police but also its organisation and management. This process continued into the 1990s with the Sheehy Inquiry and the Police and Magistrates' Courts Act. The possibility of contracting out certain functions as a means of saving money was the focus of the Inquiry into Core and Ancillary Tasks. As ever, privatisation remains a favourite weapon.

Increasing managerialism has been accompanied by a process of growing centralisation of control over the police. Although the 1964 Police Act in theory established a tripartite structure for police governance, even then the reality was that the local police committee was very much the least powerful player of the three. The changes that have taken place since then have on the one hand confirmed the chief constable's relatively autonomous position in relation to local police authorities and have, on the other, made it increasingly clear that the most significant policing policy agendas are actually set by the Home Office, with support from HMIC and the Audit Commission (Jones *et al.*, 1994).

Whilst the degree of centralisation that will result from the changes brought about by the Police and Magistrates' Courts Act has yet to be seen, the trends visible not only in other parts of the criminal justice system, but also in other public services, suggest that it may be quite significant.

CHAPTER 4

The probation service: The dilemma of care and control

The origins of the probation service

The probation service as we know it today has its origins in the Victorian temperance movement and the police court missionaries who began work in the 1870s and 1880s. Although the legal basis for alternatives to imprisonment increased during the course of the nineteenth century, it was not until the first decade of the twentieth century that probation was put on a statutory footing. The nature and scale of the work undertaken by probation officers has changed markedly during the last eighty years, with the pace of change being most marked in the past twenty years.

As far as the nineteenth century is concerned there are two developments which are central to an understanding of the origins and emergence of the probation service: the changing jurisdiction of the magistrates' courts, and increasing concern about drunkenness and the disorderly behaviour that drinking frequently led to.

In the second half of the nineteenth century the magistrates' courts moved from, as White describes it: 'administering a partial, private executive justice in minor matters . . . [to being] recognizably courts of justice' (quoted in McWilliams, 1983:130). A number of significant Acts of Parliament resulted in offences which had previously been dealt with in assizes or quarter sessions, becoming the business of the magistrates' courts. These included the 1847 Juvenile Offenders Act (extended in 1850) which allowed certain larcenies committed by juveniles to be dealt with by magistrates, the 1855 Criminal Justice Act which extended these powers to cover adults faced with similar charges, and further legislation in 1868 which extended the provisions to some cases of embezzlement.

In addition, several pieces of legislation made provision for offenders 'to enter into recognizances' with the court. Beginning with the Juvenile Offenders Act 1847, and following it the Criminal Law Consolidation Act 1861 and the 1879 Summary Jurisdiction Act, magistrates' courts were given the power 'where the offences were thought so trifling as to make punishment unnecessary, to discharge the offender on his own recognizance, with or without sureties, to appear for sentence when called upon, to keep the peace and be of good behaviour' (Jarvis, 1972:10). It was against this background that the idea of supervision of such offenders emerged. However, before considering supervision in more detail there is one other development that needs to be considered.

The second half of the nineteenth century saw a dramatic rise in concern about drunkenness, and in the numbers convicted of and imprisoned for drunkenness and for disorderly behaviour. McWilliams (1983) notes that there were over 88,000 offenders convicted of such offences in 1860 and by 1876 this had risen to over 200,000. In the same period the numbers imprisoned rose from just under 4,000 to almost 24,000. Indeed, McWilliams suggests that in London arrests for drunk and disorderly, drunkenness, and disorderly prostitutes and disorderly characters represented over half of all recorded crime in the capital. At roughly this time temperance movements and related moral campaigns emerged both in Britain and abroad (on the case of the United States see, for example, Gusfield, 1963).

In the 1860s the Church of England Total Abstinence Society was established, though relatively quickly it amended its approach in order to incorporate people other than abstainers, and in 1873 changed its name to the Church of England Temperance Society (CETS). Jarvis (1972) quotes its basis as being: 'Union and co-operation on perfectly equal terms between those who use and those who abstain from intoxicating drinks'. He argues that its large membership was its major strength, enabling a nationwide movement to develop within a relatively short space of time, though its focus on temperance and not abstinence was also crucial. The membership of the CETS had reached close on one million by the 1890s. It had three primary goals: the promotion of temperance; the removal of the causes which lead to intemperance; and, crucially for our purposes here, the reformation of the intemperate.

Reforming or 'reclaiming' drunkards through a mission to the police courts was, it is suggested, initially the idea of a printer named Frederick Rainer who, in a letter to the CETS, bemoaned what he saw to be the fate of the drunk facing the courts: 'offence after offence, sentence after sentence appears to be the inevitable lot of him whose foot has once slipped' (quoted in Jarvis, 1972). The first two police court missionaries, George Nelson and William Batchelor, were both ex-Coldstream guardsmen and were appointed in 1876 and 1877. They worked in the Bow, Mansion House, Southwark and Lambeth courts in London. McWilliams (1983:134) describes their initial efforts in the courts as being 'directed to exhorting offenders to give up drink, distributing uplifting tracts and taking pledges of abstinence'. The work in the courts expanded quickly and came to dominate the activities of the missionaries within the period of a decade. The work was 'unapologetically evangelical', the aim being 'to reclaim the lives and souls of drunks appearing before the courts. They would ask the magistrates to bind individuals over into their care and they would undertake to secure their "restoration and reclamation"' (Mathieson, 1992:143).

There is one crucial further linking step between the work of the police court missionary and what in the twentieth century we associate with the probation officer. McWilliams (1985:253) describes it as follows:

It is important to recall that in their work in the courts the missionaries were not pleading for mercy for all offenders; such a course would undoubtedly have been self-defeating. Rather their pleas were reserved for those offenders deemed suitable for moral reform and this ensured, at least at the beginning, that in addition to intrinsic worth a missionary's plea also had a sort of novelty value. Even with selective application, however, the strong possibility existed that special pleading would become a routine . . . The missionaries began to depend upon a form of justification for their pleas and this was that offenders worthy of mercy could reform under kindly guidance; that is to say that the missionaries' pleas in court began to be linked to the notion of *supervision*, and in particular to the idea that some offenders were suitable for reform under supervision.

As supervisors of offenders deemed to be deserving of mercy, the missionaries increasingly played a part in the process of determining which offenders were to be considered 'suitable for moral reform'. This meant undertaking inquiries prior to sentencing and although it is not clear when they first undertook such work for the courts, it is likely that they were doing so by the time that the extension of supervision from 'licence holders and habitual criminals' to first offenders at risk of imprisonment was made by the Probation of First Offenders Act 1887.

The previous year, Howard Vincent MP had introduced a Bill into the House of Commons which would have extended very significantly the powers to release offenders on recognizance. The dissolution of Parliament brought the end of the Bill, and a much amended version was passed a year later. Although it was the first point at which the word 'probation' was entered onto the statute book, the Act represented only a moderate extension to the system of supervision that was emerging. Though the Act only applied to first offenders, it covered a broader range of offences than had the 1879 Act, for example – including those convicted of larceny, false pretences and other offences punishable with not more than two years' imprisonment. In addition, the courts 'were required to have regard not simply to the triviality of the offence, but to the youth, character and antecedents of the offender, and to any extenuating circumstances' (Jarvis, 1972:13).

Jarvis notes that by 1907 – the point at which the modern probation service originates – there were 124 male and 19 female missionaries from the CETS working in the courts, together with a small number of missionaries from other bodies. Despite the central role played by the police court missionaries in the nineteenth and early twentieth century, most commentators are agreed that it would be a gross oversimplification to suggest that the probation service grew directly from such work (see for example Bochel, 1976). The missionaries provided a model for work with offenders and established the ground whereupon a welfare organisation could work in the courts, but 'the idea which led directly to the passing of the Probation of Offenders Act in 1907 stemmed from American experience and practice, and was actively supported in this country, not from a concern for adult offenders, but from a profound anxiety over the treatment of children by the courts' (Jarvis, 1972:9).

The 'American experience' is a reference to an experiment in the State of Massachusetts at the turn of the century. The Howard Association, as it was then called, provided the Home Secretary with an account of the Massachusetts system, together with evidence that it had been collecting about a variety of methods of dealing with juvenile offenders. Bochel (1976) notes that the 'situation was ripe' for a decision to be taken to introduce a system of probation. A Liberal government had just come to power, Herbert Gladstone, who had been Chairman of the Departmental Committee on Prisons, had become Home Secretary and there was quite widespread public concern about the treatment of juveniles (see chapter 6).

The Probation of Offenders Act

In 1906 the CETS, sensing that change was in the air, had visited the Home Office to offer the services of the police court missionaries as probation officers. The Probation of Offenders Bill was described in its Second Reading in the House as a proposal: 'of a non-controversial character. The government has not heard a whisper of opposition to it from any quarter of the House. Its purpose is to enable the courts of justice to appoint probation officers, to pay them salaries or fees, so that certain offenders whom the court did not think fit to imprison, on account of their age, character or antecedents, might be placed on probation under the supervision of these officers, whose duty it would be to guide, admonish and befriend them' (Jarvis, 1972:15). The Bill received Royal Assent in August 1907.

Section 2 of the Act is perhaps its most important element. It says that where an offender has been released on condition of their recognizance, they should: 'be under the supervision of such person as may be named in the order during the period specified in the order.' Such an order was in future to be referred to as a probation order. Conditions could be attached prohibiting the offender from frequenting with undesirable persons or in undesirable places and requiring abstention from alcohol. Petty sessional divisions were given the power, but not compelled, to appoint probation officers for their area. The duties of such officers were:

'To visit or receive reports from the person under supervision at such reasonable intervals as the probation officer may think fit;

To see that he observes the condition of his recognizance;

To report to the court on his behaviour;

To *advise, assist and befriend* him and, when necessary, to endeavour to find him suitable employment.' (emphasis added).

This was the point, then, when a probation service started to emerge. The Act came into operation at the beginning of 1908, by which time it was assumed local authorities would have had time to make appointments and establish pay scales. The Home Secretary remained responsible for the Metropolitan Police court area and, in the event, many of the standards and operations established there became models for practice elsewhere. Crucially it gave the Home Office direct experience of establishing, maintaining and administering a local service.

Although the legislation was, in Jarvis's words 'a great advance', there were a number of limitations to the new system it introduced. As was suggested above, probation officers were to be appointed by justices on a petty sessional division basis. However, many of the areas were too small to provide enough work for a probation officer. Because the legislation as drafted was permissive and there was no regional or national machinery for co-ordinating work in PSDs, there was little onus upon, or support for local areas in establishing a probation presence in court. The establishment of a more bureaucratic form of organisation did not occur until the 1920s.

With the accommodating position adopted towards the new system of probation by the CETS, and the experience that the police court missionaries had gathered by this point, it is perhaps not surprising that in the vast majority of cases in which a missionary was already working in a particular local area, it was they who were appointed as a probation officer. This was not universally popular, however, and Jarvis (1972:22) quotes the Howard Association's Annual Report of 1908 as saying: 'large numbers of persons, male and female, have been appointed probation officers, some it is to be feared not possessing the personal qualities that fit them for the delicate and important work . . . The Committee . . . feel that the wholesale appointment of volunteers, regardless of training and capacity, is likely to bring discredit upon a most useful Act and jeopardise its efficient working and ultimate success.'

A Home Office Departmental Committee which reported in 1909 was the first sign that some form of central oversight of the new probation service was thought to be necessary. The Committee stayed well short of recommending a full-scale central co-ordinating body, but it did nevertheless suggest that there should at least be one official whose function it would be to furnish 'any information with regard to (probation work) that may be asked for' (quoted in Jarvis, 1972:24).

The numbers placed on probation at this time remained relatively low. Indeed, the number dropped between 1913 and 1919 from just over 11,000 to 9,655 (though it varied somewhat between these dates). The role of the CETS was undiminished, though the concern expressed by the Howard Association just after the introduction of the Act was becoming increasingly widespread. There was a growing dissonance between the CETS's emphasis upon temperance, and the more secular philosophy held by the court-based social work agency which was slowly but surely emerging.

There was relatively little emphasis on training for probation officers at this point. Some training for the non-missionary probation officers was provided in the university settlements and the Charity Organisation Society, but relatively little training was provided for the missionaries; the schemes which existed were run for parochial workers by a variety of religious bodies (Bochel, 1976). Juvenile crime in particular continued to rise throughout the war years and criticism of the police court missionaries was undiminished.

The emergence of bureaucracy

The position remained unchanged for some while despite the establishment in 1920 of a Home Office Departmental Committee to 'enquire into the existing methods of training, appointing and paying probation officers, and to consider whether any, and if so what, alterations are desirable in order to secure at all courts sufficient number of probation officers having suitable training and qualifications, and also to consider whether any changes are required in the present system of remuneration.' The Committee recommended that government should meet half the cost of providing probation officers, and that it should do so via a central government grant. In doing so it was careful to state that the new system of finance and control should be established 'without direct interference with the organisation along local lines' (quoted in May, 1991:11). The establishment of local probation committees made up of representatives from the Bench was also recommended.

It was in the mid-1920s that the basis of a national, bureaucratic probation machinery was established. Central were the Criminal Justice Act 1925 and the Criminal Justice Amendment Act 1926. These laid the foundations for an administrative framework for the probation service. PSDs were designated as probation areas and, crucially, for the first time it became mandatory for the PSD to employ one or more probation officers.

The Home Secretary was given powers to combine PSDs into a single probation area in order to overcome the work limitations outlined above. Such combined areas would have a (combined) probation committee. Probation officers were to be appointed by the probation committee, which would also pay them, oversee their activities and receive regular reports from them. The work was to be financed by the local authority and by central government. Finally, it would be the duty of probation officers to supervise offenders placed on probation by assize courts and quarter sessions as well as courts of summary jurisdiction.

The next step was the issuing by the Home Office of the 1926 Probation Rules which introduced the distinction between principal probation officers and others, and enabled probation committees to appoint such officers at a higher salary than other probation staff. Later on posts such as senior probation officer, and deputy and assistant principal (subsequently chief) probation officer were introduced, but none of this happened quickly (McWilliams, 1981). It was thus the introduction of more formalised methods of financing, regulating, and organising the probation service, beginning in earnest in the 1920s, which really began to transform it into something akin to the service we recognise today.

The rise of the 'diagnostician'

In a series of articles, McWilliams (McWilliams, 1981, 1983, 1985, 1986, 1987) charts the changes in the philosophical basis of 'probation practice' from the earliest days of the police court missionaries onwards. At about the period under discussion here, he suggests that a gradual movement began away from the 'missionary ideal' towards what he and others have referred to as a more therapeutic or diagnostic approach to work with offenders (see also May, 1991) [doc 10]. Crudely stated, the argument advanced by such authors is that in selecting those offenders deserving of mercy, the missionaries employed the 'doctrine of the stumbling block', this being the impediments (such as drink) to the offender's understanding of the gospel. The offender could either work towards or be coerced into removing such stumbling blocks. Once these impediments became the reason why individuals behaved in the way they did, then there was little philosophical difference between such a view and the views held by the growing band of diagnosticians with a more scientifically informed medical model of individual failings. The change – and this of course was very gradual – was from a system dominated by missionaries whose task it was to reform the wicked, to one run by professionals who wanted to 'heal the sick' (May, 1994).

Two documents published in the 1930s are quite central in understanding the rise to prominence of the diagnostician. The first of these is *A Handbook of Probation and Social Work of the Courts* (Le Mesurier, 1935) which was produced by the National Association of Probation Officers (NAPO) in the year prior to the publication of the second document, the *Report of the Departmental Committee on the Social Services in the Courts of Summary Jurisdiction* (Home Office, 1936). Both dealt with court work and social enquiry reports at some length, though the emphasis in each is somewhat different (McWilliams, 1985). The NAPO Handbook attempted to establish the link between scientific diagnosis and professional practice, whereas the Departmental Committee went little further than outlining the importance of the provision of information before the courts. It said in its report, however: 'There are no doubt some defects in the provisions of the law, but the neglect of so many courts to carry out the intentions of the legislature either in the letter or the spirit has contributed to the failure of the probation service to meet adequately the increasing responsibilities placed upon it at the present day' (quoted in Jarvis, 1972:51). Its recommendations were, in the long term, influential. They included the proposal that, despite the enormous contribution of the police court missionaries, probation should become a wholly public service. Crucial in this was the very strong view held by NAPO, including its missionary members (who made up about half those employed), that it should no longer be a part of the Mission:

> . . . whilst both the Handbook and the Departmental Committee moved decisively away from the concept of a service founded on vocation and missionary spirit and towards a basis in science, diagnosis and treatment, both texts made considerable efforts not to lose the missionary element . . . . The foregoing may appear contradictory, but that is not actually the case; we must remember that the issue was clearly seen as administrative rather than ideological; it was the *Mission* which was to be rejected, *not* the missionary zeal. (McWilliams, 1985:271)

The Committee also recommended an increase in the central control of the probation service and in the creation of a separate probation branch in the Home Office. Of the Committee's recommendations that could be acted upon without the need for new legislation, many were set in train without much delay. Others were incorporated in a Criminal Justice Bill, but the outbreak of the Second World War prevented its passage, and it was some ten years before a new Act was passed. The emergence of a fully-fledged public service was not far off, however, and in 1937 Sir Samuel Hoare, the then Home Secretary, said that 'the system under which candidates for the Probation Service are nominated so far as the adult courts are concerned, by the London Police Court Mission, can no longer be defended, and . . . there is a need to bring the whole of the probation staff under unified public control' (quoted in Jarvis, 1972:56).

From its somewhat precarious beginnings, probation had by this stage become quite firmly established. As has already been noted, there were under 10,000 people placed on probation in 1919. This rose to 25,000 in 1936, and 35,000 by 1943 (with 50,000 in total under supervision). In 1945 the 1936 proposal to create a division in the Home Office with responsibility for probation was put into practice, though administratively the division was still located within the Childrens' Branch.

A new era was signalled by the passage of the Criminal Justice Act 1948 which repealed the 1907 Act and all other legislation dealing with probation. It established a new administrative structure for the service, provided for an increase in the central government grant to a maximum of 50%, set out in full the powers of the courts as far as probation was concerned, and extended the responsibilities of probation officers to include after-care. Three years later NAPO was arguing for an extension of the after-care responsibilities of its members on the basis that officers were 'specialists in casework with offenders in the community' (quoted in McWilliams, 1981:102). As we shall see below, the Advisory Council, to whom NAPO had been giving evidence, rejected the idea of a separate after-care service and plumped for 'an enlarged probation and after-care service' on the grounds that there was 'clearly a strong case for concentrating in a single service social work in the community with delinquents, whether they are probationers or offenders released from correctional establishments' (McWilliams, 1981).

A further review of the service was established in May 1959 under the chairmanship of Ronald Morison QC. His Committee's terms of reference were to inquire into 'all aspects of probation in England and Wales and Scotland and the approved probation hostel system'. It took three years to report and was not particularly radical in the vision it offered. It concluded that: 'The present functions are, with a few minor exceptions which we have specified, appropriately and desirably performed by the service. Almost all types of work are increasing or likely to increase and . . . the service must be organised, recruited and trained to meet this situation' (Morison Report (I) para.157).

Writing in 1978, Haxby said that 'the service today looks very different from the service which was reviewed and discussed in the Report of the Morison Committee in March 1962' (Haxby, 1978:15). Many of the changes in probation policy and practice stem from the work of two further committees that reported in the early 1960s. The first of these was the Streatfield Committee which reported in 1961, the second the Advisory Committee on the Treatment of Offenders which reported in 1963.

The Streatfield Committee in attempting to clarify the role of the probation officer in court said that 'whatever the circumstances in which the probation officer gives evidence he (sic) appears as a witness of the court and not as a witness for the defence or prosecution. He provides the court with relevant background information which is not necessarily for the defence or against it' (Streatfield Report, para.367). The primary consequence of the Streatfield Committee's report was to strengthen the emphasis placed upon national rather than local policies, and to move the focus from particular offenders to particular classes of offender. As McWilliams (1987:104) notes: 'This was a profound change, but one which was apparently unnoticed in these terms at that time.'

As has already been briefly mentioned, in 1963 a report of the Advisory Council on the Treatment of Offenders (ACTO), *The Organisation of After-Care* (Home Office, 1963), reviewed the arrangements for the organisation of statutory and voluntary after-care. In short what it recommended was an expansion and reorganisation of the probation and after-care service. Those organisations which were at that time involved in after-care – whether compulsory or voluntary – were to be wound down, and replaced by a common service, and all after-care in the community should henceforward become the responsibility of the new expanded and re-organised probation and after-care service. As a result a new probation and after-care department was created in the Home Office. The report framed its conclusions in the following manner:

An expansion of the probation service in England and Wales to deal with after-care on the lines we have recommended must be accompanied by a reorganisation of that service. The probation service would . . . extend beyond its hitherto accepted role of a social service of the courts, that part of its work concerned with after-care would be carried out, not upon the court's directions, but as a continuation in the community of the treatment begun in custody.

ACTO thus emphasised the development of welfare work within prisons, and initially suggested that such work should be undertaken by people with the same professional standing as probation officers. Eventually it was decided that the work should be undertaken by probation officers on secondment, and by 1966 the expanded probation and after-care service assumed responsibility for this work from the Discharged Prisoners' Aid Societies. As May (1991:17) puts it: 'Administratively at least this changed the "long-standing antipathy" probation officers had towards prisons.'

Similarly, probation officers were also given responsibility for the after-care of detention centre trainees in 1964, though for the first time the new arrangements were announced in a Home Office circular. This pattern was repeated when responsibilities for borstal trainees and young prisoners were introduced in 1967, and for those sentenced to life imprisonment from 1968. By the same process that had occurred in prisons, social workers in borstals, remand and detention centres also became probation officers on secondment.

The changes brought about in the 1950s and 1960s were, not surprisingly, reflected quite starkly in the work undertaken by probation officers. McWilliams (1987) shows that in the 1950s the (criminal) supervisory caseload increased by over 35,000 cases, though the categories of work remained largely unchanged. During the decade from 1961 that caseload increased again, but there was a major redistribution of work with the proportion of probation cases declining, whilst the proportion of after-care cases rose. These changes are summarised in Table 4.1.

Haxby (1978:17) summarises these sweeping changes by suggesting that taken together they 'represented a major shift in the focus of the service. In the future many probation officers could expect to spend some part of their career working in a penal institution, and a large part of the field officer's work would not in future derive directly from the decisions of judges and magistrates.'

It was not necessary to introduce legislation to bring in such changes,

Table 4.1   *Offenders supervised by the probation service (England and Wales) by type of supervision, 1951–81*

Type of supervision	Percentage of offenders			
	1951	1961	1971	1981
Probation	82.4	75.5	56.5	31.9
C&YP Acts 1933–1969	5.8	7.1	11.4	10.9
Money payment supervision	2.0	3.8	5.7	5.0
After-care	9.9	13.5	26.4	37.6
Susp. sentence supervision	–	–	–	1.9
Community service	–	–	–	12.8
Number	55,425	90,459	120,613	157,350

Source: McWilliams, 1987.

though it was novel for the executive – in the shape of the Home Office – to take such a directive role. Nevertheless, there was new legislation soon after: the Criminal Justice Act 1967 formalising the status of probation and after-care 'areas' and 'committees'. It further cemented the role of the probation officer in prison through the introduction of parole and, perhaps most notably, it introduced the first 'totally new sentencing option for the adult offender since the statutory creation of probation sixty years earlier': the suspended sentence of imprisonment (Bottoms, 1980). Although the government initially argued that the suspended sentence and probation ought to be kept separate, suspended sentence supervision orders were introduced following a recommendation by the Advisory Council on the Penal System in 1970.

The Children and Young Persons Act 1969 (which is dealt with in greater detail in chapter 6) ended the use of probation for juveniles, the responsibility for supervising such offenders passing in many cases to social workers. Nevertheless, two pieces of legislation in the early 1970s further extended the functions of the probation service. The 1972 Criminal Justice Act, later amended by the Powers of Criminal Courts Act 1973, empowered probation committees 'to provide and carry on day training centres, bail hostels, probation hostels, probation homes and other establishments for use in connection with the rehabilitation of offenders'. It attempted to discourage the courts from using custodial sentences by requiring them to consider an SIR before imposing a custodial sentence on an offender under the age of 21, and on those over 21 who had not previously served a term of imprisonment. In addition, it introduced community service orders (CSOs), allowing courts to order offenders to undertake up to 240 hours of unpaid work as an alternative to a short custodial sentence, and this was to be run by the probation service. Similarly, day training centres (as opposed to Day Centres which were introduced by the Criminal Justice Act 1982) – which offenders could be required to attend for up to a maximum of

60 days for full-time, non-residential training – were also to be run by the service.

Community Service has become a central part of the work of the probation service since this point, and it is worth looking at its introduction in somewhat more detail. The Advisory Council on the Penal System, chaired by Baroness Wootton, had been set the task not only of expanding the range of non-custodial disposals, but also devising new alternatives to imprisonment. Its 1970 report examined the possibility of introducing some form of community service which would require adult offenders to undertake unpaid work for the community. It was introduced in six experimental areas in 1973, and CSOs could be imposed on offenders convicted of offences punishable by imprisonment, though offenders had to consent to the order being made. The experiment was evaluated by the Home Office which concluded: 'that the scheme is viable; orders are being made and completed, sometimes evidently to the benefit of the offenders concerned. However, the effect on the offenders as a whole is not known; the penal theory underlining the scheme is thought by some to be uncertain; it has not made much of an impact on the prison population' (Pease *et al.*, 1975, quoted in McIvor, 1992). Nevertheless, in 1974 the government announced that community service would be extended to the rest of England and Wales and the extent to which they were used grew throughout the decade.

From 'alternatives to custody' to 'punishment in the community'

If the 1960s witnessed a number of quite far-reaching changes to the nature and operation of the probation (and after-care) service, the backdrop was one of a continuing emphasis on scientific treatment and diagnosis. The rate of change in the 1970s was no less rapid than that in the 1960s, but it was qualitatively different in that the philosophical basis of probation practice began to face a series of challenges. Harris (1994) identifies three sources of attack on the established systems and values.

The first change, as should already be clear, was that the government began to identify the probation service as a vehicle for the management of more serious offenders in the community, including increasing numbers on post-custodial and parole licence. Although increased resources were part of the package, one of the consequences, he suggests, was a diminished degree of officer autonomy. In other words, a further move away from judicial power towards that of the executive was underway. Crucially, initiatives had been introduced by government which, some believed, compromised the traditional welfare philosophy of probation. Thus, for example, whilst parole 'was intended not only to reduce the prison population, but to assist in the process of resettlement of the offenders in the community . . . it also incorporated elements of "public protection" in the community, through the monitoring of the parolee's progress by a probation officer' (May, 1994:864). Day training centres and bail hostels were also introduced with the intention of stiffening up the public image of community-based sanctions by adding conditions to probation orders. There was, in short, declining confidence in the potential of the standard probation order.

Secondly, at around this time there emerged the 'new criminology': at its heart a sociology of deviance that questioned the functions of the criminal justice system, including the 'nature' of probation. Could it be, as Harris puts it, 'that the service, far from acting in a humane manner, was a repressive arm of the state' (1994:935–6). Insights derived from such a sociology of deviance led to a questioning of the role of the 'neutral' professional and, as one consequence, to the development of radical social work practices and groupings. The third challenge was to the very idea that intervention by probation officers might have some effect on the individual's propensity to offend. An increasing body of research at this time cast doubt on the effectiveness of a variety of approaches. The dominant position occupied by the 'rehabilitative ideal' which had formed the basis for the introduction of many non-custodial initiatives, was no more, and a form of penal pessimism developed. As Bottoms and McWilliams (1979:159) put it:

The reformation of the criminal . . . has been central to the English approach to criminal justice since the end of the nineteenth century . . . But penological research carried out in the course of the last twenty years or so suggests that penal 'treatments', as we significantly describe them, do not have any reformative effect, whatever other effects they may have. The dilemma is that a considerable investment has been made in various measures and services, of which the most obvious examples are custodial institutions for young adult offenders and probation and after-care services in the community. *Are these services simply to be abandoned on the basis of the accumulated research evidence?* Put thus starkly, this is an unlikely proposition but one which, by being posed at all, has implications for the rehabilitative services concerned. *Will this challenge evoke a response by . . . probation officers* by the invention of new approaches and methods?

Part of the answer to this is that a significant proportion of the energies of the probation service have gone into adapting to the increasing responsibilities and changing circumstances in which they have been operating in the past 25 years. If anything the pace of change has increased during this period and the service itself has had less and less control over its working environment as central government has progressively intervened. As one indication of its seriousness, the government grant for the administration of local services was increased from 50 to 80% in 1971. It is the consequences of the decline in confidence in the treatment model that had the most profound effect on the probation service in the 1970s and, indeed, thereafter. The service no longer felt itself to have a coherent sense of mission and purpose. The traditional function as set out in the 1907 Act, 'to advise, assist and befriend', was increasingly being challenged by the requirement on probation officers that they administer what they perceived to be ever more punitive community-based sanctions, thus turning them into 'screws on wheels' (Haxby, 1978:162). Toughening-up the form and the content of community sanctions has been perhaps the major characteristic of policy in this area since the early to mid 1970s.

This change of emphasis has stimulated an extensive and sometimes heated debate within the service itself and, as early as 1969, Murch argued that it had a choice; either it could become 'some form of correctional service linked to the penal system (a crime treatment service) or a less symptom specific, more general social work agency linked to the courts (a court social work service).' He went on to argue that if the treatment of offenders was identified as the primary function of probation, then other more general social work activities would increasingly be seen as being of secondary importance.

Table 4.1 summarised the changes in the service's caseload between 1951 and 1981. Expansion and diversification is primarily what happened in the 1970s (McWilliams, 1987). The criminal caseload grew markedly, though the level of probation orders fell to an all-time low by 1977. The expansion came via continuing increases in after-care, together with the introduction of CSOs and, though less marked, SSSOs.

In parallel with the development of policy in relation to policing (chapter 3) the key element of the probation narrative for the past fifteen to twenty years has been the increasing involvement of and direction from the Home Office. The election of a new government on a 'law and order' ticket in 1979 ('We will spend more on fighting crime, whilst we economize elsewhere') is widely associated with a sea-change in criminal justice policy. The 1980s witnessed massively increased expenditure on criminal justice (Fowles, 1990; NACRO, 1992) and, after a slight delay, significantly increased emphasis on 'value for money'. At the heart of government policy was an avowed determination to 'crack down', to be 'tough on crime'. Such a project, however, was not without its contradictions, for as Brake and Hale (1992:11) point out: 'on the one hand [the government] favoured a firm hand concerning law and order, but on the other this was limited by the overcrowding of the prisons, forcing it to rethink and disguise "soft options" as *punishment in the community*' (emphasis added).   As we have already seen, however, moves to stiffen community sanctions and to present them as a tough alternative predate the 1979 election by some years. Thus, although it had a somewhat different meaning from the Intensive Probation initiative launched in 1990, experiments in intensive counselling – involving significant increases in the amount of contact between client and counsellor – were taking place in the early 1970s (for details of the IMPACT experiment (Intensive Matched Probation and After-Care Treatment) see Folkard *et al.*, 1974 and 1976).

In a semantic affirmation of the spirit of the times, the Criminal Justice Act 1982 removed 'After-Care' from the Probation Service's title. It introduced day centres and also included a provision that would allow courts to add requirements to probation orders: either requiring offenders to engage in or refrain from certain activities for a maximum of 60 days, thus increasing the surveillance and social control aspects of supervision.

Statement of National Objectives and Priorities

Rather than 1979, it is most clearly 1984 that represents the watershed in the recent history of the probation service (McLaughlin and Muncie, 1994; Mair, 1995). It was the year in which the Home Office published its *Statement of National Objectives and Priorities* (SNOP) for the probation service (Home Office, 1984c). When it was published as a draft document it had the rather less fearsome title of 'The Future Direction of the Probation Service'. The published version, however, 'represented the most penetrating government intervention ever in the affairs of the probation service and required each probation area to respond with its own local statement, to be measured against the Home Office's national statement. The process of tighter control had begun' (Mathieson, 1992). The National Audit Office (NAO, 1989:2) in describing this process said very simply 'the Home Office are taking more direct and positive action to secure improvements in local management and performance'.

SNOP outlined how the resources available to the service might be 'effectively and efficiently' used, and suggested that this was the responsibility of both the local probation committee and the Chief Probation Officer (CPO). Indeed, as the degree of Home Office direction increased during the course of the decade, so CPOs were progressively targeted as the focus for official 'advice'. Given that local probation committees are autonomous this is perhaps not surprising, but it puts CPOs in the difficult position of ensuring that the local service meets national guidelines whilst simultaneously being responsible to the local committee for the efficient use of local resources. The balance in this emergent tripartite structure is different from that which governs local constabularies, but some of the tensions are very similar.

SNOP was the first visible outcome of the application of the government's Financial Management Initiative (FMI) to the probation service. A similar process was taking place in relation to local policing budgets in the early 1980s, despite the spend, spend, spend policy that had been announced prior to the 1979 general election. SNOP was an agenda-setting document. May (1994:873) summarises its approach as follows:

Along with statutory changes in the Criminal Justice Act 1982, it was intended as a means for achieving the government's aims. SNOP prioritized the work of the probation service in both the provision of alternatives to custody and the preparation of social inquiry reports, the theme being to target offenders who were 'at risk' of imprisonment. This clearly represented a change of focus away from the traditional probation client, who was 'in need' of a social work service, towards those thought to represent such 'a threat' to society that a period of incarceration would be a justified response on the part of the courts. As such, SNOP stipulated that the probation service prioritize these ends in areas of its activity, even if this meant diverting resources from other areas of probation work such as prisoner through-care and divorce court welfare work.

One of the intentions behind SNOP then was to encourage a degree of uniformity and consistency between individual probation services. Although this in itself was not uncontentious – hitherto diversity had generally been celebrated in the service (Mair, 1995) – it was the prioritising of work that caused the greatest furore. SNOP elevated the provision of alternatives to custody above all other aspects of probation work, followed by the preparation of SIRs. In relation to through-care it required no more of local services than the commitment of sufficient resources to ensure that the statutory minimum was undertaken. Even lower priority was accorded to community work and to civil work.

Individual probation services responded with *Statements of Local Objectives and Priorities* (SLOP) and one review of these documents (Lloyd, 1986) found great diversity in the responses. Crucially, Lloyd suggested that it was differences in philosophy which underpinned this diversity. During 1986 and 1987 the Home Office, through Her Majesty's Inspectorate of Probation (HMIP), also monitored the implementation of SNOP. It too noted considerable variation in responses with only a minority of areas identifying improvements in management practice as a result of implementation. Some areas continued to refuse to prioritise their activities (National Audit Office, 1989). Perhaps the significance of SNOP is that it was part of a raft of initiatives which increased central oversight and control of local service provision, in particular through the increasing amount of information that was required from, and was kept on, individual services.

The Probation Information System (PROBIS), which was developed within the Home Office, standardised the information kept by probation services. Information gathering, the development of performance indicators, questions of measurement and financial administration and management – the development, for example, of resource management information systems – have come to dominate much official thinking about probation. The provision of better information for the courts was the subject of Home Office circular 92/1986, Social Inquiry Reports, which examined the purpose and content of such reports. This followed on from two circulars published in 1983 (nos. 17 and 18) and emphasised the point that the SIR should contain impartial professional judgement and not special pleading; that it should be concise and not contain jargon; that it should, wherever possible, contain supporting evidence for the information provided; and that reports should be costed carefully and should be targeted where there was either risk of custody or the likelihood of a probation order. This led Harris (1992:147) to conclude that the 'Home Office approach to the social inquiry report is a microcosm of its approach to criminal justice more generally: the articulation of broad brush policies involving prioritisation, economy of content and relevance to major sentencing concerns, but with policy implementation left to local negotiations'.

A further Home Office report (the Grimsey Report) on the Probation Inspectorate recommended 'efficiency and effectiveness' inspections (Home Office, 1987), and in 1989 the Audit Commission issued a report entitled *The Probation Service: Promoting Value for Money*. This is discussed in greater detail below in connection with government policy as set out in the 1989 Green Paper.

In 1987, a joint publication from ACOP, CCPC and NAPO, entitled *Probation: The Next Five Years*, attempted to provide some sort of unified approach in the face of rapid change. The document affirmed the service's commitment to civil work and to through-care, both of which had been accorded a low priority by the Home Office in SNOP. It also, as the majority of subsequent documents in this area were to do, made the point that community sanctions were significantly cheaper than custody and therefore could be supported on 'efficiency' grounds as well as in terms of their 'effectiveness'. The debate within the probation service rumbled on, however, and within a year ACOP had published its own document which reflected, in both its title and its approach, the increasing punitiveness of the times. The document, *More Demanding Than Prison* (ACOP, 1988), suggested that the service concentrate its attentions on those most at risk of custody. In addition to outlining the demanding nature of the community sanctions being proposed it also followed the growing trend and emphasised the relative economy of using such an approach.

The line taken by ACOP was not greatly dissimilar from that espoused for the service by the Home Office when it published the *National Standards for Community Service Orders* (Home Office, 1988a). The National Standards made great play of the need to ensure that community penalties such as the CSO are viewed with confidence by sentencers, and that this was to be achieved by 'ensuring that CS makes uniformly stiff demands on offenders' (quoted in May, 1991:47). The culmination of all the government's initiatives in relation to the probation service and community sanctions throughout the decade was its 1988 Green Paper: Punishment, Custody and the Community (Home Office, 1988b). As one commentator put it: 'the implications of this document are particularly profound, although its ideas and proposals do not represent any sudden change with regard to probation' (Mair, 1989:35).

Punishment, Custody and the Community

The government's thinking was summed up in this document. The approach adopted in it can be crudely summarised as one in which it is acknowledged that custody is not the most appropriate penalty for the majority of offences and that it should be reserved for the most serious offences. The majority of offenders would, by contrast, be dealt with in the community. This approach has been described as one of 'bifurcation' (Bottoms, 1980) or even, given the increased emphasis on stiff punishments in the community, as 'punitive bifurcation' (Cavadino and Dignan, 1992).

The Green Paper was direct in its views on imprisonment. It pointed out that in 1987 over 69,000 offenders were sentenced to custody and it questioned whether this was the most effective sanction for all those offenders. It suggested that custody was most likely the right punishment for the majority of violent offenders, but pointed out that 95% of recorded crime was non-violent. For less serious offenders, custody might not be the right option:

> Imprisonment restricts offenders' liberty, but it also reduces their responsibility; they are not required to face up to what they have done and to the effect on their victim or to make any recompense to the victim or the public. If offenders are not imprisoned, they are more likely to able to pay compensation to their victims and to make some reparation to the community through useful work. Their liberty can be restricted without putting them behind prison walls. Moreover, if they are removed in prison from the responsibilities, problems and temptations of everyday life, they are less likely to acquire the self-discipline and self-reliance which will prevent reoffending in future. *Punishment in the community would encourage offenders to grow out of crime and to develop into responsible and law abiding citizens.* (Para 1.1, emphasis added)

Community-based sanctions were to be thought of as punishments which restricted liberty, but which enabled offenders to face up to the effects of their crimes, thus potentially being of benefit to the victim, and economical for the tax-payer.

The Green Paper made a variety of recommendations not only for the introduction of new measures, but also for changes that were felt might improve existing arrangements. It referred to the fact that national standards for CSOs were already being introduced, and that the intention was that these standards should ensure that the orders were 'more rigorous and demanding'. It pointed to the Criminal Justice Bill which was then before Parliament which contained a provision which, it was argued, would make it more likely that compensation would be paid to victims (see chapter 7 for details).

In relation to probation orders it suggested that written statements of an agreed programme of activities, including the courts' requirements, should be available to the courts, the supervising officer and the offender. It reinforced the importance of targeting the work of the probation service on those most at risk of custody (possibly using risk prediction scales) and, in particular, on young adult offenders (then 17–20 year olds). Young adults not only had high rates of offending, but also accounted for about one fifth of the custodial population and it was hoped that some of the impact that had been visible in relation to the juvenile custodial population (see chapter 6) could be transferred to young adults.

As far as proposals for the future were concerned, the Green Paper began by setting out the three principles underpinning alternatives to custody where a fine alone, given the seriousness of the offence, would be inadequate. First, that it should restrict freedom of action – as a punishment; second, that it should involve action to reduce the risk of further reoffending; and third, that it should involve 'reparation to the community and, where possible, compensation to the victim'.

The Green Paper set out a number of possibilities in relation to restricting the liberty of offenders. These included: introducing curfew powers for the courts to require offenders to stay at home at specified times; extending and formalising the existing experiments in 'tracking' – where ancillary probation staff are used to maintain frequent contact with the offender; and the introduction of electronic monitoring – which could be used as a method of enforcing curfews or supplementing the process of tracking – though the Green Paper suggested that it could most appropriately be used to keep offenders out of custody.

The economics of punishment and the fiscal imperative behind the Green Paper was spelt out very clearly:

It costs about £1,000 to keep an offender in prison for four weeks. The cost of punishment in the community should not exceed the cost of imprisonment, which is a more severe sentence. If the courts are to have a wide discretion with powers to place a range of requirements on offenders, they should take account of the costs to the taxpayers of carrying out the requirements. The courts will therefore need regular and up-to-date information about the cost of imprisonment and that of the individual components of the new order, e.g. the cost of a day's attendance at a day centre (now about £30), the cost of 10 hours community service (about £35), the cost of tracking an offender (about £15 a day). While the suitability of a penalty cannot be measured solely in terms of cost, the total cost of the requirements for an individual offender could be a useful check on whether the penalty is proportionate to the offence. (para 3.37)

The proposals were presented as being a great opportunity for the probation service, though given what has been said above about the history and philosophy of the service, a less than entirely positive reaction was undoubtedly anticipated. The Green Paper therefore concludes by exploring whether there are other agencies which might become involved in providing 'punishment in the community'. The police – with the exception of those officers working in attendance centres in their spare time – have no role in punishment or supervision of offenders; the prison service, it suggested, is not geared up to providing supervision in the community; and the private sector, though it might play some part in monitoring curfews, would find it difficult to take on wider-ranging responsibilities. The Green Paper therefore suggests the possibility that the probation service might contract with one or more of these other agencies, including the voluntary sector, to organise punishment in the community, but that it would continue to supervise the order.

Just in case the probation service did not like this new role being shaped for it, the Green Paper went on in bullish manner to say: 'Another possibility would be to set up a new organisation . . . It would not itself supervise offenders or provide facilities directly, but would contract with other services and organisations to do so . . . The new organisation could contract for services from the probation service, the private or voluntary sector and perhaps for some purposes from the police or the prison service . . . A new organisation would be able to set national standards and to enforce them, because they would be written into contracts' (para4.4).

Enter the auditors

When we come to look back from the perspective of the mid-1990s on the changes that have taken place in the outlook of the probation service, it is as well to remember the far-reaching structural reforms that a radical government with a broad policy of privatisation was willing to consider in the mid to late 1980s. There was no let-up for the probation service after the publication of *Punishment, Custody and the Community*. The previously mentioned inquiries by the Audit Commission and the National Audit Office were also underway, and the former used the Green Paper as its yardstick for evaluating the role and performance of the probation service.

The Audit Commission's press release provides an interesting summary of their diagnosis of the situation facing the probation service in 1989. Under the heading: 'The probation service needs to re-target its activities and develop new skills', the release read:

Britain's prisons are grossly overcrowded and courts are under pressure with record numbers of people remanded in custody. The probation service needs to re-target its activities and develop new skills if, as the Government intends, it is to play a greater role in solving the problem.

The 'market share' of the Probation Service has already grown from 9% of all sentences in 1977 to 16% in 1987. But that growth has not been matched with a reduction in the proportion of offenders going to prison, rather with a reduction in the number fined. It seems that many magistrates and judges lack confidence in probation and community service orders as alternatives to custody. It is in changing their perception that the Probation Service faces its single most important challenge.

Indeed, there is evidence to suggest that more effort by local probation services (e.g. more social inquiry reports) now results directly in offenders being given more serious sentences – probation rather than a fine – which makes them more likely to end up in prison if they reoffend. There is also little evidence that probation reduces the propensity to reoffend.

All this means that unless changes are made, increased emphasis on probation could have the opposite effect of that intended.

As a consequence, the Audit Commission recommended that the probation service should focus its activities by targeting more serious offenders; should evaluate the impact of that supervision; should work more closely with other agencies, particularly sentencers; and should establish more robust management procedures. It therefore downplayed casework skills –   the bedrock of probation practice for the previous forty or fifty years – and emphasised the centrality of intensive supervision and management of the offender. Predictably, the response in the service was critical with NAPO, for example, rejecting outright the Commission's proposals.

A parallel study was conducted the National Audit Office (NAO), looking at the Home Office's control and management of the probation service. The NAO affirmed the general process that was taking place saying that although the primary responsibility for the management and delivery of probation work had hitherto lain primarily with local probation committees and probation officers, 'increasing demands, finite resources, and *the need to harness probation work more closely to central policy objectives* mean that Home Office oversight and monitoring will inevitably assume greater prominence' (National Audit Office, 1989:6, emphasis added). It recommended improved information gathering and provision in relation to probation service work generally, about the use of resources and the costs and benefits of different interventions, and greater exchange of information with other criminal justice agencies.

Crime, Justice and Protecting the Public

Following on some time after the Green Paper, a White Paper containing the government's proposals for legislation was published in 1990 (Home Office, 1990c). It was a provocative document, and an editorial in the *Criminal Law Review* noted that: 'the proposals may be said to go further than any statement by a modern British Government in setting out aims of sentencing and in foreshadowing legislation which is designed to structure the sentencing discretion of the courts. The White Paper also contains declarations of intention on a range of other penal issues. The Home Office requests comments [within three months], but the proposals are so far-reaching that the debate will inevitably continue well beyond' (CLR [1990] 217).

One of the most interesting aspects of the White Paper is that it set out the grounds of the government's interest in sentencing policy.

Though reaffirming the independence of the judiciary – 'no government should try to influence the decisions of the courts in individual cases' – it nevertheless declared that 'sentencing principles and sentencing practice are matters of legitimate concern to Government' (para 2.1)

Underpinning the White Paper was the principle of 'proportionality' or 'just deserts'. Wasik has described the desert approach to sentencing as one which 'emphasises the moral requirement of maintaining a proper proportion between offence and punishment' (1992:124). The sentence should therefore be commensurate with the harm caused by the offender, and the degree of culpability involved. The emphasis that was therefore placed on deterrence was considerably diminished. The White Paper outlined a whole set of sentencing reforms and early release arrangements with the aim of creating 'a coherent framework for the use of financial, community and custodial punishments'. The White Paper was, with an important exception described below, quite clear about the priority of desert over deterrence:

Deterrence is a principle with much immediate appeal . . . But much crime is committed on impulse, given the opportunity presented by an open window or unlocked door, and it is committed by offenders who live from moment to moment; their crimes are as impulsive as the rest of their feckless, sad or pathetic lives. It is unrealistic to construct sentencing arrangements on the assumption that most offenders will weigh up the possibilities in advance and base their conduct on rational calculation. Often they do not. (para 208)

As was suggested above, the White Paper made one exception to its advocacy of just deserts. It advocated a 'twin-track' policy of sentencing (Ashworth, 1994) and separated out the sentencing of offenders convicted of a violent or a sexual offence from all others. In essence, the White Paper argued that there was an overriding need for public protection which meant that desert principles had to be suspended in such cases, with the consequence that the sentence passed could be significantly longer than that justified on the basis of just deserts.

The White Paper reiterated the disadvantages of imprisonment that had been outlined in the Green Paper (that it encourages dependence; may encourage criminal tendencies; and is expensive) and made a number of recommendations in relation to community penalties including the proposal that the probation order become a sentence in its own right, together with a 'combined order' of community service and probation. These proposals for further stiffening of community sanctions were accompanied by another Green Paper, *Supervision and Punishment in the Community: a Framework for Action* (Home Office, 1990a), which outlined recommendations for standards of probation practice. This signalled to the probation service that the national standards that had been introduced for CSOs in 1989 were to be extended to report-writing, probation orders, supervision orders – and any new orders – the management of hostels and supervision before and after release from custody [doc 11].

The legislative outcome of *Punishment, Custody and the Community* and *Crime, Justice and Protecting the Public* was, of course, the 1991 Criminal Justice Act. It was the product of a decade of consultation, proposal and counter-proposal and, seen from today's perspective, was unusual, though laudable, for this very reason. One set of commentators who were closely involved in the process said that: 'these policy initiatives by the Home Office were accompanied by extensive consultations, training exercises and "special conferences" across the criminal justice process. Unprecedented efforts were made closely to consult senior members of the judiciary, although officials later appeared to regret that more could not be done during the actual drafting stage' (Gibson *et al.*, 1994:81).

The Criminal Justice Act 1991

The key underlying principle of the sentencing provisions is that: 'The court should try to arrive at a sentence which is commensurate with the seriousness of the offence, taking account of aggravating and mitigating circumstances'. The so-called theory of 'proportionality' – the punishment fitting the crime – or 'just deserts'. (John Halliday, Deputy Under Secretary of State, Home Office, quoted in Gibson *et al.*, 1994:33)

Following the general thrust of the White Paper, the Act encouraged greater use of community sanctions within a sentencing framework informed by just deserts but not completely constrained by it. In its original form the Act sought to restrict the courts' powers to sentence 'on record', reduce the power of the executive in relation to discharge from prison, and to introduce 'unit fines' which, it was argued, would ensure greater equality through being related to offenders' disposable income. It also included provision for curfew orders and for electronic monitoring or 'tagging'.

Prior to the 1991 Act, the probation order was made instead of sentencing the offender. From this point onwards, the probation order became a sentence of the court, a change of significant symbolic importance for the service. Perhaps most far-reaching for the probation service was the introduction of what now became known as the 'combination order': the power of the court to sentence an offender to probation (with requirements if considered appropriate) and community service for the same offence. The intention clearly was to give the courts confidence that there were sentences at their disposal which were appropriate for use in relation to offenders who might otherwise have been incarcerated, i.e. that were sufficiently punitive. Specifically, it combined the probation order 'with its emphasis on the rehabilitation of offenders, with community service with its emphasis on punishment' (May, 1994:876). This is a combination that ten years previously might have split the probation service in two. Such had been the success of the process of consultation (or the long, slow process of culture change), however, combined with the very real threat contained in the 1988 Green Paper, that relatively little fallout from the Act was visible.

The just deserts approach of the Act was intended to have a profound effect on the probation service, indeed to put it 'centre-stage'. One of the keys to this was the intended role of the service in helping the courts determine the seriousness of the offence prior to sentencing. This meant a somewhat new role for the SIR – now renamed the 'pre-sentence report' or PSR. Following the Act, PSRs were to be one, if not the key source of information for assessing not only seriousness but also suitability – whereby a community order must be the one that is most suitable for the particular offender. It became mandatory for courts to obtain a PSR before the vast majority of custodial or community penalties could be passed.

Section 12 of the 1991 Act created a new order, the curfew order. These orders which were to be available for offenders aged 16 or over, require the offender to be at a place specified in the order for the period specified in the order – usually the offender's home. The curfew could operate from a minimum of two hours to a maximum of twelve hours per day for up to a total of six months. In addition – and a particular difficulty for many probation officers – such orders could henceforward be monitored using electronic 'tags'. As far back as 1987, the House of Commons Home Affairs Committee in a report on the *State and Use of Prisons*, had suggested that the Home Office should be examining the use that was being made of electronic tags in the United States. The possibility of such tags being used in the UK was raised in the 1988 Green Paper and later that year the Home Office had set in train plans for experiments in this area. The conclusions from this experiment were, to say the least, mixed. The rate of time violations recorded was quite high as was the level of equipment failure. Sentencers reported little confidence in tagging as an alternative to remands in custody, and overall most of those involved in the trials were sceptical of electronic monitoring and thought that if it had a place in the future of criminal justice in the UK, then it was probably a relatively small place (Mair and Nee, 1990:68).

The final major change brought about by the 1991 Act – though this is dealt with in greater detail in chapter 6 – is the introduction of the youth court. This replaced the juvenile court and deals with offenders aged 10–17, as opposed to 10–16 as was the case in the juvenile court. Consequently this brought together elements of the juvenile and adult court systems which previously had had separate practices and procedures. A joint Home Office/Department of Health circular issued in 1992 said that the new provisions would 'need to be carefully planned locally, in order to make the best use of opportunities and resources for constructive work with offenders in this age group and to avoid conflicts in objectives and working methods, duplication of effort, or failure to provide the necessary support'. In practice, this meant close co-operation between the probation service and social services, with an assumption that the two organisations would produce local action plans for dealing with 16 and 17 year olds.

Partnership has in fact become somewhat of a buzz word in recent years. As one example from a different area, as it has become progressively clear that the police cannot be held responsible for the overall level of crime in society, or indeed in a local community, so more and more emphasis has been placed on the role of other agencies, organisations and individuals in the prevention and detection of crime. 'Community policing' is one initiative that has developed as a result (Rosenbaum, 1994) and as an element of this, the notion of 'partnership' has become one of the most frequently used ideas in relation to modern policing. In a by no means dissimilar manner, the links between the probation service and other agencies working with offenders have increased markedly in recent years.

This has been supported by government and, according to the decision paper *Partnership in Dealing with Offenders in the Community* (Home Office, 1993b) approximately five per cent of each probation service's budget should be allocated to partnership work (Mair, 1995). This in many ways merely reflects the government's continuing commitment to a mixed economy in criminal justice. This has sometimes been presented as a policy of privatisation and, when certain developments are focused on narrowly, this is how it can appear. However, in almost all the areas of criminal justice in which the private sector has gained ground, the public sector and the voluntary sector have also been involved. Thus, for example, the above-mentioned decision document not only signalled the possibility of putting the running of bail hostels out to tender, i.e. potentially privatising them, but also encouraged greater involvement on the part of the voluntary sector in bail accommodation, prisoner welfare work, skills training and so on (McLaughlin and Muncie, 1994). Of course, underlying all this is the continuing concern with economy, efficiency and effectiveness. The core task and method of the service, at least as far as the government is concerned, is no longer the application of social work skills with offenders in the community, it is the strategic management and administration of punishments in the community.

The emphasis on information, measurement, management and administration can perhaps be seen at its clearest in the national standards which were first issued in relation to CSOs in the late 1980s, and then in relation to the rest of the work of the probation service not long after the Criminal Justice Act 1991 which came into force in October 1992. Covering five main areas of activity – pre-sentence reports, probation orders, combination orders, hostel management, and pre- and post-release supervision of prisoners – central oversight of the service is at unprecedented levels. The centre has, however, more recently changed its mind, not only in relation to the role and centrality of the probation service, but on criminal justice policy generally.

It has long been known that a change of minister, or ministers in a government department may have quite a profound impact on the direction and thrust of policy (Bottoms and Stevenson, 1992; Downes and Morgan, 1994), but it is probably fair to say that the extent, the speed and the manner of the reversal of criminal justice policy after the passage of the 1991 Act took virtually everybody by surprise. The appointment of Kenneth Baker brought the first signs that a more prison-oriented approach might be on the horizon, a view that his successor Kenneth Clarke was all too happy to confirm. The details of the reversal of policy are discussed in more detail in chapter 5, but the key elements allowing sentencers once again to look at all the offences before it (and not simply one offence and one associated offence as specified in the 1991 Act), and to take into account previous convictions have forced the probation service to change certain practices. More importantly, the renewed emphasis on prison, and the consequent demotion of community penalties means, at least in theory, that far less emphasis is placed on the work of the service. Furthermore, as part of the process of increasing central managerial control, in 1992 probation budgets became cash-limited. Whilst the probation service was centre-stage with increased resources promised cash-limiting was not a major problem, but now as probation drops down the list of government priorities, the means are in place to impose significant cuts in probation budgets and, indeed, such cuts are promised.

Concluding comments

What can be said, briefly, about policy in relation to the probation service and community penalties? A number of themes have been identified – several of them by no means confined to this area of criminal justice policy. The first theme of managerialism could actually be described in a number of ways, but it includes bureaucratization, performance measurement, and administrative control. The role of the probation service 'is now no longer welfare inspired but driven by court advocacy and the coordination of voluntary and private agencies' (McLaughlin and Muncie, 1994:124)

There is more to it, however, than merely the subjugation of professional skills to management ideals and the primacy of value for money. The second major theme is centralisation. Though the trajectory has not been entirely consistent, or the pace uniform, perhaps the overriding feature of change in this area has been the increasing power and control exercised by the centre. Just the increasing frequency of criminal justice legislation in relation to probation in the last twenty years, not to mention Home Office circulars, Green Papers, White Papers, consultation documents, decision documents, national objectives and priorities followed by national standards, computerisation, and the resource management information system suggests that in the tripartite structure of probation governance, it is the Home Office rather than the Chief Probation Officer or the local probation committee which is driving probation policy.

Managerialism and centralisation have had a profound impact on the underlying philosophy of the probation service. Crudely put, the probation service has, during its relatively short history, 'moved from a theologically to a psychiatrically driven discourse and then to what has been termed a post-psychiatric paradigm based less on therapy than on system involvement and offender management' (Harris, 1994:34).

Finally, out of a governmental distrust of public monopolies, a desire to encourage limited forms of privatisation, and a growing belief in the efficacy and economy of partnership, there has developed a *mixed economy* in the provision of certain services hitherto assumed to be the preserve of the probation service. What the future holds is unclear. One commentator has already noted that the combination of what has been described here as managerialism, centralisation and privatisation, could lead to a development of a gap in welfare provision for offenders and their families sufficiently large to encourage the re-emergence of some form of voluntary court and community-based *missionary*.

CHAPTER 5

Sentencing and non-custodial penalties

It is often suggested that one of the basic conventions in British criminal justice is that, as a result of the principle of judicial independence, sentencing policy is a matter for the judiciary rather than for the executive. As a consequence, sentencers have had 'a wide discretion to impose whatever sentence they deemed appropriate, subject to the maximum penalty' (Clarkson and Morgan, 1994: 105). However, commentators such as Ashworth (1992) challenge the idea that the principle of judicial independence can be so broadly defined, and he suggests that rather than being a constitutional principle, it has in fact been merely a policy preference. Nevertheless, as has been suggested, the idea that such a separation actually exists has a certain currency, a currency it acquired 'largely as a result of parliamentary abstention which had its origins in the late nineteenth century and reached its zenith in the third quarter of this century' (Ashworth, 1992:41).

As a number of writers have pointed out, however, the policy preference identified above has begun to be challenged in recent years: 'government ministers have with increasing frequency addressed remarks to sentencers, and the judges have declared that they are taking account of the gross overcrowding in the prisons' (Ashworth, 1983:98). Not only is it being challenged, but Ashworth (1983) among others has argued that it is right that it should be challenged, for those responsible for the formulation of penal policy have, he believes, tended to have too little regard to sentencing, and that what is required is some means of improving coordination of policy in the criminal justice system. Though Ashworth's (1992) preferred option of a sentencing council has not come to fruition there was a period, as we shall see, around the time of the Criminal Justice Act 1991, in which an attempt was made to impose a structure on courts' sentencing powers.

As will by now be clear, if one concern has dominated penal policy over the past twenty-five years it has been the aim of reducing the prison population (see chapters 2 and 4). Equally, it has been the overriding concern with prison numbers which has led to gradual breaking down of the previously existing convention that sentencing policy was not a matter for the executive. As Clarkson and Morgan (1994;107) summarise it: 'The use of custody is always an expensive penal option and the expense is called into question if the incapacitative, deterrent and rehabilitative benefits are doubtful and if control or reduction of public spending has a high priority'. In seeking to limit custody, the key method that has been utilised during the last two to three decades has been the introduction and use of an increasing array of alternatives to immediate custodial sentences. The assumption has been that such alternatives would help 'exert some influence over the number of occasions on which courts resort to immediate custody' (Ashworth, 1983:116).

The focus of this chapter is upon the introduction and use of alternatives to custody, and the impact of such changes on the size of the custodial population. As we move on to look at the recent trends in the use of non-custodial penalties by the courts the reason for beginning this chapter with a brief discussion of the ideas of sentencing policy and judicial independence will become clear. The reason, in short, is that the ever-increasing range of alternatives – what Ashworth (1992:242) calls the *policy of proliferation* – has not been a success. There has been no marked fall during the past twenty-five years in the use of custodial sentences – indeed, quite the reverse. What are the reasons for this failure? The first reason, according to Stern (1989), is that already alluded to: there is a 'taboo' which inhibits discussion of sentencing policy. The taboo prevents or limits the extent to which politicians feel able to recommend changes in sentencing policy. Indeed, 'the whole idea of sentencers being influenced by Home Secretaries is highly contentious' (Stern, 1989:41). Secondly, the practice of sentencing is highly individualistic and subject to wide geographical variation. Given the absence of consistency in sentencing 'it is no wonder that . . . the intentions of the policy-makers, even if they were accepted as legitimate, are thwarted' (Stern, 1989:42). Finally, even if recommendations are made there is no formal mechanism for translating them into practice. Sentencers are not government officials, they use their personal judgement in applying the law in each case they are faced with. 'Undoubtedly all those who pass sentences on offenders use prison as a "last resort" – it is just that for some the "last resort" comes more readily than for others' (Stern, 1989:42–3). In beginning to unpick what has happened since the late 1960s, it is worth beginning by looking at the use and impact of some of the major non-custodial sentences in turn.

The probation order

The probation order was dealt with in detail in chapter 4 and it will be sufficient here merely to review the changing pattern in its use over the past three decades. From the mid-1960s, and through the 1970s, there was an almost continual decline in the use of the probation order (see Table 5.1). Whilst there is no simple explanation for this decline, the introduction of the suspended sentence of imprisonment and of community service orders clearly played a part. Bottomley and Pease (1986) have also suggested that some of the decline in the 1970s may have been due to a tendency on the part of sentencers to fine rather than use probation, a tendency which itself declined in the 1980s as unemployment rose and financial penalties became an apparently less appropriate option in many cases. The low point for the probation order came in 1978 when only 5% of people aged 21 and over sentenced for indictable offences received probation. This had risen back to 8% by 1989 (the figure had been 15% in 1938).

The six month probation order was introduced in 1978 and it proved popular, as did shorter orders more generally. Approximately one quarter of probation orders in the early 1970s were of three years in length, but the proportion had declined to under one in twenty by the mid-1980s. By contrast the proportion of one year orders increased from one in ten to one in three during the same period. The trend in the period immediately before the Criminal Justice Act 1991 was towards greater use of probation, and the Act sought to reinforce this process. However, the whole nature of the probation order has now, of course, changed. Prior to the Criminal Justice Act 1991 a probation order was made 'instead of sentencing' the offender. Since the passage of the Act probation has become a sentence of the court, i.e. a punishment. The Act states that the court may not impose a community sentence, for example probation, unless the offence 'was serious enough to warrant such a sentence'. Consequently, therefore, the court must be satisfied that the offence was too serious to warrant, say, a fine or a discharge.

Community service orders

Community service orders (CSOs) were introduced by the Criminal Justice Act 1972, but were not in operation nationwide until the mid-1970s. CSOs were, in part, the product of the deliberations of the Advisory Council on the Penal System. The ACPS had produced a report in 1970 on Non-Custodial and Semi-Custodial Penalties (known as the Wootton Report) which recommended the introduction of CSOs as an alternative to custody, though it suggested that it also had the potential attraction of being different things to different people:

To some, it would be simply a more constructive and cheaper alternative to short sentences of imprisonment; by others it would be seen as introducing into the penal system a new dimension with an emphasis on reparation to the community; others again would regard it as a means of giving effect to the old adage that the punishment should fit the crime; while still others would stress the value of bringing offenders into close touch with those members of the community who are most in need of help and support. (ACPS, 1970, quoted in Ashworth, 1992:267)

However, as Ashworth points out, no attempt was made either by the ACPS or by the government to locate CSOs within courts' broader sentencing practices. Indeed, Ashworth (1983) describes community service as a good idea (the fact that its meaning is intrinsically ambiguous has made it popular with sentencers) but in many ways a vague idea: 'It stands as a prime example of the failure of those concerned with penal policy-making to pay sufficient attention to the sentencing implications of what they do' (1983:118). Crucially, although the CSO was introduced essentially as an alternative to custody, this was not made clear in the 1972 Criminal Justice Act which simply restricted their use to imprisonable offences.

Under a CSO an offender is required by a court, assuming that the offender consents, to undertake between 40 and 240 hours of unpaid work. The work is organised and supervised by the probation service. The CSO became an established sentence fairly rapidly, accounting for 4% of sentences received by persons aged 21 and over convicted of an indictable offence in 1980, rising to 7% in 1987 and 9% in 1993. Approximately one in six young adult offenders are dealt with in this way and it has always been a sentence that is used disproportionately on this age group. As to its impact as an 'alternative to custody', research by Pease (1980; 1985) suggested that only something in the region of half of those receiving CSOs would otherwise have been sentenced to custody. In a similar fashion, Young (1979:140) concluded: 'the hope that the community service order would divert a substantial number of offenders from custodial sentences may have been unduly optimistic . . . It might have been hoped that, in the courts which made greater use of imprisonment there would have been more scope for the use of the community service order as an alternative to it; in fact, in general the reverse was true.'

The fine

The most long-standing of the non-custodial penalties which currently exist is the fine. Initially, courts required that fines be paid in full and it was not until 1914 that paying by instalments became possible. One consequence of this was a very sharp reduction in the number of offenders imprisoned for non-payment of fines. The major increase in the use of fines took place after the Second World War when the range of indictable offences that could be punished in this way was considerably broadened. By the 1970s, over half of adult offenders convicted of indictable offences were fined and it has incontrovertibly been the most successful community penalty at displacing custody. Part of the success of the fine has been at the expense of probation (Bottomley and Pease, 1986; Cavadino and Dignan, 1992) and the conditional discharge. As was suggested above, the increasing popularity of the fine seemed to tail off in the 1980s, a time when the use of other non-custodial penalties and indeed custody itself was rising quite dramatically. Undoubtedly unemployment and the consequent inability of many offenders to pay substantial financial penalties was a significant factor in this transformation.

Varying ability to pay, and how this ability should be assessed and the level of fines set has been an ever-present difficulty with this penalty. Many European countries have sought to solve such difficulties by using a system known as the 'day fine' where the level of the fine is linked to the offender's weekly disposable income. Such a system – known as 'unit fines' – was introduced by the Criminal Justice Act 1991 and subsequently withdrawn by the Criminal Justice Act 1993. Ostensibly, the introduction of the unit fine system was an object lesson in 'good government'. Possible changes were widely canvassed, significant consultation took place with the majority of interested parties, a rigorous evaluation of an experimental system in four Crown Courts was undertaken and published, and yet the new system was barely in operation before it was dismantled. We will return to this remarkable penal *volte face* below when the Criminal Justice Act 1991 is discussed in greater detail.

The suspended sentence of imprisonment

The suspended sentence of imprisonment was introduced at the same time as parole, by the 1967 Criminal Justice Act. As was suggested in chapter 2, it had been considered and rejected twice in the 1950s by the Advisory Council on the Treatment of Offenders, and interest in the measure was reawakened in the 1960s – indeed, as with many criminal justice measures at the time it received cross-party support. Ashworth (1983:116) argues that 'the popularity of the suspended sentence with the government of the time was strongly connected with their desire "to find ways of emptying the prisons."' In addition, however, it was also believed that it would prove to be a useful extra non-custodial penalty.

Up until 1972 courts were required to suspend the majority of prison sentences of under six months. The situation now is that courts are empowered to suspend prison sentences of two years or less, for a period of between one and two years. If during the period of the suspension the offender is convicted of commiting a further offence, the court is obliged to send the offender to prison.

The problem with the suspended sentence as a method of controlling the use of custody is that it seems clear that its use has by no means been confined to those cases in which immediate custody would otherwise have been ordered. Though estimates vary, it is suggested that up to half of those given suspended sentences would not have been sentenced to immediate custody had the suspended sentence not existed. Research by Bottoms (1981) points to a number of reasons for this state of affairs.

Table 5.1 Percentage of offenders sentenced for indictable offences, by selected sentences (all courts), 1963–93

	Probation order	Fine	CSO	Imprisonment Suspended	Immediate
1963	20	40			14
1968	15	44		9	9
1973	7	51		6	8
1978	5	51	3	7	9
1983	7	43	7	7	9
1988	9	39	8	8	11
1993	10	34	11	1	11

First, in addition to the aim of avoiding imprisonment it appears that there was a more generalised 'special deterrent' theory associated with the suspended sentence which encouraged courts to use it in place of certain non-custodial sentences in some circumstances (Bottomley and Pease, 1986) despite legal rules to the contrary. Second, some courts have tended to impose longer sentences when the sentence was suspended than they would have done when ordering immediate imprisonment (Bottoms, 1981). Bottomley and Pease (1986:91) sum up the limited impact of the suspended sentence on the prison population in the following way:

'Three in ten of all offenders given suspended sentences are reconvicted of a new offence before the period of suspension has expired. Judicial instructions specify that under these circumstances the suspended sentence is usually activated (i.e. you go directly to jail). They further specify that any prison sentence in respect of the new offence be served consecutive to, and not concurrent with, the activated suspended sentence. In consequence, many of those reconvicted after a suspended sentence eventually go to prison for longer than they would if the original sentence had not been suspended. When it is also remembered that no more than half of those given suspended sentences would previously have been given a custodial sentence, it is clear that any contribution made by the suspended sentence to the reduction of the prison population can only be marginal. More importantly, the operation is unfair.

The general trends in the use of the major custodial and non-custodial penalties over the past 30 years are contained in Table 5.1 above.

Recent history in sentencing practice can be divided into a number of periods. Ashworth (1983) distinguishes two periods: 1967–72 and 1973–81. To this may be added the periods up to and just beyond the Criminal Justice Act 1991 and, finally, the period since 1992. Ashworth has argued that the main characteristic of penal change between 1967 and 1972 was the introduction of a series of new penalties for the courts to use in the sentencing of offenders. In the period following this up until the early 1980s it 'was the orchestration of changes in the sentencing practices of the courts' (1983:132). As we have seen above, there had been significant statutory change in the late 1960s and early 1970s, and even though there was very little legislative change between 1973 and 1981 there was nevertheless quite considerable change in sentencing practice (see Table 5.1). Thus, in the mid-1970s the use of immediate and suspended imprisonment were at their lowest proportionate level and the fine was at its highest. From that point onwards the fine and probation have taken a smaller share, whereas the use of immediate imprisonment and community service has increased. As we saw in chapter 2, with the decline of the rehabilitative ideal the principal justifications for imprisonment changed during this period.

In addition to changes in penal policy and sentencing practice, Ashworth (1983:132) also suggests that the way in which penal policy was made and promulgated also changed. Indeed, he distinguishes between two periods, 1973 to 1978, and the period 1979 to 1981. In the first of these the Advisory Council on the Penal System 'assumed a much more assertive role than it had hitherto thought appropriate . . . The use of the ACPS as a vehicle for formulating and promulgating policy passed away in 1979 with the demise of that body. In its place rose government ministers and the Lord Chief Justice, a combination peculiarly appropriate to the kinds of change which were thought necessary – changes in sentencing practice rather than legislative structure.' What were these changes in sentencing practice that the government wished to encourage?

The policy advocated by government ministers was one of 'bifurcation': whereby long custodial sentences would be reserved for the violent, the dangerous and those from whom the public need protection; and shorter sentences or non-custodial sentences would be increasingly used for the more run of the mill offenders. Indeed, in considering penal policy in detail in this period, Hudson (1993) suggests that three themes or trends, each of which can be considered as a dichotomy, can be identified. Thus the first of these, bifurcation, is set against 'continuum', the other two trends being informalism/formalism, and corporatism/individualism. It is worth considering each of these briefly in turn, before moving on to consider penal policy in the 1990s.

The first trend – continuum/bifurcation – is based partly around the proliferation of sentencing options that developed in the 1970s and 1980s. Continuum refers to the idea that there should be some consistency in the nature of punishments. Hudson refers to an influential book by the American criminologist, James Q. Wilson, in which he suggests that the deprivation of liberty should be the common feature of all punishments for criminal acts. The continuum would range from those disposals which had only a marginal effect on the offender's liberty on the one hand to imprisonment on the other. 'The continuum principle can be seen at work in many of the innovations of the 1970s and 1980s: weekend or part-time prison in continental European countries; the more rigorous day centre requirements in England, as well as residential blocks in intermediate treatment programmes for juveniles' (Hudson, 1993:33). The opposite trend to this is the aforementioned 'bifurcation', which can be seen in the increasing sentence lengths for certain serious offences – and consequent increasing custodial population despite the declining proportionate use of imprisonment – during this period.

The second dichotomy is that of informalism/formalism. One of the responses to the feeling that the increasing expenditure on criminal justice and the increasing array of sanctions available to the courts was having precious little effect on levels of crime was to move away from formal processes for dealing with offenders. Particularly in relation to juvenile justice policy (see chapter 6) a policy of 'diversion' was increasingly advocated. By this was meant, at its most minimal, diversion from custody and, at its most far-reaching, diversion from formal criminal justice processes. This might mean, amongst other things, the *de facto* decriminalisation of certain offences; informal cautioning rather than charging, or referral to mediation schemes rather than charging and prosecuting. During the 1980s, however, there developed a fairly full-blown critique of the proliferation of diversion schemes and alternative forms of dispute resolution. The majority of the arguments gelled around Cohen's (1979) 'dispersal of discipline' thesis [doc 12]. Crudely, Cohen's argument was that there has been a dispersal of discipline and social control via the increasing use of community-based penalties and the policy of diversion. One of the unintended consequences of informalism was to draw into the criminal justice system people who would not otherwise have been dealt with under formal procedures. In addition, 'diversion schemes also formalised the informal by giving quasi-official powers to new people – parents, social workers, colleagues became parties to contracts, treatment, reporting' (Hudson, 1993:40). In his critique of Cohen, Bottoms (1983) suggests that an analysis of the period since the war shows that both imprisonment and probation declined as a proportion of all offences and that, in fact, it was the penalties not involving supervision – such as the fine and the suspended sentence – which flourished. This, as we have seen, was reversed in the 1980s with a significant decline in the proportionate use of the fine, and a commensurate increase in the use of probation, community service and imprisonment.

One of the consequences of the critique of informalism was the development of the contradictory trend towards formalism. Formalism involved a desire to return to type of classical or formal justice model. The most influential of these were based on the 'just deserts' principle which would link sentencing to the seriousness or gravity of the offence under consideration. At its core, however, Hudson (1993) suggests that this model contained a desire to curb professional discretion through sentencing guidelines (generally via the Court of Appeal). In addition, the Criminal Justice Act 1982 imposed limiting criteria for imposing custodial sentences on offenders under the age of 21 and on any offenders not previously sentenced to custody. Hudson (1993:45–6) concludes that 'The innovations of informalism have been maintained, but have been incorporated in the formal justice system. They have been subjected to more and more control by the state, to more formal procedures and criteria, so that the combined effect of the seemingly contradictory impulses to formalism and informalism has been aggregative rather than counter-balancing'.

The final trend Hudson identifies is that of corporatism/individualism. She suggests that there was an increasing trend throughout the 1980s to individualise penalties, particularly non-custodial penalties, by specifying programmes tailored to the needs of the individual offender. However, 'this greater differentiation and individualisation which can be demonstrated in criminal justice policy and practice is largely, however, a tactic in a strategy which is anything but individualistic' (Hudson, 1993:47). The 'corporatist' approach within which this individualisation has occurred has, for example, refocused attention on crime rates rather than individual offenders, and on prison numbers and overcrowding rather than the effects of punishment on the individual.

Much of what happened in the 1980s appears to have occurred despite the absence of a well developed or articulated penal policy. Nevertheless, the primary driving force remained the crisis in the prison estate. Despite the proliferation of alternatives to custody in the 1960s and 1970s, the policies of bifurcation and informalism and, crucially, increasing attempts to limit judicial discretion throughout the 1980s, the prison population continued to rise (see chapter 2). This, together with the collapse of faith in reductivist goals, and increasing recognition of the sentencing disparities which existed in different parts of the country (see Ashworth, 1984), led to pressure for reform of sentencing policy. As Wasik (1992:127) argues 'the apparent ineffectiveness of the Court of Appeal in persuading sentencers to send fewer offenders to custody, and for shorter periods of time . . . persuaded the legislature that this objective ha[d] to be achieved by legislative reform to fetter the discretion of sentencers.' The result was the Criminal Justice Act 1991.

The Criminal Justice Act 1991

Out of the variety of competing sentencing principles still around during the 1970s and 1980s, it was desert theory which by the end of the decade had won the day. The desert approach to sentencing puts the emphasis upon the moral requirement to maintain proportionality between offence and punishment. The primary assumption behind the punishment is that it should be what is deserved for the offence, having regard to the seriousness of the harm caused or risked by the offender and their degree of culpability. Desert theory treats the sentencing of offenders as something that is quite distinct from either tackling the causes of offending or attempting to do something about overall crime levels in society.

It would be wrong, however, to present the ascendancy of just deserts at this time as if it were merely the triumph of one principle over another. Whilst there was certainly waning confidence in the reductivist strategy which placed so much emphasis on deterrence, the placing of faith in just deserts and subsequent Criminal Justice Acts barriers to the use of custody 'owed just as much to pragmatic considerations about the costs and benefits of punishment in prison as to any weakening of resolve to be "tough on crime"' (Raine and Willson, 1993:39). Perhaps the clearest indication that desert principles were in the ascendancy was in the publication of the 1990 White Paper, *Crime, Justice and Protecting the Public*. It was very clear about the limitations of deterrence as a basis for penal policy:

Deterrence is a principle with much immediate appeal . . . But much crime is committed on impulse, given the opportunity presented by an open window or unlocked door, and it is committed by offenders who live from moment to moment; their crimes are as impulsive as the rest of their feckless, sad or pathetic lives. It is unrealistic to construct sentencing arrangements on the assumption that most offenders will weigh up the possibilities in advance and base their conduct on rational calculation. Often they do not. (Home Office, 1990c, para 2.8)

The White Paper proposed reforms both to sentencing and early release arrangements, with the aim of creating 'a coherent framework for the use of financial, community and custodial punishments'. In doing so it proposed that proportionality should be the basis upon which decisions about the severity of sentences should be made (Wasik and von Hirsch, 1990). Thus, under the new structure the courts would continue to decide both upon sentence severity in relation to individual offences and on the weight given to any aggravating or mitigating circumstances. The major recommendations in the White Paper were incorporated in to the Criminal Justice Act 1991.

Wasik (1992:131) suggests that the best way to understand the Act is 'as laying down a set of general guidelines for sentencing. There is no American style sentencing grid, so that guidance is by general principles expressed in words rather than by numbers. The Act deals with custodial sentences, community sentences, fines and discharges which can be seen as occupying four distinct levels in a pyramid, with custodial sentencing at the top and discharges at the base [see Fig. 5.1]. Selection of the appropriate level for sentencing in this hierarchy is crucially dependent upon the seriousness of the offence of

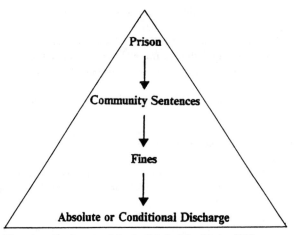

Fig. 5.1   The sentencing framework in the Criminal Justice Act 1991

conviction. Offence seriousness determines into which sentencing "box" the sentence will fit, and also at what level within that particular "box". Of course, offence seriousness has always been an important element in sentence decision making but . . . other factors have been used by sentencers to override it. The importance of the Act lies in its conceptual framework, and its emphasis upon the proportionality between offence seriousness and penalty severity.' Although in establishing a framework the Act prevented the use of custody unless the court was satisfied that the offence was 'so serious that only a custodial sentence could be justified', it did allow for an exception to this framework. Thus, in cases of violent or sexual offences, courts could impose a prison sentence if it was believed that only such a sentence would be sufficient to protect the public from serious harm from the offender. Such a sentence could also be longer than would be proportionate to the seriousness of the offence that had been committed.

It is in relation to the application of 'just deserts' to community penalties that Wasik (1992) suggests that the Act is perhaps most innovative, for up until this point such principles had rarely been applied to non-custodial penalties. The Act states that a court shall not pass a community sentence 'unless it is of the opinion that the offence, or the combination of the offence and one other offence associated with it, was serious enough to warrant such a sentence'. Thus, the only justification for imposing a community sentence under the Act is offence seriousness and, crucially therefore, community sentences are not to be considered to be 'alternatives to custody', but as distinctive penalties in their own right. Indeed, it was at this point that the probation order became a sentence in its own right rather than an order made in place of a sentence. The Act then represented a significant departure not only from previous legislation, but from the previous style of policy-making. As one senior Home Office official commented:

The Act can be seen as a first attempt to construct a truly comprehensive piece of legislation governing sentencing. It covers the whole process: virtually the whole range of disposals available; the reasoning to be applied when reaching decisions; the methods by which sentences can be calculated and implemented; and, in the case of custody, the whole process from reception, right through to the expiry of the the term imposed. The sheer scale of the attempt, taken as a whole, is probably unprecedented. Previous reforms have been more piecemeal . . . The Act breaks new ground in another way. This Act – as distinct from any others on the subject – seeks to incorporate a clearly stated set of principles about sentencing – a sentencing philosophy if you like . . . Governments habitually explain their policies in White Papers – in this case, the White Paper 'Crime, Justice and Protecting the Public'. If this is the case, the Act seeks to incorporate the policies in statutory form. (Quoted in Gibson *et al.*, 1994:33)

In what ways, then, does the 1991 Criminal Justice Act alter the range of non-custodial penalties outlined at the beginning of this chapter? [doc 13] One of the primary aims of the 1991 Act was to promote community penalties as tough and demanding, and as realistic options for courts who were to be discouraged from overuse of custodial sentences. As the Green Paper published in 1988 put it: 'Imprisonment is not the most effective punishment for most crime. Custody should be reserved as punishment for very serious offences, especially when the offender is violent and a continuing risk to the public. But not every sentencer or member of the public has full confidence in the present orders which leave offenders in the community. [Hence] . . . the Government's proposals, which aim to increase the courts' and the public's confidence in keeping offenders in the community' (Home Office, 1988b:1–2).

One consequence of the proportionate approach to sentencing is, as suggested above, that community penalties can no longer be considered to be 'alternatives to custody'. No longer was it the case that a court might consider a custodial sentence to be the appropriate one, but then decide that an alternative strategy might be pursued in relation to a particular offender. The idea in the new scheme was that community punishments should themselves be sufficiently demanding so that they could be used in all but the most serious of cases.

One of the key changes introduced by the 1991 Act was the amendment of the system of fines. Largely in response to perceived difficulties and inequities in the operation of the system of financial penalties, the 1991 Act contained provision for the introduction of what has been called the 'unit fine'. In essence, and using a set of guidelines, offences before the court were to be assessed in terms of their number of units of 'seriousness'. This could range from 1–50 units. Once the seriousness of the offence had been determined in this manner, the offender would be required to complete a means form which would assess their weekly disposable income. This would determine the amount to be paid per individual unit, subject to the statutory minima and maxima of £4 and £100. In principle, the intention was that fines should be equalised in terms of their impact upon offenders committing similar offences but who were of vastly differing means. A lot of effort went into piloting the new system. In the magistrates' courts in which the research was conducted fines were paid more quickly, there were fewer committals to prison for default, the poorest defendants were fined the least, and there was no extension in the use of fines (Moxon *et al.*, 1990). However, unit fines were implemented on a rather different basis from that operating in the pilot and were widely criticised almost from the outset. Raine and Willson (1993:38) suggest that 'the "professionals" were wary about their discretion being eroded and many were opposed to the scheme, especially when a serious offence by a low income defendant attracted a smaller fine than a minor one by a comparatively wealthy defendant'. We will return to unit fines below.

It has been suggested that one of the consequences of the Act was to end the status of the probation order as a conditional release granted instead of a punishment, and to make it a sentence in its own right. It became one of several 'punishments in the community'. In addition, the minimum age at which an offender could be placed on probation was lowered from 17 to 16 years, and the criteria for the making of a probation order were clarified. As has been suggested, the policy of bifurcation which underpinned the White Paper and the 1991 Act, consisted in part of an attempt to persuade sentencers to increase their use of community sanctions. In doing so the Act introduced a new, tough community penalty: the 'combination order'. This was probation and community service combined; the minimum period of supervision being 12 months, the maximum three years. Section 12 of the 1991 Act created a new order, the curfew order. In addition, there was also provision for electronic monitoring to take place, though a curfew order could be made with such 'tagging'. These orders could be made on anyone over the age of 16 and they required the offender to be in a specified place at a specified time.

What of the suspended sentence of imprisonment? How did this penalty fit into the new system? As Cavadino and Dignan (1992) argue, the suspended sentence does not fit easily into the just deserts framework established by the 1991 Act. Most importantly, the problem centres around the fact that it is in theory the most severe penalty short of immediate custody, yet many sentencers clearly perceive it to be somewhat less punitive in practice. This was clearly articulated in *Crime, Justice and Protecting the Public* (Home Office, 1990c): 'In practice, however, many offenders see a suspended sentence as being "let off", since it places no restrictions other than the obligation not to offend again. If they complete the sentence satisfactorily, all they have felt is the denunciation of the conviction and sentence, any consequent publicity and, of course, the impact of acquiring a criminal record. The suspended sentence does not fit easily into the proposed new sentencing arrangements.' The 1991 Act abolished the partly suspended sentence and in relation to the fully suspended sentence provided that courts could not impose such a sentence unless, first, the case was one in which immediate custody would have been satisfied and, second, that the suspension of the sentence could 'be justified by the exceptional circumstances of the case'. The result, Ashworth (1992:277) suggests, 'is confusion perpetuated and confounded'.

Overall, however, the Criminal Justice Act 1991 was greeted very favourably by penologists, criminologists and many criminal justice pressure groups. Paul Cavadino of NACRO writing in 1992 said: 'Taken overall, the Criminal Justice Act 1991 has the potential to bring about a more rational and coherent sentencing framework which uses custody more sparingly and community sentences more appropriately. Whether it fulfils this potential in practice will depend on the joint efforts of all agencies working in the criminal justice system to make the best use of the Act's many positive features'. In terms of sentencing trends after the Criminal Justice Act 1991 there appear to be two distinct phases (Gibson *et al.*, 1994). There was, first of all, a short period in which the use of custody fell, followed by a longer period in which the trend was reversed. As a consequence of the first phase the number of prisoners held in police cells was substantially reduced and was halted, temporarily, in February 1993. During this first phase it appears that the use of community service orders increased fairly substantially, though the number of probation orders fell. In addition, of course, there was the use of the completely new community penalty: the combination order. Finally, there was evidence from the Home Office that in the wake of the introduction of the unit fine system the overall use of the fine for indictable offences was increasing (Home Office Statistical Bulletin 25/93).

Retreat from the 1991 Act

Despite the extensive process of consultation that had preceded the White Paper, the broad degree of support for the intentions behind the legislation that there appeared to be amongst criminal justice professionals and practitioners, and some of the early positive signs visible in sentencing, it was not long before a governmental retreat from the 1991 Act began. It started with the arrival of Kenneth Baker as Home Secretary and the reintroduction of penal populism in the form of campaigns against 'bail bandits' and 'joyriding' – the latter ending with the hasty passage of new legislation: the Aggravated Vehicle Taking Act 1991. It was, however, the appointment of Kenneth Clarke as Home Secretary that signalled a more radical change in the criminal justice policy agenda (his impact on policing policy has already been noted in chapter 3). One of his first moves was to initiate, with the support of the police and the press, a campaign against so-called 'persistent young offenders' (Hagell and Newburn, 1994) and, more specifically, to recommend the possible introduction of new (custodial) measures to deal with the perceived problem caused by such offenders. This is discussed in greater detail in the next chapter.

Kenneth Clarke, whilst Home Secretary, avoided becoming personally associated with the implementation of the 1991 Act and gave every impression of being generally unhappy with it. The new Lord Chief Justice, Lord Taylor of Gosforth, entered the debate, criticising the new framework introduced by the Act:

However forward-thinking the penologists, criminologists and bureaucrats in government departments may be, their views should not be allowed to prevail so as to impose a sentencing regime which is incomprehensible or unacceptable to right-thinking people generally. If this happens, there could be a real risk of aggrieved parties taking the law into their own hands . . . I believe the fundamental error underlying the Act is a misconceived notion that sentencing should be programmed so as to restrict the discretion of the sentencing judge . . . The laudable desire to reduce and confine custodial sentencing to cases where it is really necessary has led to restrictive provisions forcing the judges into an ill-fitting strait-jacket. (quoted in Raine and Willson, 1993:90)

He was followed into the fray by the Magistrates' Association which was publicly critical of s.29 of the Act (which limited the extent to which previous convictions could be used in determining the seriousness of the offence and therefore the appropriate sentence) [doc 13] and of unit fines which were held to be causing sentencers significant difficulties (there was a major furore in the press over a case in which someone was fined £1000 for dropping a crisp packet). Clarke's response was to appear to be sympathetic to the criticisms and to promise an inquiry into the alleged shortcomings of the legislation. Whilst the subsequent transfer of the combative Mr Clarke to the Treasury might have been expected to have resulted in a return to normal business in the Home Office, his replacement, Michael Howard, soon signalled that he desired to be seen to be just as 'radical' as his predecessor. In addition to contradicting the bulk of the advice and evidence he was given on the limitations of imprisonment as a criminal justice strategy, he embarked on what appeared to be a one-man crusade to reintroduce the type of hard-line policies of twenty years previously. These included restricting cautioning, toughening bail decision-making, restricting juvenile justice agencies' work with young offenders and making prison regimes more austere. In the country at large, public worries about crime were heightened by the brutal and shocking murder of two-year-old James Bulger in February 1993, and the very high profile trial of the two ten-year-old defendants later in the year. At the 1993 Conservative Party conference the Home Secretary in outlining his criminal justice policy – a policy which he recognised would lead to an increase in the use of custodial sentences – said: 'I do not flinch from that. We shall no longer judge the success of our system of justice by a fall in our prison population . . . Let us be clear. Prison works.' This reassertion of Thatcherite 'law and order' values culminated in the passage of legislation to amend the 1991 Act, an Act which after years of consultation had only been in force a matter of months.

The Criminal Justice Act 1993 reversed some of the key elements of the earlier legislation, in particular the criteria justifying the use of custodial sentences; the role of an offender's previous record in sentencing; and the unit fine system. Whereas the 1991 Act restricted the courts to no more than two current offences when deciding whether custody was justified, the 1993 Criminal Justice Act amended this so that courts could in future consider the combined seriousness of any number of offences. Second, whereas the 1991 Act stated that an offence should not be regarded as more serious by reason of any previous convictions or any failure to respond to previous sentences, the 1993 Act states: 'In considering the seriousness of any offence, the court may take into account *any* previous convictions of the offender or any failure of his to respond to previous sentences' (emphasis added). Finally, the 1993 Act removed the system of unit fines and replaced it with a system in which fines are 'a flexible product of seriousness and financial circumstances . . . [though] what weight is given to particular factors in a given case are left to the court' (Gibson *et al.*, 1994:156).

Reflecting upon these changes, one former senior Home Office administrator said: 'The Government's change of direction in its policies on crime and criminal justice is probably the most sudden and the most radical which has ever taken place in this area of public policy' (quoted in Gibson *et al.*, 1994:84). From early 1993 onwards, and perhaps not surprisingly given the nature of the most recent criminal justice legislation, sentencing trends began to change. First of all there was a very sharp increase in the prison population, though this was partly a consequence of an increase in the number of prisoners on remand. There was some indication that commencements of both probation orders and community service orders rose, though there also appeared to be a trend towards longer orders (ACOP, 1994). The most recent information from the Home Office suggests that these trends are continuing. Thus, although there was some levelling off of the proportionate use of community sentences for indictable offences in the Crown Court, the proportionate use of custody rose by 4 per cent and 12 cent respectively in the magistrates' courts and the Crown Court during 1993 (Home Office, 1994a). Finally, the proportionate use of the fine for indictable offences at magistrates' courts, having risen after the 1991 Act, fell from 45 per cent of sentences at the end of 1992 to around 38 per cent at the end of 1993.

Despite the breadth and the speed of change in penal policy the legislative programme was, however, still not complete. In addition to reaffirming his belief in the efficacy of imprisonment, Michael Howard announced at the 1993 Conservative Party conference a 27 point package of 'emergency action to tackle the crime wave'. This included restricting the right to silence, reducing the use of cautioning and tightening bail provisions, and the introduction of secure training centres for persistent juvenile offenders. Later in the year the Criminal Justice and Public Order Bill was introduced, and it included, in some form, all the above-mentioned measures, together with a good deal more. The Bill had a fairly stormy passage in Parliament, but became law in 1994. The Act includes, amongst others, provisions for secure training orders for 12–14 year olds (see chapter 6); increases the grounds for refusing bail; allows inferences to be drawn from the use of the right of silence; and introduces a new offence of aggravated trespass. Although as a piece of legislation it has little coherence and is, in many ways, merely a mish-mash of largely unconnected provisions, it clearly belongs within the Thatcherite 'law and order' crime control tradition. It is in many ways hard to believe that it is less than half a decade since the desert-based Criminal Justice Bill was first published. It was a piece of legislation that took many years to construct, and yet it was undermined in a matter of months, at least partly because of a short-term, though highly visible populist media campaign. Despite its detractors, and the apparent ease with which it was dismantled, the Criminal Justice Act 1991 had a great many supporters. Indeed, it was the view of one former Home Office minister that that particular piece of legislation:

held out greater promise than any of its predecessors in the cycle of criminal justice legislation since 1948. For the first time, after a long and painstaking period of gestation, Parliament was presented with what was intended to be a coherent statutory framwork for sentencing ... Both the judicial and political omens were favourable. Despite some reservations about the way the sentencing provisions were expressed, there was no attempt by the higher judiciary to oppose or reject them on the grounds that their independence or prorogatives were being encroached. The discreet consultation with the judges, dating back to the first tentative approach by Whitelaw a decade earlier, paid the hoped for dividend. Politically, the Opposition parties, and the criminologists and the penal practitioners to whom they looked for specialist advice, were generally well disposed. (Windlesham, 1993:404–5)

Conclusion

The impression is sometimes given by ministers and judges that the prison population is in some sense a product of forces of nature beyond political or judicial control. Like the weather moving in from the Atlantic we can at best track its course and make reasonable preparations for its coming. The analogy is entirely false. It is true that the level of crime is not readily amenable to control by government. But there is no mechanical relationship between the level of crime and the size of the prison population. There is no objective formula for deciding what tariff of punishment should be attached to a particular offence. Nor, to put the issue the other way round, is the safety of the public greatly affected by the number of offenders in prison. No force beyond government control is involved. The size of the prison population is politically determined, *whether by government action or inaction*. It follows that the prisons debate is not just about prisons. It concerns criminal justice policy generally. (Morgan, 1992b:13–14)

Chapter four outlined the origins and history of the probation service and the probation order (amongst other disposals). This chapter has considered the more recent history of non-custodial penalties and trends in sentencing. The period from the turn of the century to the Second World War saw in many ways the high point of probation. It saw the establishment of a professional service, and the increasing use of a community-based disposal which, it was believed, would lead to the reform of a significant proportion of those sentenced to such supervision. However, the decline of the rehabilitative ideal, and the ever-increasing size of the prison population in the 1960s and 1970s led to the introduction of a bewildering array of non-custodial penalties, the intention being that they should in many cases be thought of and used as *alternatives to custody* with the aim of reducing the prison population.

The policy of proliferation was, however, generally a failure. As Bottoms (1987:198) put it: 'Some of the measures seen in certain respects to have had some modest success, yet almost all of them can also be shown to have run into severe difficulties of one kind or another.' The reasons for the failure are highly complex but they failed, at least in part, as a consequence of a perception widely held amongst many sentencers that the alternatives to custody were actually 'soft-options' and not alternatives at all. As a consequence of the process of attempting to persuade sentencers of the efficacy of these penalties there was a drift towards a more punitive period in community sentencing in the 1970s and 1980s (May, 1994). Punishment in the community, and the management rather than the treatment of offenders became the order of the day. Still, however, the prison numbers crisis steadfastly remained.

The solution attempted was a radical one and involved the introduction of a statutory framework which would constrain the use of custody and encourage increased use of community penalties. After an extended process of consultation and deliberation a desert-based framework was introduced and hopes were high that prison overcrowding, the use of police cells as overspill, and the serious rioting in prisons which accompanied overcrowding, poor conditions and loss of control, would become a thing of the past. For a short time, prison numbers declined and the use of community penalties increased. But it was not to last. The rediscovery of 'authoritarian populism' (Hall, 1979) first by Kenneth Clarke, and then by Michael Howard, resulted in the quickest and most complete U-turn in criminal justice policy this century. Just deserts as an explicit sentencing rationale was diluted by a renewed faith in the deterrent and incapacitative qualities of the prison. As a consequence, there was a 20 per cent increase in the prison population in the two years 1993–4, at the same time as the most punitive elements of community penalties were emphasised. Lamenting a process that seems set to continue for some time, Gibson *et al.* (1994: foreword) comment: 'Forward looking and considered policies – made following wide consultation and leading to the Criminal Justice Act 1991 – have been eroded without proper scrutiny. Every government has the right to legislate, but criminal justice issues are too important to be rushed through Parliament in the way that they are being at present, propelled by power politics.'

The preceding discussion of the failure of the 'policy of proliferation' and the continued, seemingly inexorable increase in the prison population provides an interesting backdrop to the next subject: juvenile crime and juvenile justice policy. The reason for this is that an alternative strategy was developed successfully in relation to juvenile crime in the 1980s – a strategy referred to above as informalism and diversion – one consequence of which was a significant decline in the use of custodial penalties for young people.

CHAPTER 6

Juvenile offending and juvenile justice policy

Introduction

It is not unusual for young people to get into trouble with the police. The majority of those that do will only have informal or transient contact, but a significant minority will go on to acquire a criminal record at some point in their adolescence. It is well established that approximately a third of male adults will have been convicted of at least one standard list offence by their thirties (Home Office Statistical Department, 1985), and most of these will have been as a result of offences committed when they were juveniles (Farrington, 1986).

Public discussion of crime, especially where young offenders are concerned, tends to be extremely emotive and characterised by more than its fair share of historical myopia (Pearson, 1983). Before moving on to consider the workings of the modern youth justice system it is worth looking further back at the history of criminal justice policy in relation to young offenders and, briefly, at juvenile crime itself.

Juvenile crime

One cannot know for certain how much crime is committed by young people. As the British Crime Survey (BSC) shows (*inter alia*, Mayhew *et al.*, 1989), a high proportion of crime is not reported to the police. In addition, only a minority of those crimes which do figure in the official statistics are cleared up with the result that the age of the offender is known. The best indicator we have of 'youth crime' is the number of young people known to have offended, that is, those who have been cautioned for or convicted of a crime. It has now become almost commonplace to argue that compared with times such as the early nineteenth century, current levels of crime are far from unusual (Pearson, 1975, 1983; Gurr, 1976). However, taking a shorter time-frame – the period since the Second World War for instance – there does seem to be some cause for concern [doc 14]. There was, for example, an almost 150 per cent increase in the number of 14–17-year-old male offenders in the population between 1959 and 1977. However, since that time the pattern of recorded juvenile crime has been rather different. In the period from 1980 to 1990 the number of juveniles cautioned for or convicted of indictable offences fell by

37 per cent, a dramatic turn-around which is discussed in greater detail below.

Nevertheless, it is important to bear in mind that a high proportion of all offences are committed by young people. Indeed, the relationship between age and offending has been the subject of considerable criminological scrutiny. The prevalence of offending peaks in the mid-to-late teens and decreases steadily thereafter (Farrington, 1990). So stable has this relationship been found to be over time and place that it has even been described as invariant (Hirschi and Gottfredson, 1983; Gottfredson and Hirschi, 1990). While such a view has not gone unchallenged (Farrington, 1986) the age-crime curve remains one of the most basic facts of criminology. In addition to age, offending is also closely associated with sex (Newburn and Stanko, 1994). The analysis conducted by the Home Office of the criminal careers of people born in 1953 which found that almost a third of males had been convicted of a standard list offence by the time of their 31st birthday, also showed by contrast that this was the case for only 7 per cent of females (Home Office Statistical Department, 1985). Although numerous, the majority of juvenile crimes are, however, non-violent in character. In 1990, for example, of all indictable offences for which juveniles were cautioned or found guilty, 10 per cent involved violence (Home Affairs Committee, 1993). The majority – 60 per cent – involved theft or handling stolen goods, 17 per cent were burglary offences, and 4 per cent were criminal damage. Finally, offending is for the majority of young people a transient phenomenon. A number of researchers have suggested that most young people commit some offences, which in the main do not lead to significant contact with the police or courts (Belson, 1975; West, 1982), and that the majority of those who are regularly arrested and prosecuted will nevertheless eventually desist. There remains, however, little rigorous data on the reasons that lie behind this desistance.

The history of juvenile justice

The last hundred years of juvenile justice have been characterised by dual tendencies best described as 'punishment' and 'welfare'. However, one need look back no further than, say, 150 years, to find a time when children were not only punished with imprisonment, but were also subjected to transportation and even the death penalty. Although there is some dispute about the extent to which adults and children were treated differently by the criminal justice system, it seems clear that during the latter half of the nineteenth century, alongside the development of the modern construction of childhood (Aries, 1962; Thane, 1981) came increasing concern about the welfare of children, parallelled by the development of the new professions of paediatrics and child psychiatry, and the emergence of the notion of 'delinquency'.

A variety of social reformers campaigned to protect children from danger and exploitation. One of their key demands was that children should be removed from the 'adult' prison system and placed in privately managed, state-funded institutions. In addition, such institutions would also be a source of succour for the orphaned and the destitute. One of the most vocal social reformers was Mary Carpenter, who argued that three types of institution were required, free schools for the deprived, industrial schools for young vagrants and beggars, and reformatories for convicted youngsters (Rutherford, 1986a).

Statutory provision for reformatories began in 1854 as a result of the Youthful Offenders Act of that year. Children under 16 could be sent there after serving a prison sentence for a period of between two and five years. The schools were inspected by the prison inspectors. Legislation in 1857 established the industrial schools, though for a few years these were part of the educational system rather than the penal system. They came under Home Office control after 1860. The initial arrangement was that children aged between 7 and 14 who had been convicted of vagrancy could be committed to an industrial school until the age of 15.

One commentator has suggested that the 'acceptance of Mary Carpenter's belief that children should not be dealt with as men, but as children, was a seminal point in the evolution of the modern child' (May, 1973). However, one of the unintended consequences of the introduction of the reformatories and industrial schools was the rapid increase in the number of young people in institutions. According to Rutherford (1986a), 'by 1858 only four years after the enabling legislation there were 45 reformatories holding 2,000 young people. Twelve years later there were 65 reformatories holding 7,000 young people.' Much of the later history of juvenile justice in England and Wales follows a broadly similar pattern of attempts at reform – often dominated by welfarist concerns – followed by an increase in the size of the incarcerated juvenile population.

It was not until almost the turn of the century that the period of imprisonment prior to reformatory school was abolished and, as Harding *et al.* (1985:242) note, 'the general trend, in so far as it can be identified, was to a less regimented school environment, emphasising the role of education rather than discipline'. By the 1880s, the number of industrial schools exceeded that of reformatories, reaching a high point in 1915 and falling away thereafter.

Most histories of juvenile justice begin near the turn of the century with the development of the juvenile court (see, for example, Platt, 1969). In the mid-1890s, Asquith, the Home Secretary, set up two departmental committees to examine the penal system. The first, the

Gladstone Committee, examined the prison system (see chapter 1), and the second, chaired by Sir Godfrey Lushington, reformatories and industrial schools. The split between 'punishment' and 'welfare' was evident in the products of these two committees, with the Gladstone Report advocating 'treatment' alongside punishment in prisons, particularly in the case of young prisoners, and the Lushington Committee, by contrast, advocating alternatives to imprisonment, looking in particular to education as one of the remedies for juvenile crime.

By the turn of the century a number of towns were operating separate juvenile courts, and the election in 1906 of a reformist Liberal government ensured that they were put on a statutory footing, at approximately the same time as the statutory creation of probation, of preventive detention and provision for 'borstal training'. The Probation of Offenders Act was enacted in 1907 (see chapter 4), followed by the Children Act 1908 (the 'Children's Charter') and the Prevention of Crime Act of the same year. The Children Act barred under-14s from prison and provided that 14–15-year-olds could only go to prison if the court issued an 'unruly' certificate. It included sections dealing with the prevention of cruelty to children, referred to begging and prostitution, but is best known for establishing juvenile courts. These courts were empowered to act not only in criminal cases but also in cases of begging and vagrancy. They remained, in essence though, criminal courts.

The Prevention of Crime Act of the same year included provision for 'borstal' institutions. These were intended to cater for the type of person (16–21-year-olds – the 'juvenile-adult category') who 'by reason of his criminal habits and tendencies or associations with persons of such character, it is expedient that he should be subject to detention for such a term and such instruction and discipline as appears most conducive to his reformation and the repression of crime' (quoted in Garland, 1985). It was some time however before any distinctive borstal regime developed. Borstal training involved a semi-determinate custodial sentence (the date of release was determined by Prison Commissioners) of one to three years and release was followed by a period of supervision for a minimum of six months. The aims of the borstal institutions were defined as 'reformation' and training', and these were achieved through 'physical exercise, moral instruction, [and] industrial or agricultural training' (Garland, 1985). As Humphries (1981:212; [doc 15]) notes:

Although it has often been assumed that penal reform was motivated by a humanitarian concern for the rights and protection of deprived children, in fact the issue that dominated public debates and government reports was that of the control and reformation of rebellious working-class youth . . . From the turn of the century onwards reformatories were controlled by a professional body of penal administrators who attempted to infuse the system with the public school ethos of Christian manliness and patriotic duty.

Just as juvenile courts had grown informally prior to the passage of legislation so, similarly as we have seen, arrangements for the supervision of offenders within the community also existed before the Probation of Offenders Act 1908. Young people formed by far the majority of probationers, and by 1920 80 per cent of the 10,000 people under probation supervision were under 21 (Rutherford, 1986a). Although the Great War shifted attention away from penal policy there was, within a few years of the outbreak of war, a significant increase in recorded juvenile crime – from approximately 37,000 juveniles charged in 1913 to over 50,000 in 1917 – and some consequent congestion in the reformatories and industrial schools (Bailey, 1987).

By the early 1920s there was also some public disquiet following media allegations of brutality in a number of the borstal institutions (Humphries, 1981). In January 1925 a Home Office Departmental Committee on the Treatment of Young Offenders (the Molony Committee) was set up. The terms of reference of the Committee were wide, being to look into the treatment of young offenders under 21 and those who as a result of poor surroundings were in need of 'protection and training'. The Committee favoured the retention of the juvenile court and recommended that magistrates should be given the fullest possible information about those who appeared before them, including their home circumstances and their educational and medical histories (Morris and Giller, 1987). The focus at this time, then, was firmly upon the 'welfare' of young offenders and the 'treatment' necessary to reclaim or reform them.

The principle that young people were not only to be dealt with separately from adults but in a way that promoted their welfare was also to be found in the Children and Young Persons Act 1933. The 1933 Act incorporated much of what the Molony Committee had to say concerning those up to the age of 17 (in fact the committee's proposals were given statutory force by the Children and Young Person's Act 1932 which was consolidated by the 1933 Act), though it did not bar 16-year-olds from borstal as the Committee had recommended. It did, however, give legislative effect to what had become administrative practice by prohibiting capital punishment for those under the age of eighteen. The reformatory and industrial schools were reorganised following the 1933 Act, thereafter being designated 'Schools approved by the Secretary of State', and they continued in this form through to the end of the 1960s.

In 1936 the maximum age for a borstal sentence was raised from 20 to 22, and these institutions constituted the only expanding part of the prison system in the inter-war years. There had been a sea-change during this period: prison numbers had declined, institutions closed, probation thrived and, as one later report claimed, 'in a variety of ways . . . Britain became the centre of the prison reform movement' (Home Office 1979, quoted in Windlesham, 1993). The borstal system was at its high point at this time. The regime that had developed 'was very much that of the boy scout ethos: outdoor pursuits and summer camps and a physically invigorating environment, away from the criminal contamination in urban cities, which would inculcate self-respect and self-reliance' (Harding *et al.*, 1985:247). The system's reputation dwindled quickly after the war, however, as did its success rates (Mannheim and Wilkins, 1955).

Between 1938 and 1945 recorded indictable offences rose by 69 per cent, and before long the prison population began to swell, and the increase in juvenile crime exposed the difficulties inherent in a system dependant on accommodation provided by charities and local authorities. In 1942 the Home Secretary, Herbert Morrison, began to push for the establishment of a committee on penal reform. Eventually in 1944 an Advisory Council on the Treatment of Offenders under the Chairmanship of Mr Justice Birkett was set up. The post-war Labour government embarked on an extensive programme of legislation and a Criminal Justice Bill was introduced in 1947. It was heavily based on recommendations made before the war[1] which 'strongly emphasised the unwisdom of sending young persons to prison' (quoted in Bailey, 1987) and, indeed, the 1948 Act did place a number of restrictions on the use of imprisonment. It also introduced remand centres, attendance centres, support for probation hostels and abolished corporal punishment. However, the Magistrates' Association had renewed their demands for a new short-term custodial sentence and this was eventually accepted by the Labour Government. The Home Secretary, Chuter Ede, told the House of Commons: 'there is a type of offender to whom it is necessary to give a short, but sharp reminder that he is getting into ways that will inevitably lead him into disaster . . . their regime will consist of brisk discipline and hard work' (quoted in Rutherford, 1986a). The detention centre order introduced by the Act was intended to be a short unpleasant sentence which would combine hard work with the minimum of amusement – a sentence not unlike the 'short, sharp, shock' experiment of the 1970s.

Although there was considerable continuity between the Criminal Justice Bill of 1938 and the 1948 Act, there were also significant differences. Thus, although in 1938 a Conservative Home Secretary rejected the idea of Detention Centres, a decade later his Labour successor accepted the idea. Indeed, the provision passed through Parliament with the minimum of debate, as most eyes were directed towards proposals to abolish capital and corporal punishment (Dunlop and McCabe, 1965; Windlesham, 1993). As will be clear from this discussion, the 1948 Act was far from being an entirely punitive piece of legislation, and the continuing concern about the 'welfare'

---

[1] Recommendations originally contained in the *Young Offenders Report* 1927, and later in the 1938 Criminal Justice Bill.

of juveniles also found expression in the Children Act passed in the same year. Influenced by a report from the Care of Children Committee, the Children Act sought to end the placement of neglected children in approved schools alongside offenders, and to that end set up local authority children's departments with their own resources for residential care and trained staff to oversee fostering and adoption, thereby creating 'the first professional social work service exclusively for children' (Harris and Webb, 1987).

The post-war period was characterised by a continued rise in recorded juvenile crime, and it was increasingly suggested that the approved school system was unable to cope with some of the hardened juvenile offenders that were coming before the courts (although provision for Detention Centres was included in the 1948 Criminal Justice Act, the first of these institutions was not opened until 1952[2]). As Windlesham (1993) has argued, from this point on 'the twin claws of the pincer that was to hold the development of penal policy fast in its grip were the remorseless increase in the incidence of crime, and the overcrowding in the prisons'.

The 1950s closed with the Ingleby Committee which was set up in 1956 to inquire into the operation of the juvenile court. In its report of 1960 the committee endorsed the structure of the juvenile court, and it rejected any merger of approved schools with other residential accommodation or the removal of responsibility for these institutions from the Home Office. At least one commentator has suggested that a close reading of the report suggests that the committee favoured the development of a local authority-based system of social service based on the Children's Departments established in 1948 as a method of decriminalising juvenile justice (Stevenson, 1989). The major focus of the committee's deliberations centred around the conflict that it felt existed between the *judicial* and *welfare* functions of the juvenile court. This, it suggested, resulted in:

a child being charged with a petty theft or other wrongful act for which most people would say that no great penalty should be imposed, and the case apparently ending in a disproportionate sentence. For when the court causes enquiries to be made . . . the court may determine that the welfare of the child requires some very substantial interference which may amount to taking the child away from his home for a prolonged period.

The solution proposed by the committee was to immediately raise the age of criminal responsibility from 8 to 12 'with the possibility of it becoming 13 or 14' (Morris and Giller, 1987), and below that age

---

[2] Provision for (Senior) Attendance Centres was also included in the 1948 Act but it was a full decade before they came into being. For a full history see Mair, G. (1991) *Part-Time Punishment: The Origins and Development of Senior Attendance Centres*, London: HMSO.

only welfare proceedings could be brought. The major proposals did not become law – the Children and Young Persons Act 1963, by way of compromise, raised the age of criminal responsibility to 10 – although one author in particular has argued that they were of considerable symbolic importance to later events (Bottoms, 1974).

The Ingleby Report polarised the two main political parties over the issue of juvenile justice; the Labour Party welcomed its proposal with regard to the age of criminal responsibility, but was critical of what it took to be the Committee's timidity, and in response set up its own inquiry under the chairmanship of Lord Longford. This recommended the total abolition of the juvenile courts on the basis that 'no child in early adolescence should have to face criminal proceedings: these children should receive the kind of treatment they need without any stigma' (quoted in Bottoms, 1974). The alternative was to non-judicial consultation between the child, the child's parents and a newly formed 'Family Service'. The Longford Report was followed by a White Paper, *The Child, the Family and the Young Offender*, which reproduced much of Longford, including proposals to establish family councils and family courts, and to abolish the juvenile courts. On this occasion, with legislation a significant possibility, the proposals were vehemently attacked by lawyers, magistrates and probation officers (Bottoms, 1974). With its small parliamentary majority to protect, the Labour government withdrew the proposals (Clarke, 1980).

Three years later a second White Paper, *Children in Trouble*, was published and this, after some relatively minor amendments, found legislative embodiment in the Children and Young Persons Act 1969. The system of approved schools, and that of remand homes or remand centres for juveniles which existed alongside them, was abolished by the 1969 Act, and they were replaced with community homes with residential and educational facilities (CHEs), though their subsequent history was far from happy. The juvenile court was retained under the Children and Young Persons Act (the proposal for a family court did not reappear), but the intention signalled by the White Paper was to increase the age of criminal responsibility to 14. Care was preferred over criminal proceedings; the circumstances under which court proceedings were possible was to be narrowed. Thus, 'care and protection' proceedings could be instituted for children between 10 and 14, but only when it could 'be established that the child was not receiving such care, protection and guidance as a good parent might reasonably be expected to give' (Morris and Giller, 1987). Juveniles between 14 and 17 could be subject to criminal proceedings but it was to be necessary in future for the police to consult with the local authority children's department before making an application to a magistrate. The intention was that the juvenile court should become a welfare-providing agency but also 'an agency of last resort' (Rutter and Giller, 1983), referral should only happen in those cases in which informal and voluntary agreement had not been reached between the local authority, the juvenile and the juvenile's parents (Morris and McIsaac, 1978).

It was also intended that detention centres and borstals for juveniles would be phased out and replaced by a new form of intervention – intermediate treatment. 'This (though) was less a policy of decarceration than a reiteration of the traditional welfare abhorrence of the prison system' (Rutherford, 1986b). Indeed, the 1969 Act was itself made up of a series of compromises:

First, in design, it promoted both diversion *from* courts and the provision of welfare *in* courts. And second, by design, it . . . perpetuated competing conceptions of juvenile offenders and of how best to deal with them . . . The full machinery of courtroom adjudication was retained for those who saw juvenile offenders as responsible and who believed in the symbolic and deterrent value of such appearances. At the same time, an emphasis on social welfare . . . was retained for those who saw juvenile offenders as the product of social circumstances. (Gelsthorpe and Morris, 1994:965, emphasis in original)

Between the passage of the Act and the putative date for its implementation there was, once again, a change of government and the new Conservative administration announced that it would not be implementing significant sections of the legislation. The consequence was that juvenile courts continued to function pretty much as they had before – criminal proceedings for 10–14s continued, powers in relation to 14–16-year-olds were not restricted, and the minimum age for qualification for a borstal sentence was not increased. Perhaps most significantly, although care proceedings on the commission of an offence were made possible, such powers were used exceedingly sparingly, and the more traditional 'punitive' disposals were used increasingly by the juvenile courts during the 1970s – the number of custodial sentences, for example, rising from 3,000 in 1970 to over 7,000 in 1978 (Rutter and Giller, 1983; Cavadino and Dignan, 1992). Indeed, this general trend led an influential group of commentators from Lancaster University[3] to comment that:

The tragedy that has occurred since (the passage of the 1969 Act) can be best described as a situation in which the worst of all possible worlds came into existence – people have been persistently led to believe that the juvenile criminal justice system has become softer and softer, while the reality has been that it has become harder and harder. (Thorpe *et al.*, 1980, quoted in Muncie, 1984)

---

[3] These authors who, themselves, advocated an approach to juvenile justice known as 'systems management', 'can claim a substantial degree of success' according to Cavadino and Dignan (1992). The authors were critical of traditional welfarism which they argued failed, despite its best efforts, to limit the degree of state social control over juvenile offenders.

Despite the fact that it was only partly implemented, the 1969 Children and Young Persons Act (CYPA69) became the scapegoat for all the perceived ills of juvenile crime and juvenile justice in the 1970s, and Rutherford (1986a) has cast doubt on the extent to which practice actually changed. He has suggested that it was 'the ideas and attitudes . . . culminating in the 1969 Act . . . on which the campaign for counter-reform was mounted.' The Act was attacked from all sides, not just those critical of its 'welfare' elements, and within three years of its implementation a sub-committee of the House of Commons Expenditure Committee had been set up to make recommendations for change. The omens were not good, however, for:

the inquiry was based on the assumption that the Act was not working although no evidence was quoted in favour of this. The membership of the Committee included at least two former magistrates and one former manager of an approved school, but nobody with close working or personal connections with the social work profession or social services departments. (Farrington, 1984)

Although treatment and welfare had been heralded as the basis for progress from the late 1960s onwards, the legislative platform on which such a programme might have been built was never properly constructed. The Expenditure Committee, while accepting that there was a class of juvenile that required care and support rather than punishment, nevertheless was much influenced by the view that there was also, as the Magistrates' Association put it in their evidence: 'a minority of tough sophisticated young criminals . . . [who] . . . prey on the community, at will, even after the courts have placed them in care. They deride the powerlessness of the courts to do anything effective' (quoted in Rutherford, 1986a).[4] This statement, it is worth noting, bears more than a passing resemblance to much of what was said in the early 1990s in relation to so-called 'persistent juvenile offenders'.

As a consequence the Committee argued that it was important to 'hasten the process in the case of certain offenders to deter others from embarking on criminal activities, to contain a hard core of persistent offenders, and to punish some offenders' (House of Commons Expenditure Committee, 1975, quoted in Morris and Giller, 1987). The aim of the Committee was, then, to make some form of distinction between children who need care and those who in their words require 'strict control and an element of punishment', and were critical of the

---

[4] Rutherford (1986) quotes two further members of the Association expressing similar views; "Sir William Addison talked of 'the hard core of young offenders – that is to say, the offenders in the youngest age group – that is now resulting in the very serious increase in the incidence of crime in the 15 to 17 age groups'. Mr RC Stranger added: 'the hard core of sophisticated young criminals hitherto considered and spoken of as small in number but which one fears [is] increasing'."

1969 Act for not doing so even though the Act deliberately attempted to obscure such boundaries.

In response the government issued a White Paper (Home Office and others, 1976) which was ambivalent in its views of juvenile justice, both recommending a shift away from residential care and towards supervision and fostering, whilst also sharing 'the widespread anxiety that is felt . . . about the continuing problem of how to cope with a small minority, among delinquent children, of serious and persistent offenders. It is in this area . . . that the present measures under the Act are felt to be falling short' (Home Office and others, 1976, para.3). Though it did not attempt to define how this hard core of persistent juvenile offenders might be distinguished from the majority, it nevertheless signalled the intention to establish different strategies and systems for dealing with each.

It is hard not to agree with Morris and Giller's (1987) conclusion that juvenile justice policy at the end of the 1970s 'bore little resemblance to that proposed in the 1969 Act.' In particular, they suggest, the police and the Magistrates' Association had been successful in establishing their model of 'juvenile delinquency' as the dominant one in operation in the juvenile justice system. Responsibility for the 'persistent juvenile offenders' that they identified as the core of the problem was increasingly placed in the hands of local authority Social Services Departments. A joint working party on persistent juvenile offending that included representatives of the magistracy and local authorities reported in 1978, but failed to agree on how the problem should be tackled. The Magistrates' Association continuing to press for short detention centre orders, a demand that was being echoed by William Whitelaw, the Shadow Home Secretary, who by this stage was calling for the introduction of 'short, sharp, shock' treatment (Harwin, 1982).

The Conservative manifesto of 1979 had promised to strengthen sentencing powers with respect to juveniles and young adults and the 1980 White Paper, *Young Offenders*, included proposals for the reintroduction of a limited number of detention centres with 'tougher' regimes, and this 'experiment' began in two centres – Send and New Hall – in 1980. The subsequent Criminal Justice Act 1982 shortened the detention centre sentence: its minimum and maximum lengths were reduced from 3 and 6 months to 21 days and 4 months (Cavadino and Dignan, 1992). Imprisonment for under-21s was abolished and the end of the road for borstals was signalled with the new order for 'Youth Custody' (the institutions becoming known as Youth Custody Centres). The Youth Custody Order was a determinate sentence whose length was fixed by the sentencing court (though with the possibility of remission and parole). The minimum Youth Custody sentence was 4 months 1 day, and magistrates and juvenile courts could impose sentences between the minimum and 6 months. The government's intention was that the shorter (though 'sharper') sentence, together with a requirement that sentencers should only impose a custodial sentence if they were

Table 6.1   Males aged 14–16
sentenced to custody, 1971–90

Year	Number
1971	3,200
1972	3,800
1973	4,400
1974	5,300
1975	5,900
1976	6,600
1977	6,900
1978	7,300
1979	6,900
1980	7,400
1981	7,700
1982	7,100
1983	6,700
1984	6,500
1985	5,900
1986	4,300
1987	3,900
1988	3,200
1989	2,300
1990	1,700

Source: Home Office Criminal
Statistics for England and Wales.

satisfied that no other alternative was possible,[5] would reduce the
number of juveniles held in custody (discussed in *Young Offenders*,
1980, para.46). There was considerable scepticism in some quarters,
however, at the extent to which the government really was committed
to the use of community-based alternatives to imprisonment, and there
were fears that custodial institutions would become ever more central
in juvenile justice (Allen, 1991).

Taken together, the White Paper and the 1982 Act represent a fairly
fundamental attack on the welfarist principles that underpinned the
Children and Young Persons Act. Gelsthorpe and Morris (1994:972)
have argued that they 'represented a move away from treatment and
lack of personal responsibility to notions of punishment and individual

---

[5] S.1(4) of the Criminal Justice Act 1982 laid down that a young offender could
only be sentenced to custody if the court was satisfied that one of the following
three conditions was met: (a) that the offender was unable or unwilling to respond
to non-custodial penalties; (b) that custody was necessary for the protection of the
public; or (c) that the offence was so serious that a non-custodial penalty could not
be justified. (The criteria were subsequently amended by the Criminal Justice Act 1988
and eventually superseded by the new criteria in the Criminal Justice Act 1991 which
also apply to adults.)

and parental responsibility. They also represented a move away from executive (social workers) to judicial decision-making, and from the "child in need" to the juvenile criminal – what Tutt (1981) called the "rediscovery of the delinquent."'

Unlikely as it may seem against this background, a significant and sustained decline in the use of custody for juveniles is exactly what happened during the 1980s (see Table 6.1). As Rutherford (1986a) commented, the paradox is that 'the decade of "law and order" was also the decade of what has been called "the successful revolution" in juvenile justice.'

One former Home Office minister has described this transformation as 'one of the most remarkable post-war achievements of deliberate legislative enactment' (Windlesham, 1993), and seen against the backdrop of 'evolution, revolution and counter-revolution' in juvenile justice (Morris and Giller, 1987) described above, it is impossible to deny that it is indeed a remarkable achievement. The extent to which it may be attributed to deliberate legislative enactment is, however, somewhat more debateable.

In the first instance, although it cannot explain the full extent of the fall in numbers, there were significant demographic changes during this period which must be taken into account. There was, for example, a 17 per cent decline in the number of males in the 14–16 age group between 1981 and 1988. Furthermore, in the same period the number of young people sentenced also decreased by about 38 per cent. The success of the general policy of 'diverting' juveniles from prosecution meant that there were far fewer candidates for custodial sentences. This policy arose partly as a result of the insight from labelling theory that involvement in the criminal justice process may, on occasion, reinforce rather than deter further offending (Taylor, Walton and Young, 1973).

One of the keys to diversion has been the increased use of cautioning by the police. The 1980 White Paper had accepted that 'juvenile offenders who can be diverted from the criminal justice system at an early stage in their offending are less likely to reoffend than those who become involved in judicial proceedings' (para. 3.8). The police clearly have great discretion in dealing with offenders, particularly so with juvenile offenders and, indeed, successive research studies have shown that there are marked variations in the use of cautioning between police forces (Tutt and Giller, 1983; Laycock and Tarling, 1985; Evans and Wilkinson, 1990). A series of Home Office Circulars (in 1978, 1985 and 1990) encouraged the police to use their power to caution. The 14/1985 Circular issued to chief constables included criteria to be applied by the police with the aim of increasing the likelihood of diversion from prosecution and the 1990 Circular included national standards and also, though it suggested they should be used sparingly, recognised the possible use of 'multiple cautions': it countenanced 'offenders being cautioned more than once, provided the nature and circumstances of the most recent offence warrant it'.

Alongside the increase in the use of cautioning there were also changes in the use of non-custodial penalties – diversion once again, this time from custody rather than prosecution.[6] The 1982 Act introduced new requirements that could be attached to supervision orders (Graham and Moxon, 1986). The following year, the DHSS issued a Circular LAC 83(3) in which it announced that £15 million was to be provided to support intensive Intermediate Treatment (IT) programmes as an alternative to custody. Monitoring of the subsequent development of schemes by NACRO suggests that this initiative may have had a significant impact on the custodial sentencing of juveniles (NACRO, 1987).

In addition to announcing the funding LAC 83(3) also recommended that work with serious and persistent juvenile offenders should be co-ordinated by inter-agency committees. Subsequently, such committees or panels have been formed, often involving sentencers as well as representatives of other relevant agencies. One of the consequences of this, it has been argued (NACRO, 1989) has been to provide a first step towards a more integrated system of juvenile justice (Allen, 1991). Pitts (1992:182) has even suggested that 'the IT initiative appears to have been the most successful innovation in the criminal justice system in the post-war period'.

In addition to the decline in the numbers of juveniles sentenced to custody during the latter part of the 1980s there was also a shift in the use of detention centre and borstal sentences. In the aftermath of the 1982 Act magistrates took the opportunity to use their new powers to send juveniles to borstal and were much less attracted to the new 'short, sharp, shock' detention centre regimes. In fact the experiment was, largely, a failure; evaluation by the Home Office's Young Offender Psychology Unit concluded that the new regimes seemed to be no more effective than the previous ones. More than half of those sent to detention centres had been reconvicted within a year, irrespective of the type of regime in the centre they served their sentence at (Home Office, 1984d). Despite this, the experiment was, briefly, extended to all detention centres, though aspects of the regime were modified. 'The political damage was limited,' suggests Windlesham (1993), 'but it is hard to avoid the verdict that sound penal administration was made to serve the needs of a defective icon of political ideology.'

In the longer term the government decided to abolish the separate Detention Centre sentence. The Criminal Justice Act 1988 included

---

[6] This is not to ignore the quite extended debate that has taken place about the possibility that some of these changes – increased use of cautioning and non-custodial penalties, for example – may have resulted in a degree of 'net-widening', i.e. bringing into the criminal justice process children who would not otherwise have been there (cf. Ditchfield, 1976; Farrington and Bennett, 1981; Giller and Tutt, 1987).

a new sentence of 'detention in a young offender institution', and separate Detention Centres ceased to exist, being amalgamated with youth custody centres to become Young Offender Institutions (YOIs). Courts were given the power to decide on the length of sentence, though the location where the sentence was to be served was to be determined by the Home Office. Detention in a YOI is available for people aged 15 and above.

Before moving on it is important to mention the existence, and demise, of the s.7(7) care order. This was an order created by the CYPA69, which could be used by the juvenile court in criminal proceedings to place a juvenile in the care of the local authority. The local authority then placed the juvenile where it thought most appropriate, including back in the parental home. During the 1970s practice in relation to care orders was criticised by magistrates on the one hand for tending to undermine the intentions of the court by failing to place offenders where they could be controlled and, on the other hand, by academic critics concerned at the potential criminogenic consequences of using a care order early on in an offender's 'career' (see, for example, Thorpe *et al.*, 1980). Significant claims have been made about the impact of this academic critique (Cavadino and Dignan, 1992) though, whatever the reality, the use of s.7(7) care orders declined rapidly during the 1980s and they were eventually abolished (from October 1991) by the Children Act 1989.

For the purposes of this discussion here, there is one final significant change that has taken place in juvenile justice since that point. The Criminal Justice Act 1991 changed the name of the juvenile court to the Youth Court and extended its jurisdiction to include 17-year-olds. The clear aim was to extend the gains made with the younger age group to 17-year-olds and, indeed, as early as 1988 in the Green Paper *Punishment, Custody and the Community*, the Home Office signalled its intention to transfer the lessons learnt in juvenile justice to policies in relation to offenders more generally, though it recognised that modifications would need to be made (Home Office, 1988b, paras 2.17–19). It did, however, emphasise the reasons for seeking to restrict the use of custodial sentences for young offenders:

most young offenders grow out of crime as they become more mature and responsible. They need encouragement and help to become law abiding. Even a short period of custody is quite likely to confirm them as criminals, particularly as they acquire new criminal skills from the more sophisticated offenders. They see themselves labelled as criminals and behave accordingly.

The 1991 Criminal Justice Act, in tandem with the Children Act 1989 which was part of the same general development (Faulkner, 1992), continued the by now well-established twin-track approach of punishment and welfare. The Children Act gave statutory recognition to the need to avoid prosecution, and the 1991 Act and subsequent Home Office Circular (30/92) explaining the changes brought about by the legislation reminded sentencers of s.44 of the Children and Young Persons Act 1933 which states that 'all courts must have regard to the welfare of children and young people who appear before them'. The Act extended this consideration to 17-year-olds. The legislation also gave magistrates new sentencing powers within the overall framework created by the 1991 Act (including unit fines, community sentences and custody) along with a new scheme of post-custody supervision. The Act reduced the maximum term of detention in a YOI to 12 months, and brought 17-year-olds within the ambit of s.53 of the Children and Young Persons Act 1933 which gives the Crown Court the power to order longer terms of detention in respect of certain 'grave crimes'. Finally, again reinforcing lessons learnt from developments in practice over the past decade, the 1991 Act signalled the importance of inter-agency and joint working by giving Chief Probation Officers and Directors of Social Services joint responsibility for making local arrangements to provide services to the Youth Court.

The history of juvenile justice, though relatively short, is an extremely complicated one. It has been characterised by the co-existing approaches of 'welfare' and 'punishment': a tendency on the one hand to wish to support and protect those children who for a variety of reasons may find themselves on the wrong side of the law and, on the other hand, a determination to ensure that those who continually offend despite efforts to stop them receive a punishment that makes clear that their behaviour is unacceptable. The tension between these two approaches is seen at its starkest in the debates over how best to respond to that 'hard core' of young people whose offending, it is believed, continues unchecked irrespective of the interventions of criminal justice agencies.

Persistent offending

Against this background there developed in 1992 and 1993 a rise in concern about juvenile offending and, in particular, about so-called persistent juvenile offenders. This concern about juvenile offending, though these concerns are something of an extent ever-present in our society (Pearson, 1983), was fuelled by one or two very specific factors in the early 1990s. The first of these was the well-publicised urban disturbances of 1991. Though they were not on the scale or, indeed, similar in their causes or style to the riots of the early 1980s, the disturbances at Blackbird Leys (Oxford), Ely (Cardiff) and on the Meadowell estate in Tyneside focused attention on young men in large-scale violent confrontations with the police in many cases as a consequence of attempts by the latter to put a stop to the very public displays of 'joyriding' so popular with young men and with the journalists who increasingly turned up to capture their activities (Campbell, 1993).

From mid-1991 onwards stories started to appear in the press about youngsters who, it was believed, were so involved in crime that they accounted for a significant proportion of juvenile crime in the areas in which they lived. It was suggested that the police and courts were powerless to deal with these offenders. The issue was taken up in a speech to the Federated Ranks of the Metropolitan Police in October 1992 by the then Home Secretary, Kenneth Clarke. A small number of children, he suggested, 'are committing a large number of crimes. There is a case for increasing court powers to lock up, educate and train them for their own and everyone else's interest. We will certainly be taking a long hard look at the options which are available to the courts in dealing with serious offenders of this age. If court powers need to be strengthened or new institutions created, then they will be.'

Public concern about the level of juvenile crime and the perceived ineffectiveness of the criminal justice system to deal with the problem remained high in the following months, and in early March 1993, Mr Clarke announced that the government proposed to introduce legislation that would make a new disposal available to the courts. These 'secure training orders', were to be aimed at 'that comparatively small group of very persistent juvenile offenders whose repeated offending makes them a menace to the community' (HC Deb 2 March 1993, col.139).

The new order would apply to 12–15-year-olds (later amended to 12–14-year olds) who had been convicted of three imprisonable offences, and who had proved 'unwilling or unable to comply with the requirements of supervision in the community while on remand or under sentence'. The order was to be a custodial one and would be served in a 'secure training unit' which, he suggested, would provide 'high standards of care and discipline'. Regimes would include provision for education and training for inmates; after release individuals would be subject to 'rigorous, consistent and firmly delivered' supervision until their supervising social worker or probation officer felt that he or she was no longer a threat to society.

Somewhat earlier, in the autumn of 1992, the House of Commons Home Affairs Committee (HAC) had announced that it would be inquiring into issues affecting juvenile offenders and the particular problems of persistent offenders. In explaining its reasons for doing so the Committee said: 'We decided on this inquiry both because of public concern about the level of juvenile crime in particular, and because of the apparent inability of the criminal justice system to deal adequately with it' (HAC, 1993).

Given what has been said above about recent trends in juvenile crime – a relatively sharp decline in recorded juvenile crime during the 1980s and early 1990s – it is worth briefly considering what the Home Affairs Committee made of the fact that there existed significant 'public concern about the level of juvenile crime'. The Committee received much evidence which backed up the picture presented by official criminal statistics of a general decline of recorded juvenile crime. The word 'recorded' is important here, for a number of witnesses made much of the fact that the same period may well have seen a significant rise in the use of informal warnings by the police (sometimes referred to as informal cautions), and that because such warnings are not recorded, they may account, at least in part, for some of the dissonance between what official statistics suggested and what the public and politicians felt.

In addition, evidence was presented by the Association of Chief Police Officers (ACPO) which challenged the view that there had been a decline in juvenile offending during the 1980s. They argued that, given the decline in the juvenile population, the increase in crime more generally and the generally reduced rate of detection, the period from 1980 to 1990 had in fact witnessed a 54 per cent rise in juvenile crime. Indeed, they were given some support from the Shadow Home Secretary and one of the Shadow Home Affairs ministers who also suggested that it was 'difficult to believe Home Office claims that offending by young people has actually gone down across the country' (Home Affairs Committee, 1993, para 7). The Home Affairs Committee in seeking an explanation for this apparent disagreement suggested that it was in part due to the fact that the official criminal statistics referred to numbers of offenders whereas ACPO were referring to the number of offences. As ACPO then said, whilst it did not challenge the proposition that the number of known juvenile offenders had fallen, that is not the same as saying 'that the amount of crime committed by juveniles has not increased'. The Home Affairs Committee was, not unnaturally, unable to resolve the issue, but it did suggest that:

one possible explanation for the apparent discrepancy between ACPO's picture of greater juvenile offending and the decline in the number of juvenile offenders is a growth in the numbers of persistent offenders . . . If there is a small but growing number of juvenile offenders responsible for many offences (some of which they may be convicted or cautioned for and some of which may go undetected) it is possible to reconcile the indisputable fact that the number (and rate, to a lesser extent) of known juvenile offenders has fallen over time with the more speculative assertion that the number of offences committed by juveniles has risen. (Home Affairs Committee, 1993, para.15)

Having identified this possibility, the Home Affairs Committee then went on to consider the issue of persistent offending and received a generally uniform picture from the majority of agencies. ACPO, for example, talked of a 'small hard core who have absolutely no fears whatsoever of the criminal justice system', and continued, 'society is entitled to expect a degree of protection from the ravages of the persistent juvenile offender'. Although there were few other witnesses quite so certain in their descriptions, there were few who took exception to the idea that there existed a small group of offenders that might, as the Home Affairs Committee put it, be described as 'persistent juvenile trouble makers'. The Committee went on, 'the Association of Chief Officers of Probation (ACOP) told us that there might be, for example, 10–12 such individuals in Hampshire, while NAPO suggested that there were 12–20 in Newcastle. This may only be, as ACOP said, "a very, very small handful", but there is clearly a significant group of individuals country-wide who cause a disproportionate amount of the crime attributed to young people.'

As has been suggested, the government's response to the 'problem' of persistent offending by juveniles was to include clauses in the Criminal Justice and Public Order Bill which provided for the introduction of a new 'secure training order'. Five new secure training centres were to be built, each housing approximately 40 inmates. The new sentences would be determinate sentences, of a maximum of two years, half of which would be served in custody and half under supervision in the community. Section 19 of what eventually became the Criminal Justice and Public Order Act 1994 also allowed for the new institutions to be managed by public, voluntary or private organisations, though such was the antipathy towards the new provisions by public and voluntary organisations that it was 'clearly envisaged that in practice they will be built and operated by the private sector' (NACRO, 1994).

At the time of writing arrangements are being made for the construction of the first of the new secure training centres. By and large the proposal to introduce this new penalty met with relatively little political hostility within Parliament, and other elements of the Criminal Justice and Public Order Act received far more attention and sustained criticism. The 'punitive solution' to the issue of persistent offending by young people, whilst running counter to much of what had been learnt in youth justice in the 1980s, is set to proceed.

CHAPTER 7

Victims and criminal justice policy

The bulk of this text so far has focused upon offenders and the agencies tasked with detecting and recording their offences together with those that have the job of administering punishment. Little has been said about victims and this reflects the offence- and offender-centred nature of British criminal justice. One consequence of such a focus is that it has long been suggested that 'the victim' is the forgotten party in the criminal justice process. However, the development of a variety of victim services over the past two or three decades have begun, albeit slightly, to address this oversight. In fact, a veritable industry of 'services' has developed and so strong has this growth been, that a number of authors have referred to the emergence of an all-encompassing 'victims movement' (*inter alia* Pointing and Maguire, 1988).

Nevertheless, it would still be a mistake to describe the criminal justice system as victim-friendly. The victim of crime is by no means the central focus of the criminal justice system and a variety of studies have shown in some detail how victims are often poorly treated by criminal justice agencies, sometimes to the point where it is suggested they may suffer some form of secondary victimisation. There is evidence from the late 1970s, for example (Berger 1977; Katz and Mazur, 1979) and early 1980s (Chambers and Millar, 1983) that women who reported sexual assault to the police often had their character and morality questioned in such a way as to imply some responsibility for their victimisation. The treatment of rape and sexual assault victims has changed in many respects in recent years and this reflects a growing recognition of the needs if not the rights of victims. The position of the victim in the modern criminal justice system is the focus of this chapter.

At this stage it is worth saying something briefly about 'victimology' (the sub-discipline of criminology devoted to the study of victims) as it has, in part, been responsible for the increasing attention that has been devoted to victims in recent years. The term 'victimology' was first used in the late 1940s by Frederick Wertham and the classic early studies in the genre appeared at about the same time. Beginning with Von Hentig in the late 1940s and Marvin Wolfgang in the 1950s, early studies concentrated on the role of the victim in the causes of crime. At this point, criminologists were still searching for 'grand theories' that would explain crime, and victims of crime became, in part, another focus of that concern. For Von Hentig and others, the specific focus was upon the role of the victim in the precipitation or perpetration of the crime.

It was not until the mid-1960s and the early 1970s, however, that victims 'attracted any serious public attention' (Pointing and Maguire, 1988). The mid to late 1960s saw the first murmurings of the nascent victims' movement and in its wake academic victimology, which was about to be radically transformed by the utilisation of large-scale survey techniques, moved its focus to the victim population in general rather than the individual (Fattah, 1992). This gave rise to what one author has characterised as a 'lifestyle' approach to victimology or, alternatively, as 'conventional victimology' (Walklate, 1989). In this approach it is argued that there is a link between routine daily activities and exposure to circumstances in which the risk of victimisation is high. Whilst this constituted a significant advance on the work of Von Hentig, it tended to fail to take account of those structural constraints which were not easily observable or measurable. Furthermore, in its concentration on the public domain and its avoidance of the private, it merely reinforced conventional views of victimisation (that is, for example, it paid relatively little attention to domestic violence) and through its policy emphasis on individual lifestyle engaged in, at least implicit, victim-blaming once more.

The shortcomings of 'conventional' victimology were thrown into sharp relief, however, by the re-emergence of feminism and its impact on criminology generally. Feminists were critical of both the theory and methodology associated with the lifestyle approach, and they stressed the importance of the experience of victimisation. Focusing in particular on rape and domestic violence, a number of authors were able to illustrate the limitations of the social survey as a method of uncovering either the incidence of these forms of victimisation or the reality of the experience of victimisation. Central to their account was the issue of power for as Stanko (1988:46), for example, has argued 'unless policing and crime survey researchers lend credence to the concept and reality of gender stratification, violence against women will, on many levels, remain a hidden, but all too real part of women's lives'.

Crucially, the work of feminists, and particularly activists rather than academics was essential to the transformation in understanding about the frequency and impact of rape, sexual assault and domestic violence. One simple but important historical lesson, therefore, is that certain forms of victimisation only become visible when they do, because of campaigning work of representative groups.

In a short essay on the 'victims' movement', van Dijk (1988) has, for the sake of clarity if not always historical accuracy, identified three waves in its development which he distinguishes chronologically: first, state compensation and initiatives by probation officers, 1965–75; second, rape crisis centres, shelter homes and the first victim support schemes, 1975–80; and third, institutionalisation of victim support and the call for justice, 1980 onwards. These general distinctions provide a useful structure for considering victims and criminal justice policy. This chapter will follow a roughly similar course, beginning by considering the introduction not only of the state compensation scheme but also court-based compensation. It will then focus on the re-emergence of the feminist movement and services for victims of rape, sexual assault, domestic violence and child abuse and, finally, will consider the history of victim support.

It is worth bearing in mind at this stage, and we will return to this point on a number of occasions below, that there has been no reference so far in this chapter to a 'victims policy'. The reason for this is that for the bulk of the period under discussion here neither of the major political parties – whether in government or not – has had a particularly coherent policy on crime victims. Indeed, it is probably true to say that victims have for the most part been used by government as means of justifying or, occasionally, even diverting attention from broader criminal justice policies or trends in crime. It is rare for much consideration to be given to victims of crime in their own right.

Compensation by the offender and the state

Compensation by the state

In many respects the story of the 'victims' movement' in the UK begins with the introduction of criminal injuries compensation, for it was through the introduction of that scheme that the needs of victims were first formally recognised. Rock (1990)[1] suggests that two groups of people were influential in the campaign that eventually led to the development of the criminal injuries compensation scheme (CICS). The first were what he calls a group of 'general reformers' drawn from the major political parties; the second a narrower group of penal reformers drawn from bodies like the Howard League and Justice. More particularly, however, the development of the CICS is associated with the penal reformer, Margery Fry.

A Quaker, Margery Fry had been the first secretary of the Howard League for Penal Reform, a magistrate, the chairman of a juvenile court bench, Vice-President of the Magistrates' Association, and a member of the Advisory Council on the Treatment of Offenders. Fry became convinced of the idea that restitution and reconciliation were preferable and more constructive than the more punitive process of arrest, charge, prosecution and punishment that tended to characterise the criminal justice system. However, the range of problems associated with a system

---

[1] Paul Rock's book, *Helping Victims of Crime*, is one of the few explorations of the development of a particular area of British criminal justice policy. It is a most comprehensive account and much of what is contained in this chapter – especially in relation to victim support – is drawn from or informed by Professor Rock's work.

based on restitution and reconciliation – the large proportion of cases in which no offender is apprehended; the limited financial circumstances of the majority that are arrested and prosecuted; and, the difficulties associated with enforcing some form of restitution order – convinced her that compensation from the state was a more realistic option. Furthermore Fry and others made the assumption that compensation was what victims wanted: 'In the absence of a demand from victims, without any knowledge of what victims might want, compensation was in effect a solution devised to solve the imagined ills of an imagined population' (Rock, 1990:52).

In 1958, before her campaigning could bear fruit, Margery Fry died. In the year prior to her death, she had made contact with Justice – the British section of the International Commission of Jurists – and it was they that took up the campaign from then on. In 1959 Reg Prentice introduced a Private Member's Bill – the Criminal Injuries (Compensation) Bill – which, though it made no progress, did help keep the subject on the table. Another identical Bill was introduced a year later with the same effect. Also in 1959, the government published *Penal Practice in a Changing Society*, which although focusing primarily on the penal measures did consider obligations to the victims of crime and resulted in the setting up of a working party to examine the proposal to introduce a scheme for the payment of compensation to victims of crimes of violence. Although in its report it actually considered two possible methods of making compensation available, as far as reformers were concerned there appeared a lack of appetite for any such ideas within the Home Office.

One result was that Justice set up its own working party to consider the Home Office report. Once again Justice, like other organisations before it, did not feel it important to consult victims – the assumption that their needs and desires were predictable. The report (Justice, 1961) proposed that compensation should be available for a specified range of offences. Importantly, the notion of victim culpability was introduced, the effect of which would be to reduce the size of any awards made. A little after this time a Committee set up by the Conservative Political Centre also produced a report recommending the introduction of a compensation scheme – this time to be based on common law damages (Conservative Political Centre, 1962). Pressure was kept up and in 1964 a second White Paper was published (Home Office, 1964) which made reference to the flurry of reports that had come out in the previous few years, but also to the criminal injuries scheme that had been introduced in New Zealand in 1963. The White Paper advocated an 'experimental and non-statutory' scheme be introduced in Britain, that payments be *ex gratia*, and that the scheme be administered by an independent Board. There was to be a minimum payment of £50.

Two elements of the subsequent debate in Parliament are worth mentioning briefly. First, the proposed scheme was justified by reference to the argument that for too long the criminal justice system had ignored the needs of victims and that such a scheme would begin to right this imbalance. Second, there was much discussion of the idea of victim culpability and therefore of the process of attempting to make the distinction between deserving and undeserving victims. There was virtual consensus around these issues. Rock (1990:83) notes: 'No one inside or outside Parliament was reported to have dissented from those arguments. There was such an overwhelming agreement about principle that debate centred entirely on practical matters of costings, definitions, and applications. Within that consensus, the authority and assumptions of the groups that had championed compensation were never examined.' The Criminal Injuries Compensation Scheme came into operation on 1 August 1964 and in its first year of operation received over 500 applications for an award. In its first full year of operation the scheme paid out almost half a million pounds in compensation.

As soon as the scheme had been successfully set up, those campaigners who had been most centrally involved in bringing about the change turned their attentions to other matters. Rock (1990) suggests that even Margery Fry, had she lived, would most likely have moved on to other things once the scheme was underway. The crucial point here is that the campaigns to bring in criminal injuries compensation never once involved victims themselves – such a thing does not seem to have been considered – nor did it presage the beginnings of a more concerted campaign on behalf of victims of crime more generally: 'No organization of victims had emerged. None had been sponsored. On the contrary, compensation was designed precisely to prevent such a coalescence' (Rock, 1990: 86).

The reform that had taken place had come about as part of a process of penal reform; it was perceived to be the righting of a wrong in the criminal justice system, not as the start of a long-term programme on behalf of victims. At this time, doing things for the victim was, as Rock remarks, an oblique way of doing something for the offender: '[Victims] were to become a working projection of the politics of penal reform, a figment of the reforming imagination, shaped by the concerns and purposes of their creators. Their character never seemed to be a problem, a thing to be investigated and considered. It was invented and bestowed, and the result was a contradictory creature' (Rock, 1990:88). This schizophrenic creature was, on the one hand, desirous of retribution and therefore to be placated by compensation and was, on the other hand, considered to be helpless, innocent and, therefore, *deserving* (Newburn, 1990). As the Home Office White Paper (1964) itself described:

Compensation will be paid ex gratia. The Government do not accept that the State is liable for injuries caused to people by the acts of others. The public does, however, feel a sense of responsibility for and sympathy with the *innocent victim*, and it is right that this feeling should find practical expression in the provision of compensation on behalf of the community. (emphasis added)

The new scheme operated on the basis that compensation should only be paid to the 'deserving', and there should be safeguards to ensure that public money would not be wasted on fraudulent or unmerited applications. In particular, this referred to those who failed to report crimes to the police, who provoked the crime or were in some way related to the offender.

The scheme was amended five years later in 1969, and again in 1979 following a review by an Interdepartmental Working Party. In December 1983, during a debate in the House of Lords, Lord Allen called attention to the need to put the scheme on a statutory footing, and the government conveyed its intention to introduce legislation for precisely such a purpose. Following another Working Party, provision for placing the scheme on a statutory footing was included in the next Criminal Justice Bill, but this was halted by a General Election. The Criminal Justice Act 1988 eventually provided the means for amending the status of the scheme but, as yet, this has not been acted upon. Meanwhile, the number of applications for compensation and the cost of the scheme increases year on year. There were, for example, approximately 26,000 applications in 1981/2 and this had risen to just under 66,000 by 1992/3 (Home Office, 1993a). The amount of compensation paid out rose from approximately £22 million in 1981/2 to over £152 million in 1992/3 [doc 16].

Over the years a number of means of limiting the increase in the cost of the scheme have been introduced. One of the most frequently used tactics has been to increase the financial minimum below which awards are not made. When the scheme was introduced in 1964 the lower limit for payments was £50. This was raised to £150 in 1977, £250 in 1981, £400 in 1983, £550 in 1987 and then to its current level of £1000. In 1994 a much more severe set of restrictions was put forward by the Home Secretary, Michael Howard, who proposed to introduce a tariff which would have severely limited payments, particularly to victims of especially violent crimes. However, a legal action brought by ten trade unions and the TUC resulted in the Court of Appeal ruling that the Home Secretary had 'acted unlawfully and abused his prerogative and common law powers' in flouting the will of Parliament (*Guardian*, 10/11/94) and that he was under a duty to put the old scheme on a statutory footing. Spending is likely to continue to rise and a further full review of the scheme is by now probably overdue.

Compensation by the offender

Compensation via the courts has quite a long history in England and Wales. The Larceny Act and the Malicious Damage Act of 1861 gave magistrates' courts the powers to order compensation for loss or damage to property, and the Forfeiture Act 1870 provided further powers to the courts to order convicted felons to pay for loss of property.

The Probation of Offenders Act 1907 enabled courts discharging an offender or releasing him on probation to award damages for injury or compensation for loss.

It was, however, the Criminal Justice Act 1972 which broadened the circumstances under which compensation could be ordered and which forms the basis for court-ordered compensation which still exists today. Section 1 of the Act gave magistrates' courts and the Crown Court a general power to order offenders to pay compensation for loss, damage or personal injury resulting from a criminal offence. Crucially, it dispensed with the need for an application for compensation to be made to the court and it introduced powers to order compensation for offences taken into consideration.

The changes made by the Act resulted in large part from the recommendations of a report of the Advisory Council on the Penal System chaired by Lord Justice Widgery (Home Office, 1970). Very much like the case of criminal injuries compensation in the 1960s, the impetus behind the introduction of the compensation order was cast in terms of the potential effect on the offender rather than the victim. As Mawby and Gill (1987:51) note: 'The context within which the working party operated is notable. While compensation orders could be justified as having an intrinsic moral value, or as a means of reform, their main appeal to the committee was as a means of preventing the offender enjoying the fruits of his crime; reparation was thus "an essential element in the punishment of crime" (Home Office, 1970:3).'

At this point the compensation order was an ancillary order which had to be made in conjunction with another penalty. Furthermore, there was a certain lack of clarity about how such orders were to be used, and Viscount Colville in the House of Lords debate on the Criminal Justice Bill had stated that the circumstances for compensation should not be made overly precise (Wasik, 1978; Shapland *et al.*, 1985). In 1975 Lord Widgery had pronounced that 'A compensation order made by the [criminal] court can be extremely beneficial as long as it is confined to simple, straightforward cases and generally cases where no great amount is at stake' (quoted in Davies, 1992: 23). Because of the restricted nature of the order, the lack of clarity about how it was to be used, the inherent limitations in imposing financial penalties on offenders (the majority of offenders do not come before the courts; many do not have sufficient means to pay compensation; some will be incarcerated and therefore not be in a position to pay any financial penalty) and the fact that many victims continued to remain ignorant of their 'right' to compensation, meant that orders were only made in a minority of cases in which, in theory, they might have been made (Softley, 1978; Newburn, 1988).

In an effort to overcome some of these problems, the Criminal Justice Act 1982 modified the position of the compensation order so that it could be used either as an ancillary order or as a penalty in its own right. The 1982 Act also required courts to give preference to the compensation order where it considered both compensation and a fine to be appropriate sentences. In reality these changes only had a limited impact on the way such orders were used by the courts, and magistrates (compensation orders are used very infrequently in the Crown Court) retained a degree of unease about using compensation in preference to fines or other non-custodial measures, largely because of the continuing confusion about the reparative and punitive elements in the order. Research at the time concluded: 'magistrates are generally unwilling to use compensation as a sole penalty, preferring to combine it with a fine, probation or, in some cases, absolute or conditional discharge. The rationale for this is that compensation, they feel, is not in itself a sufficient punishment, returning one only to the *status quo ante*' (Newburn, 1988:48).

The system remained in need of overhaul and a further attempt at improvement was made in the Criminal Justice Act 1988. This required courts to give reasons whenever compensation was not ordered in cases involving damage, loss or injury (Miers, 1990). Although this had the effect of dramatically increasing the proportion of cases involving personal injury in which compensation was ordered – it doubled in the magistrates courts to 46 per cent (Moxon, 1993) – it still did not overcome magistrates' reluctance to use compensation as a sole penalty.

In short, the delivery of compensation via the courts was, and most likely remains, haphazard. Only a minority of victims will ever receive compensation from an offender via the court system, and fewer still will receive anything from the CICS. In addition, the two systems of compensation do not mesh (Newburn, 1990) and, indeed, are not intended to fit together. This is an important point for it illustrates the absence of an overall strategy in relation to the needs of victims of crime. The two compensation systems cover predominantly different offences, operate at different financial levels and have quite distinct threshold criteria. Even in the area of criminal injury there appears to be little correspondence between the court system and the CICS. As it stands at the moment victims of crime tend to receive sums of compensation from magistrates' courts which, because in practice claims are generally small and many offenders have limited means, are generally far below the lower limit operated by the CICS. Although theoretically compensation orders should cover injuries up to and over the minimum threshold at CICS, in practice there exists a considerable gulf between awards from the scheme and awards from the court.

Whilst much is made of the need to do things for victims of crime, financial reparation remains a best an expensive symbolic exercise with confused aims. At least in part the confusion stems from the fact that these initiatives which are ostensibly about victims of crime were, in reality, introduced becuase of a paucity of ideas in relation to dealing with offenders. As Mawby (1988: 130) concludes: 'Of course, it would be naive to suggest that deterrence was the only pressure behind the introduction of compensation orders. Nevertheless, they, like the Criminal Injuries Compensation Scheme, clearly fail to address either the needs or the rights of crime victims. While they may, *post hoc*, be justified in terms of such principles, it makes more sense to view them as an integral part of Conservative penal philosophy of the 1960s and 1970s, representing one aspect of concern over the crime problem and balancing punishment of offenders with a carefully constrained demonstration of response to the needs of some victims.'

Duff (1988) argues that there are two discernible trends which illustrate the worldwide impact the 'victim movement' has had on the criminal justice process: the first is the introduction of state-funded compensation schemes (with the aim of strengthening the relationship between the offender and the state) and, second, the adoption of compensation by the offender to the victim into the criminal justice system (thereby increasing the importance attached to the victim–offender relationship). However, in respect of the relationship between victim and offender, it was actually the case for some time that many reformers were keener on the idea of mediation and reparation (whether material or not) than they were on financial compensation.

In part this had much to do with the fact that reparation fitted much more neatly into contemporary penal thought. Although it involved victims it was, strictly speaking, in many ways not really about victims. Many of those who were most in favour of the introduction of some form of new reparation order were primarily interested in introducing something which offenders would find challenging than they were in finding something which victims would find beneficial. This was by no means true of all commentators and campaigners of course (see, for example, the work of Marshall, 1985; Marshall and Merry, 1990; and Wright, 1982; 1991). Early developments in mediation and reparation in the UK were heavily influenced by practice in the United States, and a large number of the early projects were either court or probation service-based (Marshall and Walpole, 1985). Although reparation was often discussed, it appeared to be relatively low on the politicial agenda until, in 1984, the then Home Secretary, Leon Brittan, made a highly publicised speech at the Holborn Law Society in which he advocated the idea of reparation. Brittan said:

The idea of reparation appeals to me for three reasons. First, through reparation, the criminal justice system can concentrate its attention on the individual victim whose interests must never be ignored. Secondly, the principle of reparation can be used to ensure that the wider interests of society are better served, and thirdly, nothing is more likely to induce remorse and reduce recidivism among a certain, all too numerous, kind of offender than being brought face to face with the human consequences of crime. (quoted in Reeves, 1989:44)

He later supported requests for the funding of a number of experimental reparation projects, each of which was to be independently evaluated. In 1986 a discussion paper was issued (Home Office, 1986) which in its concentration on the possibility of a new court penalty – the 'reparation order' – proved to be 'a watershed in the development of reparation in the UK' (Davies, 1992:34). The idea of a reparation order was not popular with practitioners and, indeed, the split between the policy-makers' emphasis on reparation as a sentencing option, and practitioners' emphasis on somewhat less criminal justice-centred priorities led to a fairly full and fairly quick withdrawal of interest by government. By 1988, reparation had, as Davies (1992:39) puts it: 'resumed its place at the margins of criminal justice', and there it remains.

The re-emergence of feminism

The last 20 years have seen a marked increase in awareness of issues surrounding the role and status of women in society. Whilst a major focus has been on sexual discrimination and disadvantage in the labour market, there is also a substantial body of research on women's experiences of the criminal justice system (Gelsthorpe and Morris, 1990). An important part of this has concerned way that the criminal justice system deals with crimes of sexual violence against women. The same period has also witnessed increasing recognition of the vulnerability of children to criminal victimisation (Morgan and Zedner, 1991). During the 1980s, there were a series of public scandals involving incidents of child sexual abuse. One in Cleveland, perhaps the best known of all, led to a major public inquiry and an official report which provided a number of recommendations for procedures to be adopted by the agencies involved in such cases (Butler-Sloss, 1988).

Rape and domestic violence

The increasing recognition of women victims of sexual assault or domestic violence and the changes this has brought about have their roots in the re-emergence of the feminist movement in the 1970s (Coote and Campbell, 1987). It has been argued, for example, that the agents of the criminal justice system tend to treat women complainants in a way that amounts to 'secondary victimisation', especially in the case of sexual assault. As was suggested above, there is evidence from the late 1970s (see, for example, Berger 1977, Katz and Mazur 1979) and early 1980s (Chambers and Millar, 1983) that women reporting sexual assault to the police were, on occasion, treated as if they were responsible for their own victimisation. Public attention was focused sharply on such issues in early 1982, when a judge imposed a fine rather than a prison sentence on a man convicted of rape on the grounds that the victim was guilty of what he called 'contributory negligence'. This was followed shortly after by a BBC television 'fly-on-the-wall' documentary about Thames Valley Police, one episode of which concerned the interview of a woman who was reporting that she had been raped. So intimidating was the investigating officer's approach that a considerable public furore followed the broadcast. Much concern was voiced about the lack of sensitivity and sympathy being given to the victim's rights and feelings. As Adler (1987) put it some time later: 'All but the most transparently flawless victim was liable to be bullied by interrogators and prosecutors, exposing her to a form of secondary victimisation'. The process is summed up by one practitioner (Anna T., 1988:62–3) who said:

Barristers play upon the sexist prejudices of society in order to undermine what the woman is saying as a witness. She is often cross-questioned in an aggressive or accusatory way . . . There is a rule that women should not be questioned about their sexual relations with anyone except the accused, but judges often waive that rule at the request of defence barristers, who then use these kinds of questions to discredit women.

The Women's Movement has been particularly influential in changing this situation. A campaigning body, Women Against Rape (WAR) was established in 1976, roughly coinciding with the importation into the UK from the United States of Rape Crisis Centres. Reinforcing the point about the unattractiveness of the criminal justice system as an option for women who had been assaulted, the first of these Centres took over 600 referrals in its first two years of operation, of which under a third involved incidents that had been reported to the police.

The following year a governmental advisory group, the Women's National Commission (WNC), set up a working party to examine the issue of violence against women. Smith (1989a) suggests that the major concern of the WNC 'was to try to effect certain practical changes – for example, to help ensure that female victims receive the legal, medical, social and psychological help which they need and that their role as court witnesses be made as tolerable as possible. But it was also concerned to offer practical advice to the police and to court personnel on their procedures and to bring home to them that these procedures could be contributing to a lack of effectiveness.' The working party also reflected on broader criminal justice issues. Its report, *Violence Against Women*, criticised the police for 'reluctance to interfere in domestic disputes, and in particular, for their reluctance to arrest and prosecute the perpetrators of the violence' (Womens' National Commission, 1985). Further guidelines were issued in October 1986 by the Home Office via circular 69/1986 which dealt with victims of both rape and domestic violence. This made a number of suggestions, including the proposal that police forces should consider setting up special victim examination suites, more advice and information for rape victims, follow-up visits, and enhanced training for officers who deal with rape victims.

An increasing body of research during the 1970s and 1980s questioned the role of criminal justice agencies in relation to women victims of crime. Studies, for example, suggested that the effect of arrest in domestic violence cases may be to exacerbate the violence experienced by women rather than reduce it (Sherman *et al.*, 1992). Research in the UK context has also provided support for a more active arrest policy in the police response to domestic violence (Edwards, 1989). It has also been argued that inadequate police responses result in only a very low proportion of incidents of sexual assault and domestic violence being reported to the police. This is supported by evidence from victim surveys, which suggest very low levels of reporting for these crimes (Hough and Mayhew, 1985).

There have been a number of practical developments in response to these issues. The Women's Movement has been instrumental in setting up rape crisis centres and women's refuges in many towns and cities in the UK. The first refuge was set up in 1971 (Pizzey, 1974) and there were over 150 by 1978 (Binney *et al.*, 1981). The centres operate telephone counselling services and offer emergency and, to some extent, continuing support and advice for any woman or girl who has been raped or sexually assaulted – irrespective of whether or not the offence is reported to the police. Although referrals are taken from a number of agencies most women refer themselves to RCCs and on the whole the centres rely on volunteers although there are a small number of full-time posts (Anna T., 1988).

It was, however, the Parliamentary Select Committee on Violence in Marriage that heralded the beginnings of change in public policy and the Committee's Report, according to Dobash and Dobash (1992), signalled government support for refuges. The Working Party's survey of police forces found that domestic violence was not perceived by them as an area where their procedures fell down or where new measures were necessary or important. However, 'despite criticism of law enforcement stressed by activists and some fairly pressing questioning of the police by MPs when taking oral evidence, this concern virtually disappeared in the text of the Report and from the recommendations.

The ineffectiveness of the criminal justice system – and especially the police – was one of the major focuses of the women's movement in this area. The central and most often voiced criticism of the police was that they remained reluctant to intervene in domestic incidents, and that this reluctance was underpinned on the one hand by the perception that the threat to officer's personal safety was high (Parnas, 1972) and on the other the widespread belief that such work was not 'real' police work (Pahl, 1982; Smith, 1989b).

Pressure for change remained high and, as far as the police were concerned, it was the Metropolitan Police that led the way. During 1985, they set up a working party to look into the problems of policing domestic violence. Reporting in 1986 it recommended a more active arrest and prosecution policy, better collection of statistics on the nature and extent of domestic violence, and the introduction of improved training for the police officers who deal with such incidents. It was particularly critical of existing training which, it said, 'perpetuate[d] current terminology ('domestic dispute') which . . . trivialise[d] marital violence rather than treating it as an allegation of crime'. A Force Order encouraging arrest was issued in 1987, and the Metropolitan Police quickly set up a number of specialist domestic violence units, being followed in later years by a small number of provincial forces. The Home Office issued further guidance to police forces about domestic violence in 1990, and senior ministers made a number of public statements drawing attention to the seriousness of the problem and the need for action to address it.

Child abuse

The issue of child abuse, in particular child sexual abuse, is one in which the criminal justice agencies have been required to review policies and practices over recent years. Early work on child abuse focused its attention upon physical assaults or neglect of children. In 1962, C. Henry Kempe, a US-based paediatrician, and his associates coined the term 'battered child syndrome'. This described the process leading to physical assaults by parents on their young children. Kempe went on to argue both that the abuse was more common than was generally recognised and that professionals had been turning a blind eye to the phenomenon. His view was that child abuse stemmed from emotional or psychological problems with the parent(s) and the response should involve therapy for the parent(s) combined with temporary protection for the child. This model of child abuse was extremely influential in the USA during the 1960s and 1970s and, largely thanks to the efforts of Kempe and his colleagues to publicise the subject, it became a major social issue there. Developments in the UK were strongly influenced by those in the USA. During the 1960s, the two main groupings involved in dealing with child abuse were the NSPCC and GPs. During the late 1960s and early 1970s, the NSPCC published a large number of studies on the subject of child abuse (Parton, 1985).

However, as well as the actions of bodies working in the area of child abuse, it is the repercussions of specific highly-publicised incidents of abuse which have done as much as anything to raise the profile of the issue in Britain. A key example, and the first major case, is that of Maria Colwell in 1973. Maria was seven years old when she was killed by her stepfather. She had previously been removed from home by social services for fostering but had later been returned and had been both beaten and starved before eventually being murdered. It was this case, and the ensuing public outcry, which led to the acceptance of the term 'child abuse' and to the establishment of a new system of child protection in the UK – involving area child protection committees, inter-agency case conferences, the development of specific training and so forth. The legal framework for the treatment of children who had been abused was set out in two Acts of Parliament – the Children and Young Persons Acts of 1933 and 1969.

Certainly it was not until the early 1980s that the idea of sexual abuse of children, as opposed to physical abuse, gained any sort of real recognition. In 1984, a further notorious case involving the abuse and later murder of a young girl by her stepfather was crucial in bringing the issue to public attention. Jasmine Beckford and her sister were placed in care soon after their births because of evidence of physical abuse. They were later returned and Jasmine died, aged four, in 1984. The case led to a public enquiry chaired by Louis Blom-Cooper, which produced clear conclusions that the primary role of social work was to protect the child, rather than keep the family together.

The pressure on the police around this time to introduce more sympathetic means of dealing with adult victims of sexual violence was quickly extended to children. Once again the Metropolitan Police were at the forefront, and in 1984 established a pilot project in the Borough of Bexleyheath where training of officers was undertaken jointly with that of social workers and, subsequently, investigations of allegations of abuse were also handled jointly (Metropolitan Police and the London Borough of Bexley, 1987; for a critique see Kelly and Regan, 1990). Following the end of the pilot project the general approach was endorsed and efforts were made to introduce it universally. Home Office Circular 52/1988, for example, encouraged joint investigations by the police and social services.

Two other crucial developments in 1986 and 1987, however, did more to frame the issue of child abuse in the UK at this time than perhaps any others. The first of these was the setting up of 'Childline' in 1986. The television programme *That's Life* late on in the year had embarked upon a special investigation of child abuse. The response was huge and it prompted the programme's host, Esther Rantzen, to launch a telephone helpline for any child wanting to report abuse or seek help. Tens of thousands of calls were made on the first day of Childline, and although the service was not without its critics, the publicity that surrounded its operation did as much as anything to draw public attention to the issue of sexual abuse of children.

It was, however, the 'Cleveland affair' in the summer of 1987 which brought the issue of sexual abuse to the forefront of public debate. The scandal involved two local paediatricians who had over a period of months been instrumental in bringing over 100 children into care on place of safety orders. On the basis of a particular physical test – the anal dilatation test which later came under question – the doctors argued that many of the children had been anally abused. Before long stories of large numbers of children being taken into care in Cleveland began to surface in the national press, and parents in the area began to mobilise. The parents of the children gained the support of the MP for Cleveland, Stuart Bell, who raised the matter in Parliament and campaigned vigorously on their behalf (Bell, 1988; Campbell, 1988). The eventual outcome was the establishment of another public inquiry.

The inquiry, chaired by Judge Elizabeth Butler-Sloss, was surrounded by massive media and public attention. The Report (Butler-Sloss, 1988) made a number of detailed recommendations for the agencies involved in dealing with child abuse. These included procedures for joint investigation of child abuse cases by police officers and social workers, joint training of police and social workers, new interview techniques, and a network of communication between all the involved agencies. In contrast to the above cases of physical abuse, the main criticism of social workers in the Cleveland case was that they had been over-zealous in their desire to take action to protect children. Crucially, the Report recommended that it was the interests of the child that should form the primary focus of any policies established to deal with the problem. Indeed, it is this general philosophy that found expression in the 1989 Children Act.

This has been far from the end of the story. From 1990 onwards stories of 'ritual abuse' have appeared in the media and a number of social services departments have become involved in dealing with cases in which highly ritualised and organised abuse of children has been alleged – the most notorious of which were those in Nottingham (where police and social services disagreed publicly over an investigation of alleged 'satanic' abuse); in the Orkneys (where police and social workers had to return a number of children they had taken into care because there appeared to be little evidence of child abuse); and the more recent investigation of a large number of allegations involving childrens' homes in North Wales and Leicester (Jenkins, 1992).

Much of the focus on child victims of crime has been upon the potentially traumatic consequences for those that have to give evidence in court. Powerful arguments have been advanced in favour limiting the range of cases that come to court and thereby protecting the child (Criminal Law Revision Committee, 1984) and in favour of prosecution (Adler, 1988). Inquiries in 1989 (Home Office, 1989) and 1990 (Scottish Law Commission, 1990) highlighted the needs of child witnesses and 'cast doubt on the belief that children are more highly suggestible and less able to differentiate fantasy from reality than adults' (Morgan and Zedner, 1991:117). The 1988 Criminal Justice Act has abolished the requirement that unsworn evidence from a child be corroborated and the 1991 Criminal Justice Act introduced the use of video recordings of testimony and, more recently, screens and video links in court have been established to prevent direct contact between child witnesses and the accused. The protection of children has now become a priority for police and social services and support for child victims is now provided by Victim Support. Court procedures have been amended to take the needs of young victims and witnesses into account and, subject to reviewing how these procedures are working in practice, the Royal Commission on Criminal Justice (RCCJ, 1993) recommended that such safeguards should be extended to other vulnerable witnesses coming before the courts.

The rise of Victim Support

In the introduction to this chapter it was noted that recent decades have seen the development of a victims' movement in the UK. This movement did not, however, come about as a result of the successful campaigns for the introduction of criminal injuries compensation. It is only later with the development of victim support schemes and other forms of support or self-help groups that something approximating a movement emerged. Not only did the victims' movement emerge after the introduction of state compensation, but as has already been suggested, the campaign which resulted in the CICS must properly be described as a reform of penal policy, not the emergence of a victims' policy.

The absence of a movement, or even a recognisable pressure group, meant that further change was very slow in coming. When it did, it was supported by a relatively new organisation whose primary focus was, once again, offenders: the National Association for the Care and Resettlement of Offenders (NACRO). Rock (1990) identifies three people: Christopher Holtom, Philip Priestly and Charles Irving, respectively Deputy Chairman, Regional Organiser and Chairman of NACRO's first regional committee, and suggests that they in their activities between 1969 and 1978 'rediscovered the victim' (1990:95).

In setting up a meeting of concerned parties in Bristol, where they were based, to discuss offenders and offending, they decided that it would be interesting to have victims take part, and the result was the setting up of a victim–offender group in 1970. What of course distinguished what they decided to do from what had gone on before was that on this occasion they actually involved victims rather than assuming that they already knew what it was that victims wanted. What they found was that the emotional pain of victimisation was often as great if not greater than the physical injury or financial loss; that even supposedly trivial events might lead to trauma; that not only was the victim largely ignored by the criminal justice system, but almost any form of reparation was precluded; that victims often found that relatives and neighbours were sometimes less helpful that they imagined they might be; and that there appeared to be no statutory or voluntary body that took responsibility for looking after victims of crime (Holtom and Raynor, 1988).

Out of this work there were two main developments. A study day was organised to look at the work of the victim–offender group and, eventually, a working party was set up to look into the setting up of a pilot project providing a service for victims of crime. The second development was the establishment of the National Victims Association (NVA) whose aim was to promote services for victims and to encourage experiments in conciliation between victims and offenders. In relation to the latter development at least, the driving force once again was penal reform. Priestly, the secretary of the NVA, said in 1974: 'purely political reform, although it can achieve significant specific victories such as the abolition of hanging, can never lead to real penal reform since it leaves untouched the bedrock attitudes from which resistance to change draws its profound yet subtle strength' (quoted in Rock, 1990:113).

The NVA never really took off. Its membership remained small and it was largely unsuccessful at raising funds. Within a couple of years of its establishment it abandoned the idea of becoming a large-scale national organisation. It was not that its officers were in any way inexperienced at raising money and getting new enterprises off the ground, indeed they were extremely successful, it was simply that there was little apparent sympathy and support for groups that attempted to work in this area (Rock, 1990). In the first half of the 1970s, victims of crime were not a subject designed to attract sponsors. What NVA did do, however, was keep the issue in the public domain while others deliberated and established other initiatives.

Priestly summed up the work of the NVA in the following way:

We have been in existence since the end of 1972 and operate principally as a pressure group trying to get a better deal for the people on the receiving end of crime. We have campaigned for a drastic revision of the current Criminal Injuries Compensation scheme; for better treatment of the victims of meter thefts; . . . and to get recognition of the principle of victim-offender conciliation as a saner and more effective way of dealing with offence behaviour. We also set up the first Victim Counselling Service in this country at Kingswood and have conducted pilot conciliation sessions between violent offenders and victims. The nett effect of all this activity, I am afraid to say is rather small. (quoted in Rock, 1990: 128–9)

The study group and the subsequent working party that had been set up in Bristol, on the other hand, gave birth to the Bristol Victims Support Scheme (BVSS) and, eventually, to a national movement. In designing the new service a number of the working party's findings were acted upon and, indeed, continue to inform the work of Victim Support to this day. First of all, in recognising that although police records were significantly incomplete they were the best source of information available about victims of crime, it was obvious that the service was only likely to work if it proved to be acceptable to the police. 'This meant that in some respects a cautious and "conventional" approach was adopted as a positive policy decision' (Holtom and Raynor, 1988:19). Before he agreed to co-operate, the chief constable had to be assured that volunteers would be selected with care, and that the scheme would be run by responsible people (Rock, 1990).

Second, an 'outreach' service was planned as a way of overcoming resistance or reticence on the part of potential 'clients' of the service, and as facilitating approaches to those likely to be most traumatised by their experiences. Third, there was the question of staffing. It was felt that using volunteers from the local community would be an effective method of counteracting the feeling of ostracisation or alienation often felt by crime victims as a result of their experiences. These volunteers would be given some training in order to ensure that they were prepared to deal with the problems they would face. Finally, influenced by the crisis intervention model, the feeling was that a brief intervention by volunteers would be sufficient in the vast majority of cases, though referral on to professional help would be considered. The idea was that the project should be run on a trial basis for the first six months.

The scheme started visiting victims in January 1974 and 'within a month it was clear that a large proportion of victims faced quite severe problems and almost without exception welcomed the offer of help' (Holtom and Raynor, 1988:20). In addition, those running the scheme also found that the number of referrals was greater than they had been expecting, and the voluntary visitors couldn't cope with all the work. Seven to ten referrals a week had been anticipated. In the event, the scheme received over 500 in its first three months. If anything, 'the scheme was too successful' (Rock, 1990:143) and it was forced to recruit more volunteers. In addition, they decided to send letters to victims of thefts of or from motor vehicles, offering help rather than visiting in the first instance. This tension between outreach and limited resources continues to characterise the work of Victim Support. Perhaps more importantly, the police had already started to 'filter out' domestic violence incidents and fights in which it wasn't clear who the victim was, thereby reinforcing the gatekeeping role which they continued to occupy in relation to victim support schemes for some years.

The problem that had affected the NVA then began to trouble BVSS. It had been assumed that such a good and worthy cause would have few difficulties in attracting sponsors. After the first six months, work had to be temporarily halted in order to allow time to concentrate on fund-raising. In the interim, the opportunity arose to become involved in the making of a BBC *Open Door* programme. The role of the media in the development of social policy is rarely commented upon, though there are a small number of instances – even in criminal justice – of television in particular having an important influence on the direction of policy. In the event, the programme, entitled 'Once every twenty seconds', played a key part in ensuring the future of BVSS. The programme resulted in a flood of inquiries and even some small financial donations. Crucially what it did do was lead to the setting up of a day conference attended by like-minded people and thereafter to the establishment of a number of other victim support schemes. Some of the money that was forthcoming from charitable sources at this time was given in order to support and to co-ordinate the development of schemes nationwide.

By May 1977 there were 13 schemes in England and Wales and two years later when a National Association was set up there were 30. Thereafter the movement expanded rapidly. A national committee had been established in 1978, with Holtom as Chair, and both ACPO and ACOP were invited to join. At around this time NACRO, which was still providing support for the developing organisation in a number of ways, approached the Home Office with a view to securing some financial backing for a national association for the victim support movement. In mid-1979 this was successful, and the Home Office promised £10,000 a year for three years. More important than the money, Rock argues, was what it represented for the future of the organisation:

The Home Office's decision was a gesture whose significance reached far beyond the granting of a few thousand pounds a year. It was a major step for the Home Office to do something of this kind for the first time. It signalled government endorsement of the character and ends of the National Association, an acceptance of the duties of patronage, and the possibility of an indefinite commitment (1990:171).

A national development officer was appointed and work began to turn the fledgling movement into a fully operational national body. When the National Association (known originally as the National Association of Victims Support Schemes or NAVSS) was officially launched in 1979 there had been approximately 30 schemes. By the end of the following year there were 79. This increased to 159 by September 1983 and to over 300 by 1987. Referrals increased at a faster rate than did the schemes: from 18,000 in 1979 to 65,000 in 1983 and 257,000 in 1986–7 (Rock, 1990). The work increased not only in quantity but also in range, taking on, for example, victims of rape and sexual assault, and of serious assault and even murder.[2]

Much of the energy of the Director of National Association was taken up at this time in trying to secure funding, not only to maintain the national body, but to ensure that local schemes continued to operate. Not surprisingly, much of this fund-raising effort was directed at the Home Office. Just as those running BVSS in the early 1970s had realised that the public face of their scheme was crucial in securing co-operation with their activities and funding for their work, so the national organisation worked hard at creating an acceptable and appropriate image. There were a number of key elements to this image [doc 17].

First, it was crucial that the movement was, and was seen to be, non-party political. As Holtom summarised it: 'We'd obviously run a

---

[2] In the latter case, of course, this meant the families of murder victims.

mile from the "hang 'em and flog 'em" wing of the Tories. Similarly, we don't want to get involved with the "let's control the police" Left-wing bit' (quoted in Rock, 1990:223). Second, from the outset the organisation decided against getting involved in penal politics of any sort. It steadfastly refused to comment on criminal justice issues unless they directly affected victims or victim services. 'This single issue approach was a deliberate device to avoid distractions and to guard against co-option by the developing political theme of "law and order"; particularly, we wanted to avoid reinforcing illusions that victims benefit from tougher sentencing' (Holtom and Raynor, 1988:24).

Third, in many respects it fought shy of publicity. It certainly avoided sensationalist accounts of victimisation at all costs. Doing so was perhaps less easy than it sounds. As has already been suggested, despite the general worthiness of the work it was extremely difficult to get funding bodies interested in supporting the organisation. One of the most effective ways of galvanising support, however – as all charities know – is to seek and exploit publicity in the mass media. Because of its policy of avoiding publicity which might bring distress to victims, the National Association was therefore faced with having to turn down many opportunities for coverage which might have heightened its profile at a time when it was desperately in need of further financial support. In relation to its goal of securing funding from the state, however, this was to prove a very important strategy.

Fourthly, the National Association followed the lead established by BVSS and encouraged very close ties with the police. The fact that schemes relied upon the police for referrals meant that without their co-operation the organisation simply could not function. In addition, being a very powerful and influential body, the police also carried great weight with other agencies and bodies that NAVSS wished to influence. Early on ACPO had insisted on a policy of what were called 'indirect referrals', that is the police would act as formal gatekeepers, only passing on the names and addresses of people where they had their permission to do so. In many cases this led to a very significant lack of referrals and put the futures of schemes at risk. In the end the Home Office, which was concerned about the drop in referrals resulting from the policy, persuaded ACPO to reconsider, and the stricture requiring local constabularies to operate such a policy was removed. The early 1980s saw the development of a relationship of increasing trust between NAVSS and the police, to the point where victims support schemes were regarded 'as a reliable client and adjunct' by the middle of the decade (Rock, 1990:247).

By the mid-1980s, with the developing penal crisis (see chapter 2), and increasing scepticism about the effectiveness of the crime control role of the police (see chapter 3) politicians and administrators in the Home Office were looking for innovative policies with which to freshen the penal landscape. The Home Office had published a 'working document' – *Criminal Justice: A Working Paper* (Home Office, 1984a) – in which the possibility of finding a new role for victims was flagged up. As Rock (1990:258) summarises it: 'It was thought that little could be done to curb crime, and that increased expenditure could not be justified indefinitely. Yet the problem of crime remained, people were worried, and a public lessening of effort was politically impossible.' Into this impasse among other things entered 'the victim'. Some of this attention was devoted to the subjects of compensation and reparation; increasingly, however, it was the victim support movement which dominated the scene. Unfortunately for NAVSS this was the point at which the FMI was really beginning to bite (see chapters 3 and 4) and new expenditure within the criminal justice system was vigorously resisted. Rock (1990:330) quotes the Deputy Under Secretary in the Home Office at the time telling NAVSS:

The present Government [will not] contemplate developing a victims' support system which would in effect be a new paid social service. The Government's view is that victim support is essentially a local responsibility, ideally suited for voluntary action, and not one which should be professionalized or bureaucratized in the way which would become inevitable if it came to rely on large numbers of full-time paid staff.

Funding was, however, a major problem. The Home Office had been supporting the National Office since 1978, and local schemes had been relying on the Manpower Services Commission, on local authorities, Urban Aid and a variety of other sources of income to pay for their co-ordinators and other expenses. By the mid-1980s it was becoming increasingly clear that some local schemes were going to fold unless more secure funding could be found. In effect the whole future of the organisation rested on how the question of funding local schemes was resolved.

The Home Affairs Select Committee which published a report on *Compensation and Support for Victims of Crime* at the end of 1984 had praised victims support schemes and had recommended that the government consider providing some financial support for coordinators for local schemes. For as long as Leon Brittan was Home Secretary, however, the Home Office seemed more interested in pursuing the possibility of reparation schemes that it was in putting victim support on a sounder financial footing. By this stage, however, the Home Office had commissioned research which had illustrated in graphic detail the disadvantaged position of the victim in the criminal justice system (Shapland *et al.*, 1985) and a further study was underway investigating the work and impact of victim support schemes (eventually published as Maguire and Corbett, 1987). The research painted a positive picture of victims support, illustrated in detail the effects of crime on a wide variety of victims, and provided further impetus to substantial central funding. The decision finally came in 1986, when £9 million was set aside over a period of three years 'to strengthen the work of these local victims support schemes' said Douglas Hurd the new Home Secretary (quoted in Rock, 1990:405). One former Home Office minister commenting on this development described it as 'a clear and welcome departure from the previous policy of making contributions to headquarters' expenses, backed up by periodic hand-outs to schemes in financial difficulty. Central government has now indicated a readiness to maintain victims' support as a regular and specific commitment, rather than on an incidental or exceptional basis' (Windlesham, 1987:56).

In the first years of the organisation, the work of victims support schemes reflected the rather apolitical, unproblematic model of victimisation that was so popular with the major political parties. The schemes tended to focus their attention on the victims of 'conventional' crimes such as burglary and theft (Zedner, 1994). During the 1980s, however, they have become progressively more involved in providing support for a wider variety of victims including victims of racial harassment, families of murder victims, and victims of rape and serious sexual assault. By the time of their research in the mid-1980s Maguire and Corbett (1987) found that over half of all VSSs had taken one or more referrals in this latter area and by 1988 over 900 cases of rape were referred to VSSs. Undoubtedly one of the reasons for the development of the VSS service to rape victims, alongside and in addition to the already established Rape Crisis Centres (RCCs), was the fact that as Corbett and Hobdell (1988) have argued, the former 'tend to be more palatable to the police in style and philosophy'.

In relation to RCCs, Maguire and Corbett (1987) have argued that their great strengths are, firstly, that their existence is widely known and, secondly, that some form of help is available to any woman who requests it, twenty-four hours a day, whenever the offence occurred and irrespective of whether the offence was reported to the police. The major problem with the RCC model, Maguire and Corbett (1987) argue, is that victims are not always willing to come forward and request help (cf. also King and Webb, 1981). Maguire and Corbett (1987) argue that the major advantage of the VS model for some women is that contact is not left to the victim, as it is the scheme itself that takes the first initiative.

'Victims Support, women's refuges, and rape crisis centres are far from enjoying coherence of outlook, organization, or method,' Zedner argues (1994:1229). She goes on: 'The "victim movement" is ideologically heterogenous. Relations between the various agencies range from close cooperation to barely concealed hostility . . . Despite, or perhaps because of this heterogeneity, the combined impact of these endeavours has been enormous.'

In recent years, the work of Victim Support has broadened out in a variety of new areas. One area that was identified by researchers (Shapland *et al.*, 1985; Shapland and Cohen, 1987) in which victims required support was that of the court process itself. A longitudinal study undertaken by Shapland and colleagues charted a continuous decline in levels of satisfaction reported by victims as they passed through the criminal justice system. Crucially, they found that facilities in the courts were sadly lacking, with victims and defendants frequently having to share the same waiting spaces in court, and little information available to victims or witnesses about court dates (see also Raine and Walker, 1990; Newburn and Merry, 1990).

A working party set up by NAVSS (as it then was) in 1988 to consider the role of the victim/witness in court recommended that courts should reconsider their practices with regard to the treatment of victims (National Association of Victim Support Schemes, 1988) and, in addition, issued a circular (20/1988) to Chief Police Officers pointing out the benefits 'both for the welfare of the victim and for the police–public relationship, from making a purposeful effort to provide victims with information about progress'. One recommendation made by the working party was that a leaflet explaining court procedures should be available, and sent routinely to prosecution witnesses was accepted and acted upon by the Home Office. Indeed, the Victims' Charter, published by the government in 1990, further encouraged this process: 'The Home Office produces a leaflet called "Witness in Court" which tells witnesses who may not have been to court before, something about the procedure and what to expect. Witnesses should always receive this with the notice which tells them that they may be needed to give evidence and should attend . . . Many magistrates' courts also distribute their own leaflets showing exactly where they are, how to get there, where there is parking and so on. This is an excellent practice, to be encouraged' (Home Office 1990b:14).

By 1990, Victim Support were running a series of pilot victim/witness support programmes in seven Crown Court centres. Even getting this far was fraught with difficulties. Rock (1993:328–9) describes the process as follows: 'With some wariness, government departments had consented to mounting a trial project to assist victims and prosecution witnesses attending the Crown Court. The Home Office was to fund the project's staffing costs but not the evaluation research, which would establish its effectiveness. The Lord Chancellor's Department was to afford access to the Crown Court, but it did so only with some nervousness . . . There should be no victim impact statements, statements of the kind that had become accepted in a number of courts in North America and which listed the suffering and injuries inflicted on the victim as matters to be considered by the judge in sentencing.'

Gains such as this were limited and hard fought. They appear, however, to have been successful. The evaluation conducted as part of the pilot recommended that the system should be expanded, and this expansion is now well underway. This is potentially a particularly important development in the work of Victim Support. In many respects the work of Victim Support volunteers has been largely hidden from view, and certainly not open to scrutiny from other criminal justice professionals (Mawby and Walklate, 1994). Not only did the development of the Crown Court experiment mark a recognition of the negative experiences of many victims and witnesses in the criminal justice system, but it also signified the emergence of Victim Support as a significant 'player' in the system.

Conclusion

As even this brief overview has illustrated, there has been no shortage of initiatives undertaken 'on behalf of' victims of crime over the past thirty years. In addition, there can be no doubt that the changes that have been brought about as a result of some of these initiatives have improved, often markedly, the situation of the victim in the criminal justice system. By 1990 there was even a Victim's Charter subtitled: 'A Statement of the Rights of Victims of Crime' [doc 18]. Despite this commendable progress, however, it remains the case that the UK still lacks a coherent victims policy.

Despite the subtitle of the Charter, victims of crime continue to occupy a position which is much more likely to be defined by needs or deserts than it is by rights. While the Charter is valuable in staking out much of the territory in which victims' needs have to be addressed [doc 18] and, no doubt, provides useful leverage for those organisations attempting to respond to those needs, it falls somewhat short of guaranteeing rights. As Mawby (1988) has pointed out, acceptance of the idea of victims' rights leads to the necessity of recognising that these rights exist irrespective of need: 'victims who have not been caused serious hardship or lasting anguish still have a right to redress' (Mawby, 1988:135). Rights in relation to the four areas that he and Martin Gill identified in earlier work: the right to play an active part in the criminal justice process; the right to knowledge; the right to financial help; and the right to support and help, remain limited in important respects.

First, the various 'fiefs' (Shapland, 1988) in the criminal justice system are quick to guard their own territory and thereby limit the extent to which victims might make incursions into decision-making processes (Mawby and Walklate, 1994). Second, despite the considerable body of research that has been conducted into victims' informational needs (Shapland *et al.*, 1985; Maguire and Corbett, 1987; Newburn and Merry, 1990), the police and courts are often still slow to inform and inconsistent in keeping victims and witnesses up-to-date. Crucially, formal responsibility for such work together with sanctions for failure have never been imposed.

Third, access to financial recompense is still extremely limited: compensation orders though more effectively administered still only reach a minority of victims; the CICS still only compensates a narrow range of crime victims and continues to operate on the basis of compensating the 'deserving victim' (Newburn, 1989). Furthermore, had it not been for the Court of Appeal in November 1994 the current

Home Secretary, Michael Howard, would have instituted changes to the CICS which would have resulted in cutbacks in payments to victims of violence by up to £250 million a year. Finally, although the available services are continually bringing a greater number of victims within their ambit, the possibility of 'blanket coverage' is still some way off. As with most if not all areas of criminal justice, financial considerations are perhaps the greatest inhibitor to fundamental change. Mawby and Walklate (1994:198) in reviewing criminal justice policy in relation to victims recognise this key factor:

> To put it bluntly, *crime costs*, in both a personal and a financial sense. At the moment too much of that cost is borne by the victim of crime. In a just system it is appropriate for the state, through all its citizens, to take over that burden.

Underpinning the failures in relation to the development of a 'victims policy' is the continuing overriding concern with crime and with offenders rather than with victims. The Conservative Party – which, at least in terms of its manifestoes, has shown interest in victims since the early 1960s – nevertheless resisted all calls to provide significant funding for victim services for many years, and still seeks to cut back on expenditure when it can. As Phipps (1988:180) argues, 'in a rather paradoxical way, victims in Conservative thinking are transformed from injured individuals into symbols of injured order'. The main purpose of the techniques they use in arousing sympathy or outrage of victims of crime 'is to excite hostility against the offender or to descredit the "softness" of the criminal justice system . . . [and] . . . to promote support for deterrence and retribution'. Victims policy has in many ways therefore been a means to an end rather than end in itself.

The discussion above of the process by which the decision about funding of local victim support schemes was made, however, perhaps paints a rather too apolitical picture of the context in which it was actually taken. As I have suggested, up until the point at which the decision about full-scale funding was finally taken, the government had shown little interest in getting involved in a major way with the 'victims movement'. The Thatcher government's financial contribution had been to invest heavily in policing in the hope that this would have some impact upon crime rates. By the mid-1980s the law and order policies upon which successive Conservative administrations had been elected were beginning to look more than a little threadbare. With the criminal justice policy cupboard also looking a little bare, the announcement of £9 million of funding for NAVSS was an attractive proposition, particularly with a General Election approaching. As Phipps (1988:178) has argued, 'the change in policy remains open to the charge of political opportunism and only seems on the surface to be a major advance'. In addition, Phipps also points out that the expenditure on victims represents a very small investment when set alongside the £3 billion spent annually on criminal justice at that time.

The charge of opportunism might also quite reasonably be levelled at the Labour opposition as well. In all their manifestoes up to and including that in 1983 the Labour Party had singularly failed to show any major interest in victims of crime. By 1987, however, victims having become an established political football in Home Affairs debates, the Labour Party had developed a fully-fledged set of policies on victims support (which it promised to fund), criminal injuries compensation (which it wished to extend) and police treatment of victims and witnesses (which it wished to improve). Furthermore, although much was made in the manifesto about issues such as racism and sexism, there was an absence of policies which might have had any significant impact on the victims of racial harassment or domestic violence. What was being promised was extra cash for some of the more visible initiatives, rather than the development of a coherent and forward-looking victims policy.

Both of the major political parties have pursued half-formed and in many ways half-hearted policies in relation to victims of crime. There is little indication of change in this area. A new version of the Victim's Charter is promised. Although no doubt it will, like its predecessor, be full of good intentions, it is highly unlikely that it will confront the difficult issues involved in thinking through what the role of the victim in the criminal justice process should be, whether or not victims should be considered to have rights and, additionally, what the responsibilties of the state should be in ensuring proper treatment of victims of crime.

CHAPTER 8

The future of criminal justice policy

Crime and criminal justice policy is now accepted as being a major political issue. That is, not only do we expect politicians to spend a lot of their time talking about crime and criminal justice, but we expect them to disagree. It was not always thus. As many commentators (*inter alia*, Brake and Hale, 1992; Rawlings, 1992) have noted, for many years there existed something approximating a bipartisan consensus on issues to do with policing, crime and punishment. Although it is often assumed that 1979 marked the point at which all this ended (see Nash and Savage, 1994) as Downes and Morgan (1994:187) have pointed out, this was merely 'the heightening of a trend in relation to law and order' that had existed since the election of 1970 (see also Hall *et al.*, 1978). From that point onwards, the major political parties began to blame each other for what was happening in relation to crime, and began to look to make political capital out of their criminal justice policies.

The end of the bipartisan consensus coincided (in very rough terms) with the death-throes of the rehabilitative ideal, the emergence of penal pessimism, and a significant ratcheting up of the prison crisis. In addition, of course, from 1979 onwards, this modern period in criminal justice has seen only one party in power. The Conservative Party has therefore had a unique opportunity to leave its imprint on the criminal justice system in England and Wales. Although the focus of this book has been on a longer time-frame than merely the last decade and a half, these closing reflections are confined in the main to this most recent historical period.

It would be difficult to think of a measure that would indicate that the criminal justice policies of the Thatcher and Major governments have been successful. Certainly levels of crime and of fear of crime provide little comfort. There are a number of methods of measuring crime. The two most common – crimes recorded by the police, and incidents recorded in victimisation surveys such as the British Crime Survey (BCS) – both show a remarkable rise in crime during the 1980s. For those crime categories that can be compared, between 1981 and 1991 recorded crime in England and Wales rose by 96 per cent, whereas crime measured by the BCS (often considered to be the more reliable measure) rose by 49 per cent [doc 9].

The Conservatives had been elected in 1979 on a ticket that not only suggested that the Labour Party were responsible for the increases in crime in the latter half of the 1970s, but maintained that the extra expenditure that was promised by their opponents for criminal justice

– 'never, ever, have you heard me say that we will economise on law and order' (Margaret Thatcher in 1985, quoted in Nash and Savage, 1994:142–3) – would have a significant impact on crime levels. However, as we saw, for example in chapter 3, the hugely increased expenditure on the police in the first half of the 1980s did not lead to the hoped-for reductions in recorded offences. Far from it. Crime continued to rise, and rise at a dramatic rate as, in general, did people's fear of crime.

The 'law and order' approach to criminal justice has quite clearly failed. Indeed, this was in some respects recognised by the Conservative administration itself. Certainly, the 'spend, spend, spend' strategy was experimented with and then, fairly quickly, abandoned. As a consequence a number of other strategies have been adopted, three of which will be briefly considered here: 'managerialism' (including privatisation), increasing centralisation and, lastly and most recently, the return of a form of penal populism.

Managerialism and financial control

The continued rise in crime despite the doubling of police expenditure between 1979 and 1984 led to the ending of the apparent immunity the police had enjoyed from the financial stringencies being applied to all the other public services. From the mid-1980s onwards a policy of 'tight resourcing' was applied not only to the police, but also to the probation service and to the courts system (Raine and Willson, 1993). Thus, although the major criminal justice agencies were not cash-limited in the way that, say, the health and social services were, other limiting factors quickly came into play. One of the difficulties for criminal justice agencies is that available resources are not necessarily linked to levels of demand.

The policy solution to the combination of tight resourcing and increasing demand was in essence managerialist (Atkinson and Cope, 1994). The public services were encouraged to change their management styles. Through the application of the Financial Management Initiative, the construction of performance indicators, the use of management information systems (such as PROBIS – see chapter 4) and, later in the 1980s, scrutiny by the Audit Commission and the National Audit Office, radical changes in the management of criminal justice agencies were encouraged.

In relation to prisons, there were two principal foci: the managerialist 'Fresh Start' package, and the increasing emphasis upon and use of privatisation. Announcing the publication of a joint report by the Prison Department and a group of management consultants in 1986, the Home Secretary said that it presented 'a telling indictment of the present shift and complementing systems in the Prison Service and the working practices that surround them'. Furthermore, the report also included 'recommendations for new systems which would release large amounts of now unproductive capacity which ought to be used for other purposes' (McDermott and King, 1989:161). It was as a result of this report that the 'Fresh Start' package came into being. As part of the process of implementation of the package, new management structures were introduced which reduced prison governors' autonomy by making them answerable to area managers – indeed the new management structures were designed so that 'everybody was accountable to somebody'. Fresh Start, it is suggested, 'involved some of the most far-reaching changes to the prison system since it was nationalised in 1878' (King and McDermott, 1992:153).

No doubt a similarly radical set of changes were in the Home Secretary's mind when he set Sir Patrick Sheehy the task of inquiring into police rank structures and remuneration. Although much of what Sheehy recommended was successfully resisted by the police, many of the cumbersome managerial structures once visible in the service – many of which were identified by Sheehy – are now being dismantled. In much the same way, the professional skills of the probation service have been increasingly subject to management ideals (McLaughlin and Muncie, 1994).

Although privatisation was resisted for some years, and the policy has only been pursued in earnest relatively recently, major changes have nevertheless taken place. The first major announcement came in April 1992, when Group 4 Security won the contract to manage a new purpose-built institution for remand prisoners, the Wolds. A second prison, Blakenhurst, opened in 1993 under the management of UK Detention Services, and later that year tenders were invited for the running of existing as well as new prisons, including Strangeways. It has been suggested that up to half of the existing estate may be market-tested. In August 1994 a list of prisons to be market-tested was published, though those selected were encouraged, the Prison Service said, to make in-house bids alongside any that might come from the private sector.

In addition to the prisons themselves, contracts have also been issued to run court escort services. The first contract was awarded to Group 4 Court Services Ltd in November 1992 to run a service in the East Midlands and Humberside areas. This was followed in December 1993 when Securicor Custodial Services Ltd were awarded the contract to run the court escorting and custody service in London.

Finally, in April 1993 the Prison Service itself became an executive agency under the 'Next Steps' programme. It was suggested by some commentators that this move, including the appointment of ex-Granada TV boss, Derek Lewis, as Chief Executive of the Prison Service, would lead to further privatisation. This appeared to be confirmed by the Home Secretary who on announcing the change said the 'Chief Executive . . . will be personally responsible for the day-to-day running of the Service and will be my chief policy advisor on all prison issues. I will be looking to him to improve the performance of directly managed prisons and to increase private sector involvement to provide competition [and] a fresh stimulus for innovation'. At the same time as lauching the agency, the Prison Service published its strategic plan for the next three years together with an action plan which included eight performance indicators.

In relation to policing, the encouragement of the private sector has taken place with a greater degree of stealth. Britain is almost alone in Europe in having no statutory licensing or other form of vetting of its private security industry. Recent Home Secretaries have consistently maintained that self-regulation is the best form of regulation, despite the fact that many of the major companies – indeed the ones responsible for the voluntary system of regulation – are in favour of the introduction of statutory controls. There is evidence that the private security industry is expanding particularly quickly (Jones and Newburn, 1995) and, although there are a relatively small number of examples, private companies are increasingly moving into areas of work like patrol – which is considered to be one of the primary functions of public constabularies. In addition to encouraging the private sector by being seen not to discourage it, the government has also set in train the Inquiry into Core and Ancillary Tasks and a Review of Traffic Policing. Both of these have as their aim the identification of areas of police work that might be contracted out. Although the early signs are that the recommendations from these inquiries will not be especially radical, a further expansion of private operations is inevitable.

One of the solutions that the government has pursued in relation to the problems it has faced in crime and criminal justice has been to seek to make criminal justice agencies more business-like. 'The perceived attributes of the well-run private sector company (of high efficiency, of explicit accountabilities, of clear objectives, and of measured performance)' are increasingly applied to management in the police, prison and probation services and other agencies (Raine and Willson, 1993:23). Managerialism has impacted on all criminal justice agencies, and has become so central a part of current thinking that it even dominated the style in which the Royal Commission on Criminal Justice defined its job (see Ashworth, 1994). Part of this new management creed involves a devolution of decision-making and of budgetary control and, indeed, there have been moves – particularly within the prison and police services – to provide local managers with considerably enhanced powers. There has, however, been a process moving in exactly the opposite direction taking place at the same time. This was what was referred to above as 'centralisation'.

Local autonomy or state control?

Although the new managerialism has involved a great deal of talk about devolution, one author has argued that this is merely a front behind which the state is increasing its control over the various criminal justice agencies (Jones, 1993). McLaughlin and Muncie (1994:137) by contrast have argued that 'there has been a redistribution of decision-making powers to the new managerial strata that are now firmly in place within the criminal justice agencies' and that it is these managers who now have responsibility for delivering 'law and order'. It is too early in the process of reorienting the criminal justice system to tell how the balance between these dual processes of devolution and centralisation will work in practice. What is clear is the degree of centralisation that has already taken place.

As we saw in relation to both the long-term and more recent history of the probation service, the overriding feature of change in this area has been the increasing power and control exercised by the centre. Home Office circulars, Green Papers, White Papers, consultation documents, decision documents, SNOP followed by national standards, suggest in combination that the Home Office now occupies the key role in the tripartite structure of probation governance. In relation to the police, a similar process has been taking place and, indeed, would have gone considerably further, had key elements of the original Police and Magistrates' Courts Bill not been resisted by the House of Lords.

Despite the intentions of the 1964 Police Act local police committees have always occupied a relatively powerless position when compared with the other players in the tripartite structure. Once again it is too early to tell what the impact of the most recent changes will be, though it is almost certainly the case that the Police and Magistrates' Courts Act will in years to come be viewed as having further strengthened the hand of the Home Secretary. However, it is also possible that the newly constituted police authorities will prove to be more active than their predecessors in attempting to set targets and policy agendas for chief officers to follow. They have clearly been given the opportunity to do so. That this is the case suggests that McLaughlin and Muncie (1994) are right to argue that centralization and devolution are complementary processes.

A return to penal populism?

With the clear failure of the 'law and order' policies of the Thatcher government, the latter half of the 1980s witnessed a gradual move away from the most strident aspects of that particular form of rhetoric. More particularly, increasing attention was paid to the notion that (the by now better-resourced) criminal justice agencies could not tackle crime alone. They were encouraged to form partnerships and inter-agency groupings and, more importantly, the wider 'community' was itself encouraged to take responsibility for the fight against crime. Towards the end of the decade there was increasing recognition that the problem of crime and the 'crisis of containment' needed to be tackled in a rational manner and the eventual result, after a series of Green and White Papers, was the reinforcement of the policy of bifurcation via the passage of the 1991 Criminal Justice Act. The Act sought to impose on the sentencing process a framework which would encourage a 'coherent approach to non-custodial sentencing' (Ashworth, 1992:245), would bring about greater use of punishments in the community and reduce prison numbers. The general spirit of optimism which greeted the passage of the 1991 Act was reinforced by nature of the Report produced by Lord Woolf in the aftermath of the worst prison disturbances in the twentieth century.

Furthermore, this sense of optimism was furthered by the initial period after the passing of the legislation and the publication of the Report. Prison numbers began to fall, there was some respite from the problems of overcrowding that had bedevilled prisons for many years, there was some evidence of increasing use of certain community-based penalties, and the government, though it by no means made across the board promises with regard to Woolf's proposals, nevertheless produced a White Paper which was perhaps more progressive than many expected. The greatest of all U-turns, however, was just around the corner.

At the Conservative Party conference in 1993 the Home Secretary, Michael Howard, announced a new 'law and order' package. The description is not a loose one, for the approach taken by Howard flew directly in the face of all the major trends in criminal justice since the late 1980s. The government were by this stage under pressure from a Labour Party which appeared to be persuading voters that it could be just as 'tough on crime' as the traditional party of law and order claimed to be, whilst simultaneously implementing social policies that, as in Tony Blair's famous soundbite, would make them 'tough on the causes of crime' as well. The choice that Howard made in seeking to bolster his party's and his own fortunes was to return to the strident tones reminiscent of Mrs Thatcher's 'authoritarian populism'.

The package of measures that Howard announced were punitive, involving a reassertion of the central position of custody in a range of sanctions he interpreted as having deterrence as their primary aim. Most famously, he announced that previous approaches which involved attempts to limit prison numbers were henceforward to be eschewed. The new package of measures would be likely to result in an increase in prison numbers, an increase which he appeared to welcome: 'I do not flinch from that. We shall no longer judge the success of our system of justice by a fall in our prison population . . . Let us be clear. *Prison works*. It ensures that we are protected from murderers, muggers and rapists – and it makes many who are tempted to commit crime think twice' (emphasis added). The short-term decline in the prison population that had occurred after the introduction of the 1991 Act was quickly reversed; numbers are now back at record levels and, despite the biggest prison building programme this century, are once again due to exceed the overall capacity of the estate.

The recent history of criminal justice policy makes depressing reading. However, were this to have been written in 1992 instead of 1995 perhaps the outlook would, in part, have been more optimistic. It is not that lessons cannot be learnt, or that once learnt they cannot be put into practice. It is that with the politicisation of criminal justice issues comes the likelihood that long-term benefits will continually be sacrificed on the altar of short-term expediency. With the front bench Home Affairs spokesmen (for they are generally men) of both major parties battling to 'out-tough' each other, there appears little prospect of coherent and forward-thinking policy-making. Whilst the 1991 Criminal Justice Act may not by any means have been an ideal piece of legislation, it was at least formulated in a constructive and thoughtful manner. It was the product of considerable thought, debate and consultation. Sadly, the prospects of there being new criminal justice legislation in the near future that is a product of a similar process seem slim. Short-term electoral advantage (whether imagined or real) is once again the driving force in criminal justice policy-making.

LIST OF DOCUMENTS

Document 1
PUNISHMENT, TORTURE AND SPECTACLE

On 2 March 1757 Damiens the regicide was condemned 'to make the *amende honorable* before the main door of the Church of Paris', where he was to be 'taken and conveyed in a cart, wearing nothing but a shirt, holding a torch of burning wax weighing two pounds'; then, 'in the said cart, to the Place de Grève, where, on a scaffold that will be erected there, the flesh will be torn from his breasts, arms, thighs and calves with red-hot pincers, his right hand, holding the knife with which he committed the said parricide, burnt with sulphur, and, on those places where the flesh will be torn away, poured molten lead, boiling oil, burning resin, wax and sulphur melted together and then his body drawn and quartered by four horses and his limbs and body consumed by fire, reduced to ashes and his ashes thrown to the winds' (*Pièces originales . . .* , 372–4).

'Finally, he was quartered,' recounts the *Gazette d'Amsterdam* of 1 April 1757. 'This last operation was very long, because the horses used were not accustomed to drawing; consequently, instead of four, six were needed; and when that did not suffice, they were forced, in order to cut off the wretch's thighs, to sever the sinews and hack at the joints . . .

'It is said that, though he was always a great swearer, no blasphemy escaped his lips; but the excessive pain made him utter horrible cries, and he often repeated: "My God, have pity on me! Jesus, help me!" The spectators were all edified by the solicitude of the parish priest of St Paul's who despite his great age did not spare himself in offering consolation to the patient.'

Bouton, an officer of the watch, left us his account: 'The sulphur was lit, but the flame was so poor that only the top skin of the hand was burnt, and that only slightly. Then the executioner, his sleeves rolled up, took the steel pincers, which had been especially made for the occasion, and which were about a foot and a half long, and pulled first at the calf of the right leg, then at the thigh, and from there at the two fleshy parts of the right arm; then at the breasts. Though a strong, sturdy fellow, this executioner found it so difficult to tear away the pieces of flesh that he set about the same spot two or three times, twisting the pincers as he did so, and what he took away formed at each part a wound about the size of a six-pound crown piece.

'After these tearings with the pincers, Damiens, who cried out profusely, though without swearing, raised his head and looked at himself; the same executioner dipped an iron spoon in the pot containing the boiling potion, which he poured liberally over each wound. Then the ropes that were to be harnessed to the horses were attached with cords to the patient's body; the horses were then harnessed and placed alongside the arms and legs, one at each limb.

'Monsieur Le Breton, the clerk of the court, went up to the patient several times and asked him if he had anything to say. He said he had not; at each torment, he cried out, as the damned in hell are supposed to cry out, "Pardon, my God! Pardon, Lord." Despite all this pain, he raised his head from time to time and looked at himself boldly. The cords had been tied so tightly by the men who pulled the ends that they caused him indescribable pain. Monsieur Le Breton went up to him again and asked him if he had anything to say; he said no. Several confessors went up to him and spoke to him at length; he willingly kissed the crucifix that was held out to him; he opened his lips and repeated: "Pardon, Lord."

'The horses tugged hard, each pulling straight on a limb, each horse held by an executioner. After a quarter of an hour, the same ceremony was repeated and finally, after several attempts, the direction of the horses had to be changed, thus: those at the arms were made to pull towards the head, those at the thighs towards the arms, which broke the arms at the joints. This was repeated several times without success. He raised his head and looked at himself. Two more horses had to be added to those harnessed to the thighs, which made six horses in all. Without success.

'Finally, the executioner, Samson, said to Monsieur Le Breton that there was no way or hope of succeeding, and told him to ask their Lordships if they wished him to have the prisoner cut into pieces. Monsieur Le Breton, who had come down from the town, ordered that renewed efforts be made, and this was done; but the horses gave up and one of those harnessed to the thighs fell to the ground. The confessors returned and spoke to him again. He said to them (I heard him): "Kiss me, gentlemen." The parish priest of St Paul's did not dare to, so Monsieur de Marsilly slipped under the rope holding the left arm and kissed him on the forehead. The executioners gathered round and Damiens told them not to swear, to carry out their task and that he did not think ill of them; he begged them to pray to God for him, and asked the parish priest of St Paul's to pray for him at the first mass.

'After two or three attempts, the executioner Samson and he who had used the pincers each drew out a knife from his pocket and cut the body at the thighs instead of severing the legs at the joints; the four horses gave a tug and carried off the two thighs after them, namely, that of the right side first, the other following; then the same was done to the arms, the shoulders, the arm-pits and the four limbs; the flesh had to be cut almost to the bone, the horses pulling hard carried off the right arm first and the other afterwards.

'When the four limbs had been pulled away, the confessors came to speak to him; but his executioner told them that he was dead, though the truth was that I saw the man move, his lower jaw moving from side to side as if he were talking. One of the executioners even said shortly afterwards that when they had lifted the trunk to throw it on the stake, he was still alive. The four limbs were untied from the ropes and thrown on the stake set up in the enclosure in line with the scaffold, then the trunk and the rest were covered with logs and faggots, and fire was put to the straw mixed with this wood.

'. . . In accordance with the decree, the whole was reduced to ashes. The last piece to be found in the embers was still burning at half-past ten in the evening. The pieces of flesh and the trunk had taken about four hours to burn. The officers of whom I was one, as also was my son, and a detachment of archers remained in the square until nearly eleven o'clock.'

From: M. Foucault, *Discipline and Punish*, Harmondsworth, Penguin, 1979.

Document 2
A PROFESSIONAL POLICE FORCE AND THE END OF TRANSPORTATION

In 1861 it was reported that in the counties and most of the larger boroughs the police were considered to be efficient in numbers and discipline and equal to the duties required. 'Some of the smaller Boroughs, however, give cause of complaint, where the authorities, by neglecting to amalgamate for Police purposes with the surrounding county, appear to be opposed no less to the public benefit than to their own advantage and security.' Not only did this problem in itself prove an obdurate one, but, as a Royal Commission of our own day has put it, 'although Government intervention was constantly increasing, the leading characteristic of police conditions of service was diversity . . . it is difficult to talk in the same terms about the bewildering patchwork of local units that existed before 1919 and the standardised service to which the country has since become accustomed.' The Statute of 1856 fell far short of providing a basis for the coherent and unified system of police for the whole country of which reformers had dreamed.

Yet in its time it marked a decisive advance. At least the local authorities were required to provide professional forces. At least the central government, through inspection and the grant, could accumulate closer knowledge and experience of the nation's police, could bring some pressure to bear upon those who lagged furthest behind. For the first time it became possible to collect and publish on a national scale statistics of the offences known to the police. A break had been made in the long tradition that the provincial police was a wholly local concern. The passing of the Act implied acceptance of Grey's contention that the local police 'could not be considered as an isolated question, but that it affected the whole community and not alone the county or borough in which crime was allowed to be undetected or unrepressed'. The expenses of maintaining prisons and prosecuting prisoners had already been thrown upon the community at large: the public had thus to pay for any failure in the repression of crime in a particular locality. It was logical that national as well as local interests should be recognised.

Awareness of the police as a national responsibility was sharpened by the ending of transportation, which was abolished for the great majority of criminals in 1853. The cost of gaols and police to deal with transported offenders in Australia had been a heavy charge on the national exchequer for over half a century. Now such offenders would have to be controlled at home. This was one of the reasons advanced by Grey for the Treasury grant towards the cost of provincial police.

The ending of transportation, however, influenced more than the financial aspect of the Bill. It played a major part in securing the acceptance of a measure of compulsion which would have been rejected out of hand in the 1830s or the 1840s. Much might be ascribed to the success of those police forces that had already established themselves. Much might also be due to the liberal attitude maintained by recent governments, even in fact of grave threats to public order. Much, too, must be attributed to the growing familiarity of legislative intervention in the common affairs of life. Important, in their time, had been the fears aroused by the belief that crime was increasing fast and, even more so, to the alarm occasioned by ill-controlled outbreaks of rioting and disorder. Yet none of these had brought public opinion and Parliament to the point of conceding any general compulsion upon local authorities to provide efficient police.

When acceptance came at last, it came during a period of growing prosperity, when disorder was becoming rarer, when Chartism had ceased to be a menace, when even the levels of crime were believed to be falling. The peaks of commitments reached in 1842 and 1848 seemed things of the past. From 1849 to 1853 the figure hovered around twenty-seven thousand and after a rise in 1854 dropped to below twenty-six thousand in 1856. The reduction was partly due to extensions in summary jurisdiction, especially in 1855, but the editor of the Judicial Statistics was satisfied that this was not the only explanation. In particular he noted that the end of the Crimean War had brought no increase in crimes of violence comparable with that following the Napoleonic Wars.

It was the new factor, the ending of transportation, that introduced into this apparently satisfactory situation a sense of deep insecurity, all the more potent because it was a fear of the unknown. Chadwick had foreshadowed disastrous consequences when he gave evidence earlier to the Select Committee: 'We have now constantly under confinement, in the prisons of Great Britain, a force of able-bodied men, equal to an army of about 30,000, numerically greater than the British force which fought at the battle of Waterloo.' Many of them were depredators who would eventually be transported. But resistance to transportation, already building up, would eventually succeed. Then 'these numbers of convicts, heretofore regularly shifted from this country, will be discharged with the almost certainty that the greater proportion of them must renew their careers, which they will have extensively open to them for renewal unless preventive measures of a general and complete nature be adopted.' Superior officers of the police and other competent persons, he added, viewed the prospect of an unguarded change of practice with very serious alarm.

Some of the offenders transported in earlier times had been mere boys or others guilty only of comparatively minor crimes. But over the past thirty years the use of the death penalty for the more serious offences had been more and more restricted, both by legislation and by administrative discretion. Transportation had provided a reassuring alternative. So long as it had been available, dangerous or persistent criminals could still be eliminated. It had removed that section of the criminal classes which caused the greatest public anxiety. In future such offenders would remain in this country on their release. Certainly those discharged after serving part only of their sentences of penal servitude were to be subject to supervision under the 'ticket of leave' system, but the value of this must itself depend on the adequacy and efficiency of the police. If the country must, for the future, learn to live with its criminals, it must pay the price of protection against them.

From: Leon Radzinowicz, *A History of the English Criminal Law*, vol. 4, London, Stevens, 1968.

Document 3
TYPES OF PRISON SENTENCE

Penal servitude

The convict prisons were for prisoners sentenced to penal servitude. In 1877 these prisons were the 'depots' at Millbank and Pentonville in London and the 'public works' prisons at Portland, Dartmoor, Portsmouth and Chatham; convict labour was later used to build new prisons of this kind at Woking, Wormwood Scrubs and Borstal. The sentence of penal servitude, introduced in legislation of 1853, originated in the demise of transportation and in broad terms substituted, for the more serious offenders, a term in an English convict prison and then release on licence ('ticket-of-leave') in this country for performance of the sentence in an overseas penal colony (although for some years a small number of convicts continued to be sent to Bermuda, Gibraltar and Western Australia).

The important feature of the sentence was that it was staged. The first nine months were spent in separate confinement in either a convict prison or one of the local prisons which catered for this class of convict and the prisoner was subject to first class hard labour for the first month. In the words of Du Cane: 'The first stage is one of severe penal discipline, during which the prisoner's mind is thrown in upon itself . . . he becomes open to words of admonition and warning . . . he is put in that condition when he is likely to feel sorrow for the past and to welcome the words of those who show him how to avoid evil for the future.' In the second stage, the convict was put to associated but still 'silent' labour in a public works prison. This involved, typically, work such as farming, quarrying and land reclamation and such projects as the building of harbours at Filey and Dover. In this stage the prisoner progressed through four classes by means of a system of marks earned for exemplary industry and lost by bad conduct. John Lee, in his autobiography, recalls how the notoriously misconvicted Adolph Beck lost some privileges for a breach of the rules which forbade prisoners to talk to warders – Beck was trying to do a favour for another prisoner who was about to be released. Privileges with regard to such things as visits, letters and exercise were used as an inducement to good behaviour and promotion to a higher class and eventually perhaps remission. Finally, the prison authorities could determine the appropriate point at which to release the prisoner on licence for the rest of his term. The licence was primarily subject to a condition of good behaviour and was under a degree of police supervision (an account is presented by Joseph Conrad, in relation to his character Michaelis, the 'ticket-of-leave Apostle' in *The Secret Agent*). Any misconduct, not only the commission of a further offence, could lead to revocation of the licence. The length of the sentence of penal servitude was related to the former sentence of transportation – sentences would be for three (until 1864), five, seven, ten or fourteen years.

As already mentioned, Du Cane had claimed that the prison regime at that time was effective in reducing the level of crime and in particular he drew attention to the reduction in the number of sentences of penal servitude between 1859 and 1884 and implied that there was a related decrease in the level of serious crime. The Gladstone Committee, however, were critical of the initial stage of separate confinement and argued that virtually the whole period of confinement should be served in association in a convict prison. When this change was implemented after 1898 the real distinction was not so much between penal servitude and other imprisonment as between a term in a convict prison and confinement in one of the local prisons. Those in the convict prisons were the more serious, longer-term prisoners, moving through the progressive stages system towards release on licence. But even the rationale of the progressive stages system, that privileges and remission should be *earned* in accordance with a mathematical score, eventually came under attack.

In the course of time many of the differences between penal servitude and imprisonment were whittled away so that when the sentence was formally abolished in the Criminal Justice Act of 1948 the main surviving distinction was the release on licence for those serving the former sentence. Sir Lionel Fox commented that the legal abolition of the sentence was a recognition of a largely *de facto* situation (and the number of those sentenced to penal servitude had become very small – just over 1,300 in 1921, for example, with the result that Portland could be closed as a convict prison); but he added that it would have the beneficial result of removing the tradition among the convict class that they were 'the Horse Artillery of the convict world'.

Imprisonment, with or without hard labour

This was the term used for prison sentences other than penal servitude. The majority of offenders sentenced to imprisonment were given shorter terms, to be served in local prisons, with or without hard labour (usually the former: in 1893, for example, there were over 109,000 sentences with hard labour as compared to 41,000 without). However, the term 'hard labour' was misleading. As Du Cane pointed out:

> . . . any prisoner sentenced to imprisonment should be, and is by law, required to labour, under specified conditions, suitable to his health and his capacity; and, in fact, excepting the specific kind of labour called 'First Class Hard Labour', defined in the 'Prison Act 1865', as 'crank, tread-wheel, etc. and other like kind of labour', the term 'hard' has no particular meaning, and its employment in the sentence makes no practical difference.

Therefore, by the 1880s, it was only the first class hard labour which was distinctively hard and the Gladstone Committee a few years later inveighed against the kind of useless labour involved in that regime, with the result that under the 1899 Prison Rules first class hard labour was abolished and all prisoners were to be employed on 'useful industrial labour' from the start of their sentence. Even so, the sentence with 'hard labour' still involved an initial period of 28 days separate confinement with hard bodily or manual labour, the prisoner then proceeding to associated labour of 'a less hard description'. It was difficult, however, to work out different degrees of hard labour and in practice the work done under separate confinement contrary to the original intention, tended to be less rigorous. The period of separate confinement was abolished during the First World War — in the public interest, it was necessary for the so-called hard labour prisoners to work as hard (and usefully) as the others — and thereafter there was a more or less single regime of prison labour in the local prisons. The surviving feature of the distinct regime of hard labour was the requirement that during the first fortnight of the sentence the prisoner should sleep on a plank, and this rule was not removed until 1945.

As far as imprisonment without hard labour was concerned, there was an attempt to introduce a structure into this sentence in the 1898 Prison Act, according to which the sentencing court could specify that the imprisonment be in the first, second or third division. Placement in these divisions affected the privileges and general creature comforts allowed to prisoners, the first division being reserved for 'political' and a few other prisoners not regarded as belonging to the typical criminal type and so deserving less harsh treatment. One of the most famous prisoners to sample an earlier version of the first division was the Editor of the *Pall Mall Gazette*, W.T. Stead, haplessly convicted of an offence involving the selling of children into prostitution and for whose introduction he himself had vigorously campaigned. He was guilty only in a technical sense and this fact was acknowledged in his prison sentence. In his cell on E Wing of Holloway Prison he had papers, books and flowers, could continue to work as a journalist and received a stream of visitors: 'Never had I a pleasanter holiday, a more charming season of repose' he commented. But it was clear within a few years of the courts being given this power of classification that they were making little use of it, principally because most sentences were to be served with hard labour. From 1900 the prison authorities used certain classification for their own purposes, notably the use of the 'star' class for first offenders (a classification already used in the convict prisons) so as to separate the first and other offenders. Later on, prisoners between the age of 16 and 21 were placed in a distinct Juvenile Adult Class.

The Criminal Justice Act of 1948 abolished the sentences of penal servitude and hard labour and also the divisions of imprisonment without hard labour. Apart from the special regimes for preventive detainees and those sentenced to corrective training, discussed below, there has since that date been a single sentence of imprisonment for adult offenders, whatever the nature of the offence or antecedents of the offender.

The single sentence of imprisonment

Since 1948 these different types of sentence have been merged into a single sentence of imprisonment and the sentencer's function has been limited to deciding upon the use of imprisonment in the first place and determining the basic length of the sentence. It has been the role of the prison authorities to decide upon the placement and classification of prisoners. Leaving aside for the present penal institutions for offenders under the age of 21, four types of prisons have come into use since 1948: the local prison, as before, concerned with remand, allocation of convicted prisoners and those sentenced to shorter terms; 'training' prisons for longer term prisoners (a term brought into official use in 1969 to replace the terms 'central' and 'regional training' prisons used after 1948) — the successor to the convict prison, some of these being open prisons; a small number of prisons for female offenders; and, since 1967, a number of 'dispersal' prisons, which are training prisons with conditions of maximum security. Allocation to a particular prison depends on a number of factors but in particular, since the late 1960s, on a security rating: categories A, B, C and D, ranging between the two extremes of a maximum security dispersal prison (category A) and an open prison (category D).

At the level of sentencing, therefore, the important development over the last 100 years has been one of simplification, resulting in a single generic prison sentence. However, that statement leaves out of account the development of a number of sentences and institutions for younger offenders, best discussed separately, and tends to mask a complexity of classification once a person has been given a prison sentence. It is perhaps also fair to say that, despite the different types of sentence in existence during the last part of the nineteenth century, there was probably a greater uniformity of regime and prison experience than in more recent years, given the variable conditions of overcrowding and available facilities in present day prisons.

From: C. Harding, B. Hines, R. Ireland and P. Rawlings, *Imprisonment in England and Wales: A Concise History*, Beckenham, Croom Helm, 1985.

Document 4
THE AIMS OF IMPRISONMENT

4.21 Most of the evidence we received on objectives was unsystematic and rarely precise. None of the staff associations, including the governors, attempted to redefine penal objectives. The BAPG said that there was confusion both within and outside the prison service and suggested that priorities should be clarified, but did not offer proposals of its own, affirming that Rule 1 'was in general terms good enough and should be proclaimed as an objective, regardless of its feasibility. Some other witnesses said Rule 1 was imprecise but were unable or unprepared to say what exactly should be done. Others went further and contended that the sentiments implicit in Rule 1 had been shown to be unreal. One of the clearer statements of this character was:

'If we are right in our regretful view that the reformative effect on prisoners in minimal, and the experience of most of the staff of prisons we visited appears to confirm this conclusion, then it must be accepted that at present the main practical value of prisons is to punish serious or repeated crimes, and where necessary to protect society from dangerous criminals.'

4.22 It is possible that some witnesses hesitated to specify strictly penal objectives because they were much more concerned with getting criminal justice objectives and priorities right first. Our limited terms of reference may well have inhibited their preference for taking a wider view of the place of imprisonment both in the criminal justice system and in the context of delinquency as a whole.

4.23 One of the most thoughtful pieces of evidence we received on this as on a number of other subjects was from Dr King and Mr Rodney Morgan. They argued that, since the 'treatment' model has been shown as invalid, the only proper replacement is a system devoted to secure and humane containment based on three principles, minimum use of custody, minimum use of security, and the 'normalisation' of the prison. As they put it:

'We take the view that precisely because humane containment may fail to fire the imagination so it may prevent the excesses of the past. The function of prison *is* a limited one and its use and administration should no longer be guided by claims which it cannot fulfil.'

4.24 In general, we think that his kind of statement is representative of many informed observers' views at present. Whilst we feel it has much force, particularly in its impatience with wishful thinking, there is a great danger that it may throw out the good with the unattainable and we are sceptical about the extent to which it may justify, as is claimed, sweeping changes in the allocation of resources in penal establishments. Further, as one group of witnesses pointed out to us, 'humane containment' suffers from the fatal defect that it is a means without an end. Our opinion is that it can only result in making prisons into human warehouses – for inmates and staff. It is not, therefore, a fit rule for hopeful life or responsible management.

The future

4.25 We take it as axiomatic that imprisonment is bound to remain as the final sanction for imposing social discipline in our community under agreed rules of law. For the reasons which will appear hereafter, we are forced to the conclusion that it should be used as little as possible.

4.26 If Rule 1 is to continue to set out the objectives of the prison service, then we think it should be re-written and we suggest the following for contemporary purposes:

'The purpose of the detention of convicted prisoners shall be to keep them in custody which is both secure and yet positive, and to that end the behaviour of all the responsible authorities and staff towards them shall be such as to:
(a)   create an environment which can assist them to respond and contribute to society as positively as possible;
(b)   preserve and promote their self respect;
(c)   minimise, to the degree of security necessary in each particular case, the harmful effects of their removal from normal life;
(d)   prepare them for and assist them on discharge.'

Suitable amendments should be made simultaneously to the Borstal and Detention Centre Rules. Although strictly Rule 1 does not apply to remand prisoners, we think the spirit of the suggested new Rule 1 should. If separate Rules are made for remand prisoners, then such Rules too should appropriately reflect the suggested new Rule 1.

4.27 We think that the rhetoric of 'treatment and training' has had its day and should be replaced. On the other hand, we intend that the rhetoric alone should be changed and not all the admirable and constructive things that are done in its name.

4.28 Secondly, we hope that by suggesting this alteration to Rule 1 we make it clear that in our view mere 'secure and humane containment' is not enough. Prison staff cannot be asked to operate in a moral vacuum and the absence of real objectives can in the end lead only to the routine brutalisation of all the participants. There may be ample room for argument about the extent to which imprisonment should be used, but there can be no neutrality about it once it is imposed. We think that there both can and should be purposive objectives in imprisonment, but we do not feel that realistically they can be set any higher than we have just suggested.

From: Committee of Inquiry into the United Kingdom Prison Services (The May Inquiry) Cmnd 7673, London, Home Office, 1979,

Document 5
THE CENTRAL PROBLEMS OF THE PRISON SERVICE

1.142   The riots which the Inquiry investigated were not isolated incidents. Other lesser, but still serious disturbances occurred in April 1990. They stem from a long history of violent disturbances in the prison system. On the evidence, prison riots cannot be dismissed as one-off events, or as local disasters, or a run of bad luck. They are symptomatic of a series of serious underlying difficulties in the prison system. They will only be brought to an end if these difficulties are addressed.

1.143   There was a considerable degree of consensus among those who provided evidence as to the causes of these successive disturbances. Differences tended to be ones of degree. The emphasis frequently depended on the perspective of the person providing the evidence. If it was a prisoner or a pressure group, the focus would usually be on: (i) the insanitary and overcrowded physical conditions to which prisoners were subjected; (ii) the negative and unconstructive nature of the regime; (iii) the lack of respect with which the prisoners were treated; (iv) the destructive effects of prison on the prisoner's family ties and the inadequacy of visits; and (v) the lack of any form of independent redress for grievances.

1.144   If the evidence was from uniformed staff, it would recognise a need to improve the conditions for prisoners, but would stress additional causes which staff felt were frustrating them in performing their duties. The evidence would draw attention to the lack of staff, lack of training, a sense of being undervalued, isolation from other staff and the divide between different grades and classes of staff. It would refer also to a lack of leadership within the Service.

1.145   Evidence from governors would agree that all the causes so far identified required attention. It would also draw attention to a lack of support and assistance from Headquarters. Governors lacked confidence in Headquarters. They felt powerless to implement the changes which they know were needed within their establishment.

1.146   Some witnesses drew attention to a further problem. They identified a lack of co-ordination between the different parts of the Criminal Justice System. As the system operated at present, there was no link or established means of communication between the Judges who were responsible for sending prisoners to prison, and the Prison Service which was responsible for holding them there. Some of those giving evidence suggested that the result of this breach in the chain of communication was chronic overcrowding. Unless a link were established, overcrowding would continue. Overcrowding led to an inherently instable prison system and resulted in disruption and riot.

1.147   I accept that these lists identify the majority, but not all, of the possible underlying causes of the riots. Each of these causes contributed to the present problems of the Prison Service. In the Report, there are recommendations or proposals which directly relate to them. They are dealt with under the respective headings of the Sections in Part II of this Report.

1.148   It is possible, however, to identify one principal thread which links these causes and complaints and which draws together all our proposals and recommendations. It is that the Prison Service must set security, control and justice in prisons at the right level and it must provide the right balance between them. The stability of the prison system depends on the Prison Service doing so.

1.149   Security here refers to the need to prevent prisoners escaping. Control refers to the obligation, ultimately, to prevent prisoners causing a disturbance. Justice encapsulates the obligation on the Prison Service to treat prisoners with humanity and fairness and to act in concert with its responsibilities as part of the Criminal Justice System.

1.150   The April riots occurred because these three elements were out of balance. There were failures in the maintenance of control. There were failures to achieve the necessary standards of justice. There could easily have been a collapse in security.

1.151   These factors are each dependent on the other. If there is an absence of justice, prisoners will be aggrieved. Control and security will be threatened. This is part of what happened in April. The scale of each of the riots indicates that in each establishment there was a substantial number of prisoners who were prepared to turn what otherwise could have been a limited disturbance into a full scale riot. This was, at least in part, because of the conditions in which they were held and the way in which they were treated. If a proper level of justice is provided in prisons, then it is less likely that prisoners will behave in this way. Justice, therefore, contributes to the maintenance of security and control.

1.152   Lapses in control affect both security and justice. Prisoners did not escape during the April disturbances. But they might easily have done so. They were very close to achieving this at Long Lartin prison on 2 April 1990. The April disturbances also clearly demonstrated that, with a breakdown in control, prisoners suffer as well as the Prison Service. No-one can claim that the prisoners attacked in Strangeways, and intimidated in Cardiff, Pucklechurch and Dartmoor were at that time being treated in prison with justice. The breakdown in control led in many senses to a breakdown in justice in prisons.

1.153   Security, control and justice will not be set at the right level, and will not be held in balance, unless there are changes in the way the Prison Service structures its relations, both between management and staff, and between staff and prisoners. There is a fundamental lack of respect and a failure to give and require responsibility at all levels in the prison system. These shortcomings must be tackled if the Prison Service is to maintain a stable system.

1.154 The evidence from Part I of the Inquiry makes this clear. Industrial relations at Dartmoor were notoriously poor. The handling of the disturbance was hampered as a result. The sense of hostility by inmates at Pucklechurch was very marked. There were failures in communication among management and with headquarters which affected the handling of and which probably prolonged the Strangeways siege.

1.155 A central objective in our proposals and recommendations, therefore, is to ensure that relations within the prison system are based upon respect and responsibility. To do this we have addressed the structures and procedures which operate in the Prison Service. We have considered the nature and standard of provision for prisoners and for those who work in the Prison Service. If, through the operation of these structures, management show that they respect their staff and are ready to give them greater responsibility for their own work, then staff are the more likely to treat prisoners in the same way. At the same time, prisoners will not respect staff if they know that staff have no respect for or confidence in their managers. Headquarters must give a lead, but it has a right also to expect that leadership to be followed.

1.156 These then should be the fundamental objectives of the Prison Service. If they are to be achieved, the Prison Service will need to be an integral part of a Criminal Justice System which co-operates to meet the objectives of all parts of that system. The recommendations and proposals in this Report are directed to these ends.

From: Lord Justice Woolf, *Prison Disturbances April 1990: Report*, London, HMSO, 1991.

Document 6
HOW SHOULD PRISON RIOTS BE PREVENTED?

1.157   The Prison Service is well aware of a need to improve the present situation in its prisons. Over recent years, the Prison Service has instituted a series of fundamental changes within the Service of the greatest importance.

1.158   First, there has been a vast rebuilding and refurbishment programme which was long overdue. In 1990/91, roughly £300m is to be spent on new prisons and almost £150m is to be spent on refurbishment. That programme necessarily takes time. It will transform the physical conditions within the prisons. This will both increase stability within prisons and improve relations between prisoners and staff and staff and management.

1.159   The Inquiry has had two aims in relation to the building and refurbishment programme. The first is to stress the importance of ensuring that the progress is as fast as is practicable. The second is to ensure that, where it is not already too late, the programme takes fully into account the lessons which are to be learnt from the recent disturbances and the principles which should apply for the future. The most important of these principles are that prisoners should be accommodated in small units and in community prisons.

1.160   Secondly, the Prison Service has introduced, since 1987, two different and radical managerial reforms. The first was a package designed to reform the organisation of staff and management within prison establishments. It was sorely needed. There were undoubtedly deeply embedded work practices within the Prison Service which were grossly inefficient and which needed to be addressed. There were structural difficulties which needed attention. There were organisational problems which required change. 'Fresh Start' was an attempt to achieve the necessary changes.

1.161   Under 'Fresh Start', the excessive periods of overtime which prison officers were working, and were having to work in order to earn a reasonable wage, were to be phased out. The uniformed grades of staff and the governor grades were to be unified. The tasks within each prison establishment were to be grouped and were to be performed by teams of management and staff. These were all important changes for the better.

1.162   The manner in which the changes have been implemented, however, has meant that 'Fresh Start' has not succeeded in improving relations in many prisons. Staff feel that they were misled as to what was involved in the 'Fresh Start' package. They do not believe that the Prison Service has delivered what it promised. The objectives of the 'Fresh Start' package have been imperilled by a widely held belief that it has resulted in still more inadequate staffing levels.

1.163 Whether this last belief is justified or not can only be ascertained if some way is found of objectively ascertaining what is the proper staffing level within each prison establishment. The Prison Service is at present carrying out a process to enable this to be done. The merits of that process were in dispute before the Inquiry. The Prison Officers' Association at the present time are not prepared to be associated with the process. This is a reflection of the unhappy state of industrial relations between the Prison Officers' Association and the Prison Service. While the present approach for determining staffing levels may not be perfect, no better method of achieving the objective has been suggested to the Inquiry. If undertaken properly, the present exercise cannot but improve the position. It is for this reason that the Report urges the Prison Officers' Association to rethink their attitude to it.

1.164 The second managerial reform was implemented in September 1990. It involved the reorganisation of management above establishment level. There are aspects of this reorganisation which have been strongly criticised by governors and other staff. However, the reorganisation has been implemented. The Inquiry took the view that, this having been done, it should have an opportunity of proving its worth before its merits were assessed. The Inquiry has assumed, therefore, that, for the time being at any rate, this structure of management above establishment level will remain.

1.165 The changes which the Prison Service has already attempted and is attempting to bring about are important. However, they are primarily directed to the physical conditions within the prison system, and to the management of that system. There needs now to be greater attention paid to the way in which prisoners and staff are treated. The way prisoners are treated can often be a reflection of the way staff themselves feel they are treated by management. An important lesson of the riots is that they would either not have taken place, or, if they had, they would have been on a different scale, if a substantial body of inmates had not been prepared to support those who instigated the initial disturbance which developed into a riot at each establishment. What is now required is a planned programme of change which will address the substantial problems which remain.

1.166 The planned programme should address the lack of stability and the unsatisfactory state of relations within the prison system. The programme has to take into account the need for a balance between security, control and justice. In Part II of this Report, together with His Honour Judge Tumim, I identify such a programme:

1.167 Our programme is based on 12 central recommendations. These are that there should be:

i)   closer co-operation between the different parts of the Criminal Justice System. For this purpose a national forum and local committees should be established;

ii)   more visible leadership of the Prison Service by a Director General who is and is seen to be the operational head and in day to day charge of the Service. To achieve this there should be a published 'compact' or 'contract' given by Ministers to the Director General of the Prison Service, who should be responsible for the performance of that 'contract' and publicly answerable for the day to day operations of the Prison Service;

iii)   increased delegation of responsibility to Governors of establishments;

iv)   an enhanced role for prison officers;

v)   a 'compact' or 'contract' for each prisoner setting out the prisoner's expectations and responsibilities in the prison in which he or she is held;

vi)   a national system of Accredited Standards, with which, in time, each prison establishment would be required to comply;

vii)   a new Prison Rule that no establishment should hold more prisoners than is provided for in its certified normal level of accommodation, with provisions for Parliament to be informed if exceptionally there is to be a material departure from that rule;

viii)   a public commitment from Ministers setting a timetable to provide access to sanitation for all inmates at the earliest practicable date not later than February 1996;

ix)   better prospects for prisoners to maintain their links with families and the community through more visits and home leaves and through being located in community prisons as near to their homes as possible;

x)   a division of prison establishments into small and more manageable and secure units;

xi)   a separate statement of purpose, separate conditions and generally a lower security categorisation for remand prisoners;

xii)   improved standards of justice within prisons involving the giving of reasons to a prisoner for any decision which materially and adversely affects him; a grievance procedure and disciplinary proceedings which ensure that the Governor deals with most matters under his present powers; relieving Boards of Visitors of their adjudicatory role; and providing for final access to an independent Complaints Adjudicator.

1.168   In the following paragraphs and in the remainder of the Report we describe these recommendations more fully. They are central to resolving the problems which have been identified from the April disturbances. They are also a package. They need to be considered together and moved forward together if the necessary balance in our prison system is to be achieved.

From: Lord Justice Woolf, *Prison Disturbances April 1990: Report*, London, HMSO, 1991.

Document 7
JUSTICE WITHIN PRISONS

9.24 A recurring theme in the evidence from prisoners who may have instigated, and who were involved in, the riots was that their actions were a response to the manner in which they were treated by the prison system. Although they did not always use these terms, they felt a lack of justice. If what they say is true, the failure of the Prison Service to fulfil its responsibilities to act with justice created in April 1990 serious difficulties in maintaining security and control in prisons.

9.25 It is not possible for the Inquiry to form any judgment on whether the specific grievances of these prisoners were or were not well-founded. What is clear is that the Prison Service had failed to *persuade* these prisoners that it was treating them fairly.

9.26 It is significant that prisoners recently transferred from other establishments were centrally involved in all the incidents which precipitated trouble in the target prisons. One of the leading participants at Strangeways had, in the course of a mere 21 months in prison, been moved from establishment to establishment at least six times, usually for reasons of maintaining control in the prisons from which he was moved.

9.27 Another prisoner, serving a much longer sentence, after an initial period of turbulence in which he was moved from prison to prison, had settled reasonably well for four years at a dispersal prison. But he resumed his unsettled behaviour at the Category B prison to which he was moved on recategorisation. At the time of the riot, he had only recently been transferred to Strangeways.

9.28 The inmate whose actions precipitated trouble at Glen Parva had very recently been moved in. He was then further from home and was said to be homesick for visits from his family.

9.29 At Dartmoor, one of the leading participants in the troubles had been in at least nine different prisons in the course of a three year sentence. He had only recently been transferred into Dartmoor. He was held there under the part of Rule 43 which is used to segregate prisoners in the interests of good order or discipline (GOAD).

9.30 The riot at Cardiff appears to have been precipitated by the actions of an inmate only recently moved into the prison from Bristol for control reasons. The Bristol disturbance again seems to have been set off by men recently moved in, this time from Dartmoor. At Pucklechurch, one of the inmates whose actions seem to have precipitated the riot had only recently been transferred there for the purpose of receiving accumulated visits.

9.31   All this evidence cannot prove that the movement of prisoners is in itself conducive to riot. Many prisoners are moved, be it for reasons of control or otherwise, without a riot resulting. But the evidence is suggestive. In all the cases studied, the precipitating incidents which set off riot involved those who had been recently transferred.

9.32   The Inquiry also received theoretic evidence from several sources which suggested that frequent moves for prisoners could be a source of instability and lead to disturbance. At the first of the public seminar hearings, Dr Grubin of the Institute of Psychiatry said:

'prisons are places where people live; they are the inmates' homes'.

He reminded the seminar that moving home is inevitably a stressful experience. He argued that, wherever possible, prisoners should be controlled by the use of different small units within individual 'community' prisons.

9.33   Professor Bottoms, in some interesting theoretic papers based on research at Long Lartin and Albany prisons, stressed to the Inquiry the importance of a stable and predictable environment for prisoners. He regarded this as a form of 'social crime prevention' within prisons. Social structures depended on repeated routines of behaviour. Frequent moves for prisoners must make it more difficult to achieve such stable and predictable routines ('Situational and Social Approaches to the Prevention of Disorder in Long-Term Prisons'; Bottoms, Hay and Sparks).

9.34   The evidence before the Inquiry, therefore, suggests that a transfer against the wishes of a prisoner is one of the most resented actions which the Prison Service can take. It is made worse when the prisoner feels that he has been given no satisfactory explanation for that transfer, and when the transfer results in his being further away from his home. Such transfers can appear to the inmate to be unjust, and, in the way they are effected, may leave deep scars of resentment. In view of this evidence, in Part II (Section 12) of the Report, the issues raised by the Prison Service's use of transfers as a control mechanism for disruptive prisoners is considered in greater detail. Proposals are made which are intended to reduce the possible adverse effects of transfers.

9.35   It can also be said, on the basis of the evidence from all six disturbances, that the incidents which at the start involved only a few inmates, spread because they found ready support from many more inmates. Without that support, the disturbances would not have spread and would have been more readily resolved. Broad support for the instigators contributed to the seriousness of the incidents. At Strangeways, Pucklechurch, and possibly Bristol, although not all the inmates supported the disturbances, such support appears to have been widespread. The disturbances spread to almost all parts of each prison.

9.36   A contributory factor to the spread of the disturbances at Strangeways and Bristol was the way in which the disturbances were handled, in particular the decision by staff to vacate certain areas of the prisons. It was at those two establishments, together with Pucklechurch, that the hostility was the greatest and the damage was the most intense. At Glen Parva and Cardiff, where the disturbances were most effectively contained, the inmates were the least discontent, and the damage was the least extensive.

9.37 The evidence of prisoners is that they will not join in disturbances in any numbers if they feel conditions are reasonable and relationships are satisfactory. These are matters of justice which the Prison Service must address more closely. They are fundamental to maintaining a stable prison system which is able to withstand and reject the depredations of disruptive and violent individuals. These are matters which must be resolved if we are to have peace in our prisons.

From: Lord Justice Woolf, *Prison Disturbances April 1990: Report*, London, HMSO, 1991.

Document 8
TWO PRINCIPLES OF POLICING

4.55   Before I deal with these criticisms, it will, I think, be helpful to refer to two well-known principles of policing a free society which are relevant to my Inquiry:

(1)   'Consent and balance', words which I take, with respect and gratitude, from the written evidence of the Chief Constable of Avon and Somerset;
and
(2)   'Independence and accountability'.

(1) Consent and balance

4.56   The function of our police has been authoritatively defined as:

The prevention of crime . . . the protection of life and property, the preservation of public tranquillity.[1]

This three-fold function requires 'consent and balance', words which I take to mean that, if the police are to secure the assent of the community which they need to support their operations, they must strike an acceptable balance between the three elements of their function.
4.57   What is the balance which they would seek to achieve? An authoritative answer has again been given: the primary duty of the police is to maintain 'the Queen's peace', which has been described as the 'normal state of society',[2] for in a civilized society, normality is a state of public tranquillity. Crime and public disorder are aberrations from 'normality' which it is the duty of the police to endeavour first to prevent and then, if need be, to correct. It follows that the police officer's first duty is to cooperate with others in maintaining 'the normal state of society'. Since it is inevitable that there will be aberrations from normality, his second duty arises, which is, without endangering normality, to enforce the law. His priorities are clear: the maintenance of public tranquillity comes first. If law enforcement puts at risk public tranquillity, he will have to make a difficult decision. Inevitably there will be situations in which the public interest requires him to test the wisdom of law enforcement by its likely effect upon public order. Law enforcement, involving as it must the possibility that

---

[1] Extract from Sir Richard Mayne's instructions to the 'New Police of the Metropolis' in 1829.
[2] *The Home Office*, Sir Frank Newsam, Allen and Unwin, 1955 (2nd edition).

force may have to be used, can cause acute friction and division in a community – particularly if the community is tense and the cause of the law-breaker not without support. 'Fiat justitia, ruat caelum'[3] may be apt for a Judge: but it can lead a policeman into tactics disruptive of the very fabric of society.

4.58   The conflict which can arise between the duty of the police to maintain order and their duty to enforce the law, and the priority which must be given to the former, have long been recognized by the police themselves, though they are factors to which commentators on policing have in the past often paid too little attention. The successful solution of the conflict lies first in the priority to be given in the last resort to the maintenance of public order, and secondly in the constant and common-sense exercise of police discretion. Indeed the exercise of discretion lies at the heart of the policing function. It is undeniable that there is only one law for all: and it is right that this should be so. But it is equally well recognized that successful policing depends on the exercise of discretion in how the law is enforced. The good reputation of the police as a force depends upon the skill and judgement which policemen display in the particular circumstances of the cases and incidents which they are required to handle. Discretion is the art of suiting action to particular circumstances. It is the policeman's daily task.

(2) Independence and accountability

4.59   The independence of the police is the other principle of policing a free society to which I wish to refer. Neither politicians nor pressure-groups nor anyone else may tell the police what decisions to take or what methods to employ, whether to enforce the law or not in a particular case, or how to investigate a particular offence. The exercise of police judgement has to be as independent as the exercise of professional judgement by a doctor or a lawyer. If it is not, the way is open to manipulation and abuse of the law, whether for political or for private ends.

4.60   There are, nevertheless, limitations on the power of the police. First and foremost, the law. The police officer must act within the law: abuse of power by a police officer, if it be allowed to occur with impunity, is a staging-post to the police state. But there is also the constitutional control of accountability (see Part V, paragraphs 5.55–71, infra). The police must exercise independent judgement: but they are also the servants of the community. They enforce the law on behalf of the community: indeed they cannot effectively enforce it without the support of the community. The community pays them and provides them with their resources. So there has to be some way in which to secure that the independent judgement of the police can not only operate within the law but with the support of the community. At present, outside London, that mechanism is provided by the local police authority. A Chief Constable is independent, but accountable to his local police authority. The Metropolitan Police are differently placed. The Commissioner is accountable not to a local police authority but to the Home Secretary and, through him, to Parliament. Both these arrangements have been subject to criticism in the course of the Inquiry. I examine those criticisms later (Part V, paragraphs 5.55–71, infra). Suffice it to say for the present that the second basic principle of policing a free society which is of

---

[3] 'Let justice be done, though the heavens collapse.'

essential relevance to my Report is the independence of the police, coupled with the need to ensure that the police operate not only within the law but with the support of the community as a whole. Accountability and effective consultative machinery are needed to ensure this support.

From: Lord Scarman, *The Brixton Disorders, 10–12 April 1981*, Harmondsworth, Penguin, 1982.

Document 9
CHANGES IN CRIME BETWEEN 1981 AND 1991

In comparing trends in recorded offences and the BCS comparable sub-set, there are three relevant measures:

* the number of offences recorded by the police,

* BCS offences, *whether or not* reported to the police, and

* BCS offences which *were* reported to the police.

Generally, there has been a flatter rise in BCS estimates of crime over the last ten years than in recorded offences. Figure 2.5 shows this with figures for 1981 indexed at 100. The number of *recorded* offences rose by 96% between 1981 and 1991; BCS offences, whether reported or not, rose by 49% – a difference which is well outside the range of sampling error. The number of *reported* offences rose by just over 100%, reflecting partly the underlying growth in crime and partly an increase in reporting. The result is that the dotted line in Figure 2.5, which covers reported offences, shows a similar trend to police statistics.

Between 1987 and 1991, the rise in BCS crime was 14% compared to 39% for police figures – again a statistically significant divergence.

Within sub-groups of offences the pattern is by no means consistent, however. Figure 2.6 shows the results for acquisitive crime, vandalism and violence. Where trends diverge, this may be explained by reporting changes, or changes in the extend and manner of recording by the police of offences reported to them. Estimates of the proportion of reported offences which are *recorded* should be treated cautiously, but possible changes in the proportion seem important for some offences.

Acquisitive crime

Around two-thirds of the comparable sub-set is made up of property thefts. These have nearly doubled since 1981, and have increased by a quarter since 1987. Police figures show the same increase over the last ten years, although a statistically significantly greater increase since 1987. Despite the parallel trends, the BCS shows that more property thefts are now being reported. This implies that fewer reported crimes are being recorded, or that they are being recorded under other types of crime (e.g. vandalism or other types of household theft).

There is some variation in the picture for individual offence categories within the acquisitive crime group. (Chapter 4 gives fuller details for burglary, Chapter 5 for thefts of and from cars and Appendix B for other individual offences.) In brief, thefts from motor vehicles have risen more in police figures than in the BCS since 1981, while bicycle thefts have risen less (mainly because of a steeper increase in BCS figures before 1987). Since 1987, recorded offences have risen more than BCS estimates for attempted burglary, thefts from vehicles and vandalism. (Divergences appear for other offences but are not statistically reliable.)

Vandalism

Overall, vandalism of private property has shown no significant change in the BCS since 1981, and has decreased since 1987 (Figure 2.6). Police figures indicate a doubling since 1981, and an increase of a third since 1987. Separate police-recorded estimates are not available for incidents against vehicles and against other household property, but the BCS indicates that *vehicle vandalism* (comprising 62% of vandalism offences) has been most stable. *Household vandalism*, however, increased slightly between 1981 and 1987, but has shown a more marked decline in the last four years.

For vandalism in general, reporting has increased significantly since 1981, though this masks an increase in reporting of vehicle vandalism and a decline for household vandalism. Given the low level of reporting of vandalism generally,

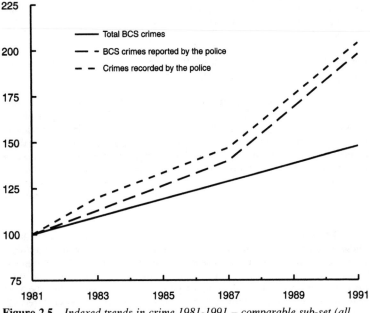

Figure 2.5   *Indexed trends in crime 1981-1991 – comparable sub-set (all 1981 numbers = 100)*

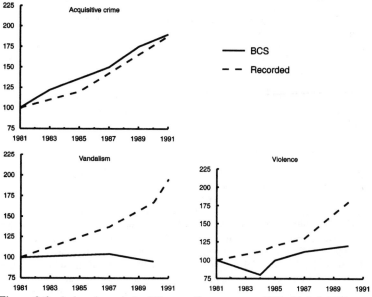

Figure 2.6 *Indexed trends in different offence groups, 1981–91 (all 1981 numbers = 100)*

any rise in reporting translates into a much larger increase in recorded crime. The increase in reporting of vehicle vandalism, then, seems to play some part in the higher rise in police figures, but does not account fully for the divergence in trends. It may be that the police are now recording a larger proportion of incidents reported to them, or are classifying incidents as vandalism that the BCS classifies elsewhere (e.g. as attempted vehicle theft).

Wounding and robbery

Wounding and robbery have together risen less than police statistics indicate, and this is statistically reliable. BCS figures have increased by a fifth since 1981, while recorded offences have almost doubled (Figure 2.6). The BCS suggests that reporting has increased somewhat, but again not enough to account fully for the divergence. This may suggest increased recording by the police. Another possibility is that the police are now giving higher priority to some types of violent crime, such as domestic crime and street robbery; and where there are two options for classification (for instance, between wounding and common assault, or between robbery and theft from the person), they may now choose the more serious.

Interpretation of the divergence between BCS and police figures is made more complex by the fact that the dividing line between 'wounding' and 'common assault' is often difficult to draw, both for the BCS and, no doubt, the police. Common assaults as measured by the BCS have increased by a quarter since 1981, and this – if accompanied by a tendency by the police to classify more of these as 'wounding' – may have contributed towards the observed rise in recorded woundings.

From: P. Mayhew, L. Aye Maung, C. Mirlees-Black, *The 1992 British Crime Survey*, London, HMSO, 1992.

Document 10
THE JUSTIFICATION OF MISSION

We may say that the service began as a straightforward enterprise intended to save offenders from harsh punishments with a view to their salvation through divine grace. The missionaries' work in the courts began as one expression of the wider mission of saving souls and, it is important to remark, their underlying purpose provided sufficient *justification* for their court work. The changes which followed the rise of 'scientific' understandings of offenders radically changed the *nature* of the original mission, but it is quite clear from the writings of the more dedicated social diagnosticians that the *sense* of mission continued unabated; its ontology had changed, its overarching objective had changed, and its justifying purpose had changed, but it remained missionary in its zeal and sense of the righteousness of its cause, the 'cure' of offenders through scientific treatment.

The decline of confidence in the treatment ethic had profound effects upon the probation service in general, but especially on its court work. The social enquiry report could no longer be a simple plea for mercy for the accused in the face of harsh punishment, the scientific ideal had put paid to that; but no longer could the report of a probation officer purport to be a vehicle of accurate diagnosis either. The answer to these fundamental problems in the phase of pragmatism was to begin to see the report to court as an instrument of the policy of diverting offenders from custody and this has been confirmed recently in the Home Office's (1984) *Statement of National Objectives and Priorities* for the probation service. Unfortunately, it is at this point that a gap between the theory of policy formulation and the reality of practice becomes apparent.

In the post-diagnostic era the probation service has not actually lost its sense of mission (although it must be noted that the conception of that mission now varies as between the different schools of thought); rather it is that the loss which the service has suffered is that of any satisfying transcendent *justification* for its present concerns with providing realistic alternatives to imprisonment. It is true (at least in most instances) that there are cost advantages in dealing with offenders outside penal institutions, and it is equally true that many non-custodial disposals can be held to be more humane than their custodial counterparts, but justifications such as these, no matter how ardently they are reiterated for public consumption, do not actually provide the sort of inspirational justifications which both the phases of special pleading and diagnosis could command.

From: W. McWilliams, 'Probation, pragmatism and policy', *Howard Journal* 26:2 (1987).

Document 11
NATIONAL STANDARDS FOR THE SUPERVISION OF OFFENDERS IN THE COMMUNITY

1.1 Why national standards?

The supervision of offenders in the community is a crucial part of any comprehensive response to crime. For *offenders* supervision can *restrict liberty* and make very real *mental and physical demands*. Effective supervision can help offenders *stay out of trouble* and become *responsible members of the community*. For *probation and social services staff,* supervision is *challenging and skilful,* requiring *professional social work in the field of criminal justice.*

2. Supervision in the community can, therefore, represent both a demanding and a constructive sentence of the criminal court. Increasingly, the value and importance of community sentences are being recognised. This is reinforced through the sentencing framework of the Criminal Justice Act 1991.

3. The *objective of these national standards* is to strengthen the supervision of offenders in the community, building on the skill and experience of practitioners and service managers:

- by setting a clear framework of *expectations and requirements* for supervision, understood by those carrying out the task and by others;

- by enabling *professional judgement* to be exercised within a framework of *accountability*;

- by encouraging *imagination, initiative* and *innovation,* and the development of *good practice*; and

- by ensuring that supervision is delivered *fairly, consistently* and *without discrimination,* and that positive steps are taken to ensure that is the case.

1.2 What is the status of these standards?

4. These standards are issued jointly by the Home Office, Department of Health and Welsh Office as required standards of practice for probation services and social services departments in England and Wales, in relation to the supervision of offenders in the community and the preparation of reports for the criminal courts. Services are expected to follow the guidance and requirements in the standards or – should that become impossible at any stage – to ensure locally that sentencers are made aware of the situation.

Relevant inspections by HM Inspectors of Probation and, where appropriate, the social services inspectorates will have regard to the satisfactory attainment of the standards.

5.   It should be emphasised that the standards seek to encourage good practice but avoid unnecessary prescription. In many respects, the standards lay down expected norms rather than outright requirements, with the clear onus on practitioners and managers to record and justify any necessary departures from these norms in individual cases. It is recognised that the attainment of the standards by probation and social services is dependent on the co-operation of others with whom they work.

1.4   What do national standards achieve?

8.   National standards are intended to achieve several purposes:

- **QUALITY ASSURANCE** – As well as setting requirements for probation and social services work, and criteria for the return to court of offenders under supervision, the national standards provide for *monitoring* to ensure that standards are met (and if not, for sentencers to be advised). They are backed by *independent review,* through internal monitoring and inspection and through external inspection by HM Inspectorate of Probation and, where appropriate, the social services inspectorates;

- **ACCOUNTABILITY** – The standards establish a clear and consistent framework, within which work can be viewed and decisions justified. The standards support and encourage local discretion and initiative. Where an officer finds it necessary to depart from a normal expectation in the standards, the case file should note the departure and explain why it was necessary. The standards provide a basis of accountability for individual cases, and for services as a whole;

- **CONSISTENCY** – No two offenders are identical. It is essential that supervision takes adequate account of the individual needs and circumstances of each person. Nevertheless, some degree of consistency, particularly of general approach, is important to ensure fairness to the individual and to give assurance to the courts and others;

- **EQUAL OPPORTUNITIES** – The work of probation services and social services departments must be free of discrimination on the ground of race, gender, age, disability, language ability, literacy, religion, sexual orientation or any other improper ground. All services must have a stated *equal opportunities policy* and ensure that this is effectively implemented, monitored and reviewed. Effective action to prevent discrimination *(anti-discriminatory practice)* requires significantly more than a willingness to accept all offenders equally or to invest an equal amount of time and effort in different cases. The origin, nature and extent of differences in circumstances and need must be properly understood and actively addressed *by all concerned* – for example, by staff training, by monitoring and review and by making extra effort to understand and work most effectively with an offender from a different cultural background. This is in keeping with the duty not to discriminate confirmed in section 95 of the Criminal Justice Act 1991, and is reinforced, in context, in each of the national standards. This is not simply a matter of fairness in what is provided to others: in the context of the firm requirements in the standards and the consequent risk of breach, effective anti-discriminatory practice is essential to avoid further disadvantaging those already most disillusioned and disadvantaged in society;

- **GOOD PRACTICE** – The framework of the standards leaves, as it should, much of the application of probation and social services work with offenders to the exercise of skill, imagination, discretion and judgement on the part of individual practitioners and services; it also provides a consistent basis for developing and promulgating good practice;

- **GOOD MANAGEMENT** – Management has a key role in formulating policy and ensuring that it is delivered effectively and consistently in individual cases, in accordance with these standards. The standards contain important guidance for management at all levels in achieving the required standards, for example, through planning, training, practice guidance, efficient use of resources, liaison and monitoring. Good management involves clear, deliberate choice over strategy; effective leadership of staff; and consistent promotion to all concerned of the value and credibility of work undertaken;

- **TARGETING OF COMMUNITY ORDERS** – All the standards relating to the supervision of community orders (probation, supervision, CS and combination orders) contain guidance on when that order may or may not be the most suitable for a particular offender, and the need to relate restriction of liberty to the seriousness of the offence, linking to the section on assessment in the PSR standard;

- **MANAGEMENT OF RISK** – Some offenders and defendants coming to the attention of social and probation services present a significant potential risk to the public. While guarantees cannot be given about offenders' future behaviour, the standards give consistent support to positive management of risk: through advice to courts (e.g. in PSRs and on breach) and careful assessment of individual offenders to devise suitable programmes of supervision;

- **SUPPORT TO STAFF** – The standards emphasise the need for appropriate support to staff, eg through training, practice guidance, health and safety procedures and line management;

- **EFFECTIVE LIAISON AND PUBLICITY** – The standards identify key areas for discussion and local sentencers and for wider consultation and publicity.

From: *National Standards for the Supervision of Offenders in the Community*, London, Home Office, 1992.

Document 12
DISPERSAL OF DISCIPLINE

Imagine a complete cultural dummy – the Martian anthropologist or the historian of centuries to come – picking up a textbook on community corrections, a directory of community agencies, an evaluation study, an annual report. How would he or she make sense of this whole frenzied business, this *mélange* of words?

There are those agencies, places, ideas, services, organizations, and arrangements which all sound a little alike, but surely must be different:

- pre-trial diversion and post-trial diversion;
- all sorts of 'releases' – pre-trial, weekend, partial, supervised, semi-supervised, work and study;
- pre-sentence investigation units and post-adjudication investigation units;
- community-based residential facilities and community residential centres;
- all sorts of 'homes' – community, foster, small group, large group or just group;
- all sorts of 'houses' – half-way, quarter-way and three-quarter-way;
- forestry camps, wilderness and outward-bound projects;
- many kinds of 'centres'; attendance, day, training, community, drop-in, walk-in and store-front;
- hostels, shelters and boarding schools;
- weekend detention, semi-detention and semi-freedom;
- youth service bureaux and something called 'intermediate treatment';
- community services orders, reparation projects and reconciliation schemes;
- citizen-alert programmes, hot-line listening posts, community radio watches and citizen block watches;
- hundreds of tests, scales, diagnostic and screening devices . . . and much, much, more.

All these words at least give us a clue about what is happening. But what of:

GUIDE (Girls Unit for Intensive Daytime Education);
TARGET (Treatment for Adolescents Requiring Guidance and Educational Training);
ARD (Accelerated Rehabilitative Dispositions);
PACE (Public Action in Correctional Effort);
RODEO (Reduction of Delinquency through Economic Opportunity);
PREP (Preparation Through Responsive Educational Programs);
PICA (Programming Interpersonal Curricula for Adolescents);
CPI (Critical Period Intervention);

CREST (Clinical Regional Support Team);
VISTO (Volunteers in Service to Offenders); not to mention
READY (Reaching Effectively Acting Out Delinquent Youths);
START (Short Term Adolescent Residential Training); and
STAY (Short Term Aid to Youth).

Then who are all those busy *people* and what might they be doing? Therapists, correctional counsellors, group workers, social workers, psychologists, testers, psychiatrists, systems analysts, trackers, probation officers, parole officers, arbitrators and dispute-mediation experts? And the para-professionals, semi-professionals, volunteers and co-counsellors? And clinical supervisors, field-work supervisors, researchers, consultants, liaison staff, diagnostic staff, screening staff and evaluation staff? And what are these parents, teachers, friends, professors, graduate students and neighbours doing in the system and why are they called 'community crime control resources'? To find our way through all this, let us begin with an over-elaborate, somewhat arch and even, occasionally, quite misleading metaphor.

Imagine that the entrance to the deviancy control system is something like a gigantic fishing net. Strange and complex in its appearance and movements, the net is cast by an army of different fishermen and fisherwomen working all day and even into the night according to more or less known rules and routines, subject to more or less authority and control from above, knowing more or less what the other is doing. Society is the ocean – vast, troubled and full of uncharted currents, rocks and other hazards. Deviants are the fish.

But unlike real fish, and this is where the metaphor already starts to break down, deviants are not caught, sorted out, cleaned, packed, purchased, cooked and eaten. The system which receives the freshly caught deviants has some other aims in mind. After the sorting-out stage, the deviants are in fact kept alive (freeze-dried) and processed (shall we say punished, treated, corrected?) in all sorts of quite extraordinary ways. Then those who are 'ready' are thrown back in the sea (leaving behind only the few who die or who are put to death in the system). Back in the ocean (often with tags and labels which they may find quite difficult to shake off), the returned fish might swim around in a free state for the rest of their lives. Or, more frequently, they might be swept up into the net again. This might happen over and over. Some wretched creatures spend their whole lives being endlessly cycled and recycled, caught, processed and thrown back.

Our interest is in the operation of this net and the parent recycling industry which controls it: the whole process, system, machine, apparatus, or, as Foucault prefers, the 'capillary network' or 'carceral archipelago'. The whole business can be studied in a number of quite different ways. The fishermen themselves, their production-iine colleagues and their managers profess to be interested in only one matter: how to make the whole process *work better*. They want to be sure, they say, that they are catching 'enough' fish and the 'right' fish (whatever those words might mean); that they are processing them in the 'best' way (that the same fish should not keep coming back?); that the whole operation is being carried out as cheaply and (perhaps) as humanely as possible. Other observers, though, especially those given the privileged positions of intellectuals, might want to ask some altogether different questions.

First, there are matters of *quantity*: size, capacity, scope, reach, density, intensity. Just how wide are the nets being cast? Over a period of time, do they get extended to new sites, or is there a contraction – waters which are no longer fished? Do changes in one part of the industry affect the capacity of another part? And just how strong is the mesh or how large are its holes, how intensive is the recycling process? Are there trends in turnover? For example, are the same fish being processed quicker or more new ones being caught?

Second, there are questions about *identity*. Just how clearly can the net and the rest of the apparatus be seen? Is it always visible as a net? Or is it sometimes masked, disguised or camouflaged? Who is operating it? How sure are we about what exactly is being done in all the component parts of the machine?

Third, there is the *ripple* problem. What effect does all this activity – casting the nets, pulling them in, processing the fish – have on the rest of the sea? Do other non-fish objects inadvertently get caught up in the net? Are other patterns disturbed: coral formations, tides, mineral deposits?

From: S. Cohen, *Visions of Social Control*, Oxford, Polity Press, 1985.

Document 13
CRIMINAL JUSTICE ACT 1991, SELECTED PROVISIONS

Custodial sentences

1. (1) This section applies where a person is convicted of an offence punishable with a custodial sentence other than one fixed by law.

(2) Subject to subsection (3) below, the court shall not pass a custodial sentence on the offender unless it is of the opinion –
(a) that the offence, or the combination of the offence and one other offence associated with it, was so serious that only such a sentence can be justified for the offence; or
(b) where the offence is a violent or sexual offence, that only such a sentence would be adequate to protect the public from serious harm from him.

(3) Nothing in subsection (2) above shall prevent the court from passing a custodial sentence on the offender if he refuses to give his consent to a community sentence which is proposed by the court and requires that consent.

2. (1) This section applies where a court passes a custodial sentence other than one fixed by law.

(2) The custodial sentence shall be
(a) for such term (not exceeding the permitted maximum) as in the opinion of the court is commensurate with the seriousness of the offence, or the combination of the offence and other offences associated with it; or
(b) where the offence is a violent or sexual offence, for such longer term (not exceeding that maximum) as in the opinion of the court is necessary to protect the public from serious harm from the offender.

3. (1) Subject to subsection (2) below, a court shall obtain and consider a pre-sentence report before forming any such opinion as is mentioned in subsection (2) of section 1 or 2 above.

(2) Where the offence or any other offence associated with it is triable only on indictment, subsection (1) above does not apply if, in the circumstances of the case, the court is of the opinion that it is unnecessary to obtain a pre-sentence report.

(3) In forming any such opinion as is mentioned in subsection (2) of section 1 or 2 above a court –

(a)   shall take into account all such information about the circumstances of the offence (including any aggravating or mitigating factors) as is available to it; and

(b)   in the case of any such opinion as is mentioned in paragraph (b) of that subsection, may take into account any information about the offender which is before it.

4. (1) Subject to subsection (2) below, in any case where section 3(1) above applies and the offender is or appears to be mentally disordered, the court shall obtain and consider a medical report before passing a custodial sentence other than one fixed by law.

(2) Subsection (1) above does not apply if, in the circumstances of the case, the court is of the opinion that it is unnecessary to obtain a medical report.

(3) Before passing a custodial sentence other than one fixed by law on an offender who is or appears to be mentally disordered, a court shall consider –

(a)   any information before it which relates to his mental condition (whether given in a medical report, a pre-sentence report or otherwise); and

(b)   the likely effect of such a sentence on that condition and on any treatment which may be available for it.

5. (1) For subsection (2) of section 22 (suspended sentences of imprisonment) of the Powers of Criminal Courts Act 1973 ('the 1973 Act') there shall be substituted the following subsections

'(2) A court shall not deal with an offender by means of a suspended sentence unless it is of the opinion

(a)   that the case is one in which a sentence of imprisonment would have been appropriate even without the power to suspend the sentence; and

(b)   that the exercise of that power can be justified by the exceptional circumstances of the case.

(2A) A court which passes a suspended sentence on any person for an offence shall consider whether the circumstances of the case are such as to warrant in addition the imposition of a fine or the making of a compensation order.'

(2) The following shall cease to have effect, namely –

(a)   sections 28 and 29 of the 1973 Act (extended sentences of imprisonment for persistent offenders); and

(b)   section 47 of the Criminal Law Act 1977 (sentence of imprisonment partly served and partly suspended).

Community sentences

6. (1) A court shall not pass on an offender a community sentence, that is to say, a sentence which consists of or includes one or more community orders, unless it is of the opinion that the offence, or the combination of the offence and one other offence associated with it, was serious enough to warrant such a sentence.

(2) Subject to subsection (3) below, where a court passes a community sentence –
(a) the particular order or orders comprising or forming part of the sentence shall be such as in the opinion of the court is, or taken together are, the most suitable for the offender; and
(b) the restrictions on liberty imposed by the order or orders shall be such as in the opinion of the court are commensurate with the seriousness of the offence, or the combination of the offence and other offences associated with it.

(3) In consequence of the provision made by section 11 below with respect to combination orders, a community sentence shall not consist of or include both a probation order and a community service order.

7. (1) In forming any such opinion as is mentioned in subsection (1) or (2)(b) of section 6 above, a court shall take into account all such information about the circumstances of the offence (including any aggravating or mitigating factors) as is available to it.
(2) In forming any such opinion as is mentioned in subsection (2)(a) of that section, a court may take into account any information about the offender which is before it.
(3) A court shall obtain and consider a pre-sentence report before forming an opinion as to the suitability for the offender of one or more of the following orders, namely –
(a) a probation order which includes additional requirements authorised by Schedule 1A to the 1973 Act;
(b) a community service order;
(c) a combination order; and
(d) a supervision order which includes requirements imposed under section 12, 12A, 12AA, 12B or 12C of the Children and Young Persons Act 1969 ('the 1969 Act').

8. (1) For section 2 of the 1973 Act there shall be substituted the following section –

Probation

Probation orders.

2. (1) Where a court by or before which a person of or over the age of sixteen years is convicted of an offence (not being an offence for which the sentence is fixed by law) is of the opinion that the supervision of the offender by a probation officer is desirable in the interests of
(a) securing the rehabilitation of the offender; or

(b) protecting the public from harm from him or preventing the commission by him of further offences,

the court may make a probation order, that is to say, an order requiring him to be under the supervision of a probation officer for a period specified in the order of not less than six months nor more than three years.

9. (1) For sections 3 to 4B of the 1973 Act there shall be substituted the following section –

'Additional requirements which may be included in such orders.

3. (1) Subject to subsection (2) below, a probation order may in addition require the offender to comply during the whole or any part of the probation period with such requirements as the court, having regard to the circumstances of the case, considers desirable in the interests of

(a) securing the rehabilitation of the offender; or

(b) protecting the public from harm from him or preventing the commission by him of further offences.

11. (1) Where a court by or before which a person of or over the age of sixteen years is convicted of an offence punishable with imprisonment (not being an offence for which the sentence is fixed by law) is of the opinion mentioned in subsection (2) below, the court may make a combination order, that is to say, an order requiring him both –

(a) to be under the supervision of a probation officer for a period specified in the order, being not less than twelve months nor more than three years; and

(b) to perform unpaid work for a number of hours so specified, being in the aggregate not less than 40 nor more than 100.

(2) The opinion referred to in subsection (1) above is that the making of a combination order is desirable in the interests of

(a) securing the rehabilitation of the offender; or

(b) protecting the public from harm from him or preventing the commission by him of further offences.

12. (1) Where a person of or over the age of sixteen years is convicted of an offence (not being an offence for which the sentence is fixed by law), the court by or before which he is convicted may make a curfew order, that is to say, an order requiring him to remain, for periods specified in the order, at a place so specified.

(2) A curfew order may specify different places or different periods for different days, but shall not specify –
- (a) periods which fall outside the period of six months beginning with the day on which it is made; or
- (b) periods which amount to less than 2 hours or more than 12 hours in any one day.

13. (1) Subject to subsection (2) below, a curfew order may in addition include requirements for securing the electronic monitoring of the offender's whereabouts during the curfew periods specified in the order.

(2) A court shall not make a curfew order which includes such requirements unless the court
- (a) has been notified by the Secretary of State that electronic monitoring arrangements are available in the area in which the place proposed to be specified in the order is situated; and
- (b) is satisfied that the necessary provision can be made under those arrangements.

18. (1) This section applies where a magistrates' court imposes a fine on an individual
- (a) for a summary offence which is punishable by a fine not exceeding a level on the standard scale; or
- (b) for a statutory maximum offence, that is to say, an offence which is triable either way and which, on summary conviction, is punishable by a fine not exceeding the statutory maximum.

(2) Subject to the following provisions of this section, the amount of the fine shall be the product of
- (a) the number of units which is determined by the court to be commensurate with the seriousness of the offence, or the combination of the offence and other offences associated with it; and
- (b) the value to be given to each of those units, that is to say, the amount which, at the same or any later time, is determined by the court in accordance with rules made by the Lord Chancellor to be the offender's disposable weekly income.

(3) In making any such determination as is mentioned in subsection (2)(a) above, a court shall take into account all such information about the circumstances of the offence (including any aggravating or mitigating factors) as is available to it.

(4) The number of units determined under subsection (2)(a) above shall not exceed

- (a) 2 units in the case of a level 1 offence;
- (b) 5 units in the case of a level 2 offence;
- (c) 10 units in the case of a level 3 offence;
- (d) 25 units in the case of a level 4 offence; and
- (e) 50 units in the case of a level 5 offence or a statutory maximum offence;

19. (1) In fixing the amount of a fine (other than one the amount of which falls to be fixed under section 18 above), a court shall take into account among other things the means of the offender so far as they appear or are known to the court.

(2) Subsection (1) above applies whether taking into account the means of the offender has the effect of increasing or reducing the amount of the fine.

28. (1) Nothing in this Part shall prevent a court from mitigating an offender's sentence by taking into account any such matters as, in the opinion of the court, are relevant in mitigation of sentence.

29. (1) An offence shall not be regarded as more serious for the purposes of any provision of this Part by reason of any previous convictions of the offender or any failure of his to respond to previous sentences.

(2) Where any aggravating factors of an offence are disclosed by the circumstances of other offences committed by the offender, nothing in this Part shall prevent the court from taking those factors into account for the purpose of forming an opinion as to the seriousness of the offence.

31. (3) In this Part any reference, in relation to an offender convicted of a violent or sexual offence, to protecting the public from serious harm from him shall be construed as a reference to protecting members of the public from death or serious personal injury, whether physical or psychological, occasioned by further such offences committed by him.

From: A. Ashworth, *Sentencing and Criminal Justice*, London, Weidenfeld & Nicolson, 1992.

Document 14
CRIMES RECORDED BY THE POLICE: HISTORICAL TRENDS

- 5.4 million crimes were recorded by the police in 1992 and notified to the Home Office. This compares with 2.5 million in 1980, 1.6 million in 1970 and 500,000 in 1950. Up to the 1920s, the annual recorded level was under 100,000. However, recording methods used up to 1930 are not comparable with those used today and therefore the apparent differences should not be over-interpreted.

- Since 1970, the average annual increase in recorded crime has been about 5 per cent.

Crimes recorded by the police

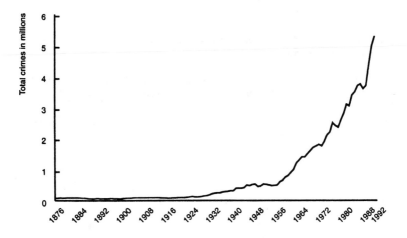

- The number of crimes has risen from about 1 per 100 of the population in the 1950's to 5 in the 1970's and to 10.6 in 1992.

Crimes recorded by the police per 100 population

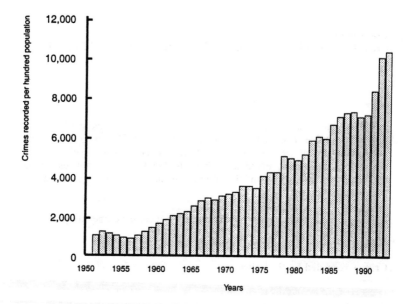

'Crime' is used here as a shorthand for 'notifiable offences', it excludes criminal damage of less than £20.

Source: Criminal statistics, England and Wales (HMSO) and Notifiable Offences 1992 (Home Office Statistical Bulletin April 1993).

From: Home Office Research and Statistics Department, *Digest 2*, London, Home Office, 1993.

Document 15
REFORMATORIES

I went to the orphanage in 1910, November 1910. I'll always remember. It was on a Monday morning, and a lady took the three of us there, me, my brother and sister. We arrived at this huge building, number 3. There were two thousand children in the five big homes altogether, and my brother was taken from us and taken to number 4. My sister was supposed to go to number 5 because she was quite young, but she wouldn't leave me – they could not part us. They were very strict, but it was no good – she was such a strong-willed child – so in the end, for the time being, they gave in. We were numbered. I was 381 and she was 382. We were taken to a changing-room and all our nice clothes that we had on were taken from us, and we put on calico chemises and calico knickers and a flannel petticoat and long black stockings. I found out eventually that we knitted them. We had to do it ourselves, and we had black in the winter and white in the summer . . . . We had to knit our own stockings and there hadn't to be a flaw in anything, and I think I'd made a little mistake in the heel, nothing much, but she made me unpick it all, and it had to be reknitted in a certain time. I was so fearful, I used to sit up in bed and knit in the dark to try and get it done in the time she allotted me to reknit it. I remember one or two girls coming in. I expect they were very nervous; they did wet the bed. And the poor dears, they were humiliated. They were just held up to ridicule. They would be put right down the end in the other dormitory, on a straw bed, and that was their punishment. Really, it was inhuman.

Ivy Petherick, together with her brother and sister, were removed from their home in Barnstaple and deposited at Muller's Orphanage, Bristol, after the premature death of their mother and father. Her recollections of the rigid classification of inmates, the formalized and regimented daily routine and the harsh discipline and brutal punishments inflicted upon working-class children are very similar to the memories of others committed to orphanages. They closely resemble the experiences of delinquent and destitute young people who were incarcerated in the complex web of reformatory institutions, such as truant schools, industrial schools, approved schools and Borstal, that developed from the late nineteenth and early twentieth century onwards. For whether a working-class child was an orphan, a vagrant, a truant, a rebel at home or school or a thief, the assumption was often made by magistrates and officials that he or she was the offspring of a degenerate and deprived class, requiring intensive disciplinary treatment in a reformatory.

From: S. Humphries, *Hooligans or Rebels? An Oral History of Working-Class Childhood and Youth 1889–1939*, Oxford, Blackwell, 1981.

Document 16
Criminal Injuries Compensation Scheme
(Historical Record)

Financial Year	Applications Made	Year on Year Increase	Resolved	Outstanding	Awards Made	Compensation Paid (£M)	Administration Costs (£M)	Total Costs (£M)	Average Award (£)[3]	Lower limit for awards (£)	GDP Deflator (@ 30-11-93)	Compensation Paid (£M)	Admin Costs (£M)	Total Costs (£M)	Year on Year Increase	Average Award (£)	Year on Year Increase	Number of Admin Staff[4]	Admin cost as % of Total cost
						At Actual Prices						**At 1993-94 Prices**							
1964-5[1]	554		130	424	122	0.033	0.016	0.05	270	50	9.864	0.35	0.17	0.51		2,831		11	32.7%
1965-6	2,452	343%	1,375	1,501	1,164	0.403	0.060	0.46	346	50	10.337	4.03	0.60	4.62	802%	3,458	22%	30	13.0%
1966-7	3,312	35%	2,717	2,096	2,404	0.914	0.094	1.01	380	50	10.770	8.76	0.90	9.66	109%	3,645	5%	40	9.3%
1967-8	5,316	61%	3,869	3,543	3,490	1.294	0.122	1.42	371	50	10.081	13.25	1.25	14.50	50%	3,797	4%	58	8.6%
1968-9	6,437	21%	5,985	3,995	5,060	1.673	0.178	1.85	331	50	11.645	14.83	1.58	16.41	13%	2,932	-23%	58	9.6%
1969-70	7,247	13%	6,817	4,425	5,614	1.992	0.208	2.20	355	50	12.253	16.79	1.75	18.54	13%	2,990	2%	65	9.5%
1970-1	7,419	2%	5,893	5,951	4,901	2.098	0.229	2.33	428	50	13.262	16.33	1.78	18.12	-2%	3,333	11%	65	9.8%
1971-2	9,886	33%	9,449	6,388	8,102	3.301	0.298	3.60	407	50	14.474	23.55	2.13	25.67	42%	2,906	-13%	79	8.3%
1972-3	10,926	11%	9,837	7,477	8,322	3.450	0.356	3.81	415	50	15.654	22.76	2.35	25.10	-2%	2,734	-6%	99	9.4%
1973-4	12,215	12%	10,564	9,128	9,024	4.048	0.441	4.49	449	50	16.720	24.98	2.72	27.71	10%	2,769	1%	99	9.8%
1974-5	14,227	16%	12,506	10,849	10,708	5.059	0.629	5.69	472	50	20.015	26.10	3.24	29.34	6%	2,437	-12%	107	11.1%
1975-6	16,690	17%	13,599	13,940	11,500	6.477	0.911	7.39	563	50	25.107	26.64	3.75	30.38	4%	2,316	-5%	120	12.3%
1976-7	20,400	22%	16,393	17,947	13,951	9.677	1.158	10.84	694	150(a)	28.499	35.06	4.20	39.25	29%	2,513	8%	117	10.7%
1977-8	20,826	2%	16,432	22,341	14,052	10.107	1.267	11.37	719	150	32.376	32.23	4.04	36.27	-8%	2,294	-9%	126	11.1%
1978-9	21,960	5%	19,607	24,694	16,357	13.046	1.578	14.62	798	150	35.994	37.42	4.53	41.95	16%	2,288	0%	133	10.8%
1979-80	22,801	4%	21,113	26,382	17,460	15.737	1.916	17.65	901	150	42.008	38.68	4.71	43.39	3%	2,215	-3%	155	10.9%
1980-1	24,679	8%	26,277	24,784	20,138	21.462	2.930	24.39	1,066	150	49.705	44.58	6.09	50.67	17%	2,214	0%	157	12.0%
1981-2	26,515	7%	22,557	28,742	17,350	21.977	3.242	25.22	1,267	250(b)	54.513	41.63	6.14	47.77	-6%	2,399	8%	163	12.9%
1982-3	29,440	11%	26,098	32,084	19,733	29.445	3.742	33.19	1,492	400(c)	58.396	52.06	6.62	58.68	23%	2,638	10%	163	11.3%
1983-4	31,939	8%	29,705	34,318	21,133	32.821	3.776	36.60	1,553	400	61.104	55.46	6.38	61.84	5%	2,624	-1%	182	10.3%
1984-5	34,890	9%	27,450	41,758	19,771	35.293	4.163	39.46	1,785	400	64.174	56.78	6.70	63.48	3%	2,872	9%	189	10.6%
1985-6	39,697	14%	29,965	51,490	22,534	41.560	4.382	45.94	1,844	400	67.734	63.35	6.68	70.03	10%	2,811	-2%	204	9.5%

Criminal Injuries Compensation Scheme (Continued)

Financial Year	Applications Made	Year on Year Increase	Resolved	Outstanding	Awards Made	At Actual Prices — Compensation Paid (£M)	Administration Costs (£M)	Total Costs (£M)	Average Award (£)[3]	Lower limit for awards (£)	GDP Deflator @ 30-11-93	At 1993-94 Prices — Compensation Paid (£M)	Admin Costs (£M)	Total Costs (£M)	Year on Year Increase	Average Award (£)	Year on Year Increase	Number of Admin Staff[4]	Admin cost as % of Total cost
1986-7	42,301	7%	29,605	64,186	21,925	48.242	5.451	53.69	2,200	550(d)	69.717	71.45	8.07	79.52	14%	3,259	16%	215	10.2%
1987-8	43,054	2%	29,153	78,087	20,991	52.043	6.759	58.80	2,479	550	73.432	73.18	9.50	82.68	4%	3,486	7%	267	11.5%
1988-9	43,385	1%	38,830	82,642	27,752	69.381	7.481	76.86	2,500	550	78.362	91.42	9.86	101.27	22%	3,294	-6%	312	9.7%
1989-90	53,655	24%	38,620	87,780[2]	27,926	72.722	9.064	81.79	2,604	750(e)	83.811	89.59	11.17	100.76	-1%	3,208	-3%	332	11.1%
1990-1	50,820	-5%	53,384	81,828[2]	35,190	109.330	10.293	119.62	3,107	750	90.568	124.64	11.73	136.37	35%	3,542	10%	368	8.6%
1991-2	61,400	21%	60,113	81,190	39,249	143.660	13.102	156.76	3,660	1,000(f)	96.303	154.02	14.05	168.07	23%		11%	380	8.4%
1992-3	65,977	7%	58,688	86,951[2]	36,638	152.490	14.249	166.74	4,162	1,000	100	157.45	14.71	172.16	2%	4,297	10%	387	8.5%
1993-4										1,000	103.25								
Totals	730,420		643,469		462,561	909.735	98.095	1,007.83				1417.4	157.38	1574.7					10.0%

NOTES

1. Scheme started 1 August 1964
2. Manual check revealed under-recording of resolved cases in previous years. Corrected 'applications outstanding' figures inserted, but earlier figures for resolved cases not now capable of correction.
   NB Resolved 'total' figure accordingly calculated by deducting 'applications outstanding' (1992–93) from 'applications made' total.
3. Average award excludes 'nil' awards.
   (a) from 1 March 1977   (d) from 7 November 1986
   (b) from 1 April 1981   (e) from 1 February 1990
   (c) from 1 February 1983 (f) from 6 January 1992
4. Complement 1964-77 Average in post 1977 onwards.

Source: Home Office/Scottish Home and Health Department
Compensating Victims of Violent Crime: Changes to the CICS,
London, HMSO, Cm 2434, (1993)

Document 17
THE AIMS OF VICTIMS SUPPORT SCHEMES

The main aims of Victims Support Schemes, as set out in the first Annual Report of the National Association, is 'to provide the best possible services to those members of the community who have suffered injury, loss, fear or distress as a result of crime. The aim is to minimize the bad effects of crime and to help people through the uninvited crisis as fully and as quickly as may be possible.' The *object* here is to help people *cope* with the crime they have experienced. There was a very early acknowledgement of the need to avoid reinforcement or imposing a 'victim' status.

Some basic principles

Members of the Association have taken the view that victims do have a need of support which would not otherwise be provided from existing sources. In planning a response, however, some basic principles have to be taken into account:

- The wide range of needs, including information, advice, practical assistance, support or therapeutic intervention suggest an equally wide range of services beyond the capacity of an individual helper or small agency.
- People are unlikely to identify themselves as 'in need' and, in this country at least, police research indicates that few people are likely to ask for information or assistance even when they want it.
- Many of the services required already exist within local communities and these should not be duplicated.
- According to current thinking, crime is the responsibility of the whole community and, as far as possible, all sectors of the community should be encouraged to play a part in dealing with the effects of crime.
- It is not possible to determine from police records which victims will benefit from assistance until an offer has been made.
- It is not helpful to encourage a 'victim identity' and long-term dependency on special victims services could be counterproductive.
- Victims should be directed towards the normal services which already exist in their communities as far as possible.

The community-based Victim Support model

The model has therefore been developed which aims at bringing together the normal resources of each local community, both agencies and individuals, who together can provide a variety of expertise, knowledge and skills. The 'Scheme' provides a focal point to which all victims can be referred and a structure in which all resources can be coordinated and developed.

Management Committees are convened from local communities, including such people as the Police, the Probation and Social Services, Solicitors and Magistrates, as well as a wide range of voluntary agencies and churches. The Committee has the responsibility for negotiating referral policies with the Police, recruiting and training volunteers to undertake the initial visiting, and appointing voluntary coordinators to ensure that all referrals receive an adequate response. The Committee is also responsible for raising and managing the necessary funds. As well as providing individual expertise, representatives of such agencies are also able to arrange back-up resources and referral facilities with their own agencies as the need arises.

Members of professions or organizations which are not represented on the Committee are normally contacted and asked to provide either help with training of volunteers or additional referral arrangements. Youth groups may do home repairs; hospitals may provide therapy referrals; Lions and Rotary clubs may be approached for individual grants, etc.

The volunteers: Men and women from a wide range of backgrounds and experience are recruited and trained to undertake the initial visits to people in crisis. They would provide whatever help and support they could at the time, but also discuss with the victim concerned what other assistance may be necessary.

Referrals to other agencies and resources can be made when appropriate, but in most cases the information required, or the amount of support needed, is well within the volunteer's capability. Training programs will take account of when volunteers should normally expect to refer for professional or long-term support. Follow-up visits will often be made to bring information which may be needed or to see how people are coping, but in general it is recommended that long-term work should be dealt with by the normal community resources.

The Coordinator: In each Scheme a Coordinator is appointed, usually voluntary but increasingly on a salary where this becomes available, to obtain referrals from the Police each day and to ensure that a suitable volunteer is appointed to visit. In many Schemes, the Police have adopted a policy of referring all victims of crime so that at least an offer of support can be made. Where there are insufficient volunteers to visit all the victims referred, letters and leaflets are sent by first-class post. The Coordinator is responsible for supervising the volunteers and ensuring that they have provided the best service available.

Advantages of the model

- By coordinating local resources, it can be demonstrated that the offer of support is from the whole community, which includes members of the criminal justice system rather than from a separate or partisan agency.
- By promoting balanced committees, no one agency is able to dominate Victims Support policy and no one agency would become accountable for the work. This ensures that Victims Support is the priority of the Committee and not a subsidiary interest to other agency priorities.

- Individual members of the community have an opportunity to participate constructively in helping to seek some solution to crime.
- By being visited by a 'good neighbour' in the first instance, the victim is protected from the necessity of having to 'ask for help'.
- There is a bonus in that agencies who would normally have very little contact are able to work together in a positive way, with mutually agreed aims.

Problems with the model

1. For certain aspects of victims' needs, adequate community provision does not yet appear to exist. Help with racial harassment and counselling for rape or bereavement are the most obvious examples. It is hoped that, by identifying the need, Victims Support Schemes will be in a position to encourage professional social work agencies to consider their role in these areas. At this stage, there appears to be little real knowledge as to what forms of counselling or intervention would be most suited to these areas of work, which is a major block to the planning of service provision. The Schemes will need to encourage more research and experimental work in these areas.

2. By bringing agencies together to share their resources, the Schemes have attempted to break the traditional mould of agencies working in isolation, and frequently even in competition. Many existing organizations, both statutory and voluntary, originally resisted this innovation. Although almost all the key groups are now giving Victims Support their full backing, there are still one or two exceptions to this rule.

3. Inevitably, there is a danger that, as soon as a group has been formed and begins work, it will take on the status of a separate organization. This is most likely to occur if the membership of committees remains static. There are signs of this occurring already in some of the early Schemes and this position needs to be kept under constant review.

From: H. Reeves, Victim support schemes: The United Kingdom model, *Victimology* 10 (1985), 1–4.

Document 18
VICTIM'S CHARTER

Part II
Guiding principles

Crime is a misfortune which anyone can suffer. The majority of victims are not to blame. They deserve to be treated with both sympathy and respect.

Crime cannot be neglected or ignored whether or not it has any individual victim. We do not leave it to the individual to act – public authorities act on behalf of us all. The public interest must come first, but the harm done to a victim is the usual cause of action and in considering the public interest no one should overlook or disregard the interests and wishes of the victim.

Many victims of crime suffer severely. Their subsequent involvement with the criminal justice system may add to that trauma. It is essential that every possible step is taken to minimise the upset and even hardship which may be caused.

We live in a free country with a free press and broadcasters. Justice is dispensed fairly and openly. In striking a balance between the private and public interests, the criminal justice services – like the law itself – should try to ensure that the victim's privacy is not needlessly violated, and that proceedings do not take on the character of a public spectacle. The media have a particular responsibility not to add to the trauma suffered by victims of crime and the criminal justice services will encourage them to exercise proper restraint and consideration towards victims. Most do so already.

Victims should always be treated fairly and without adverse discrimination. Consistently with this, the services will give particular consideration to victims who are especially vulnerable such as children, victims of sexual or violent crime, and those who are severely shocked by their experience. But all victims are special by virtue of what they have gone through.

Reporting the crime

The police should respond to complaints of crime as promptly as the circumstances require and allow, with courtesy and attention.

The police should make readily available to all victims the Home Office leaflet 'Victims of Crime' which describes how the court can order the offender to pay whatever compensation he can reasonably afford, if he is caught and convicted; and how victims who are injured in a crime of violence can claim compensation from the Criminal Injuries Compensation Board.

The police should try to give the name, station and telephone number

of the police officer dealing with the case, so that the victim can check if he or she has questions about the investigation or court case.

The police should ensure that they know what loss or injury the victim has suffered – to pass on to the Crown Prosecution Service and court if someone is charged, in order to ensure that no victim loses their right to compensation by oversight.

The police should outline to the victim the investigatory process. They should aim to ensure that he or she is told of significant developments in the case particularly if a suspect is found, if he is charged or cautioned, if he is to be tried, and the result of his trial.

Victim support

In accordance with local agreements the police should tell the local victim support scheme about the victims of crime, giving their name and address (unless the victim asks them not to). Otherwise victims can get in touch with schemes themselves. There are now over 350 schemes compared with just over 250 five years ago.

Schemes have a co-ordinator who may be paid (usually from a Home Office grant or sometimes from other contributions), or unpaid with some office expenses met, or may manage without any help. Where appropriate the police will refer crimes to the co-ordinator who will arrange for a volunteer to make contact with the victim or may do so himself or herself.

The victim may be visited, or telephoned, or written to with information and to offer advice. Victim Support volunteers should without fail carry identification approved by the police. They work to a nationally approved code of practice. There are important safeguards to protect the victim's rights and privacy. Volunteers must be careful not to do anything which might prejudice successful court proceedings. They should not talk about cases to outsiders. They should invariably act in the victim's interests, no one else's.

Victim Support volunteers cannot offer money to pay for losses. This is not their job. It is their job to bring the victim information and advice. They can help to ensure that he or she is kept in touch by the police. They can advise on claiming compensation from an insurance company, or from the offender if he is caught, or (for personal injury) from the Criminal Injuries Compensation Board. They can also familiarise the victim with court procedures.

Victim Support has set up special projects in seven Crown Court centres. These projects are funded by the Home Office and are supported by the Lord Chancellor's Department. In each court centre there is a court based co-ordinator, employed by the local victim support scheme with a team of specially selected volunteers, trained to give practical and emotional support to victims of crime and other vulnerable witnesses attending court. This includes making contact with victims as soon as possible so that help can be given where necessary with such matters as childminding, liaison with employers or transport to court.

Support for victims of property crimes and crimes of violence is widely available from victim support schemes throughout the country. For the most serious offences – such as rape and murder – very special skills are needed in supporting the victim or victim's family. Victim Support nationally has organised projects to improve skills in dealing with these most acutely distressing and sensitive cases.

Criminal proceedings

The police will try to catch the criminal, but inevitably they will not always succeed. When they have a suspect they will assemble the evidence against him. Then they must consider whether there is enough evidence to warrant charging or cautioning him. If they decide to charge, they may do so on the spot, or they may apply to the magistrates' court to issue a summons. Either way the conduct of the court case is taken over by the Crown Prosecution Service (CPS) who prosecute in the name of the Queen – showing that the prosecution is intended to meet the injury done to the *public* as well as the victim.

In making the decision whether or not to proceed with a prosecution the Crown Prosecutor will first consider the sufficiency of the evidence and whether there is a realistic prospect of conviction. Once he has satisfied himself that the evidence can justify proceedings he must go on to consider whether the public interest requires a prosecution. In deciding whether a prosecution is in the public interest the Crown Prosecutor will also take into account the interests of the victim.

The police and the CPS are therefore bound to consider the case from a different viewpoint from the victim and for this reason may not share the victim's view that a prosecution is justified; for instance, with their greater experience of criminal proceedings they may know that it will be particularly difficult to prove the accused person's guilt. If there are other charges against the person they may judge that prosecuting him for one further crime would not make much difference to the penalty the court would likely impose.

The great majority of cases are dealt with by magistrates' courts. The most serious cases have to be sent to the Crown Court for trial by jury. In other cases the magistrates can decide whether to hear the case themselves or to sent it to the Crown Court; but they must send it to the Crown Court if the accused wishes to be tried there. Nearly two million people a year are proceeded against in magistrates' courts and over 100,000 are tried in the Crown Court.

The institution of criminal proceedings is not automatic. It may be – for instance if the offender is young or mentally disordered, and the offence is not too serious – that the police will caution instead. Or there may not be enough evidence. Or a decision to prosecute may have been taken for more serious alleged offences, or the person may already be serving a prison sentence. In deciding whether to start proceedings the police will take into account the views of the victim.

Police cautioning can be an effective way of dealing with an offender without drawing him too far into the criminal justice system. But it must meet proper standards. The effect of cautioning is that the case never comes before the court, so that there is no prospect of an order to compensate the victim. In 1988 a total of 103,000 cautions were given for indictable offences and 38,500 for summary offences.

The police (and the CPS) have to consider the wider implications of the case and in doing so they will take into account the victim's view. The guidance they are given on cautioning asks them to take account of the harm done by the offence and the offender's mental condition. They should not become involved in negotiation between the victim and the offender about putting things right, but if the offender has apologised to the victim and perhaps made some amends, that is something which the police can legitimately take into account in deciding whether prosecution is called for. The final decision whether a caution is appropriate has to remain in the hands of the police and CPS, who have the duty of ensuring that the final decision is taken in the public interest.

Whenever practicable, the police will tell the victim of a decision to caution and remind the victim of how he may be able to obtain compensation by a civil court action.

If the police do decide to start proceedings, the CPS must decide whether they should be continued, and if so will conduct the case. The CPS will check that cases referred by the police include a statement of any injury or loss by the victim.

Some victims may be worried that they will suffer further attacks or retaliation. They should ensure that the police are made aware of their concern. The police will take careful note of any such fears, and communicate them to the prosecution so that any danger to the victim can be reported to the court when it comes to consider bail.

After any serious offence, particularly where personal violence has been used, the victim should be told if the accused is released on bail. It will normally be simplest for the police to tell the victim, because they will often have to tell him or her about further proceedings.

Going to court

The victim is often also an important witness in the court case. One common complaint from witnesses is that they are asked to go to court, perhaps at an inconvenient time, only to find that they are not called, and may have to go back on another day. In many cases the victim or the victim's family may not be required as witnesses. Efforts will be made to ensure that they receive information about hearing dates and the results of cases.

Organising court business is difficult. Several people have to be ready to attend at the same time. It is important that cases should not be unduly delayed because it is difficult to find a day which suits everyone.

The magistrates' courts deal with most cases. There the problem is most acute. But it can apply also in the Crown Court, where many defendants decide to plead guilty only on the day of their trial.

The victim (or any other prosecution witness) should let the police know if there are any days he or she could not manage to attend – for instance because of important job or professional commitments, or because there is a holiday which has been booked. These can then be avoided, if possible, but there may be occasions when the convenience of individual witnesses has to be subordinate to the interests of justice.

The CPS will consider carefully whether witnesses will be required and will avoid calling them unnecessarily. But it is open to an accused person who has said that he will plead guilty to change his mind on the day, so that the prosecution may be obliged – if its witnesses are not there – to ask for the case to be adjourned. On the other hand, an accused who has protested his innocence may decide on the day to plead guilty, so that witnesses are not needed. Although an accused is entitled to reconsider his position at any time until he makes his plea, it is good practice for the defence representatives to ensure that when a decision on plea is changed the court is told without delay.

It will often be helpful to the court as well as the victim and other witnesses if the prosecution and defence are in touch before the day of trial. There may be scope for the CPS, the Law Society and the Criminal Bar Association to work out better arrangements for clarifying beforehand those issues which have to be tested in court.

A witness who has to attend court can claim expenses and a contribution for loss of earnings, within the limits of a set scale.

The possibility of a contested trial means that the prosecution must be ready to produce any physical evidence if called on to do so. Sometimes the victim's property may be needed, to show to the court (for instance so that damage can be seen) or for forensic tests which can take a long time. The police will always try to return property as soon as possible. If it is needed for evidence, they will see if other ways can be found of proving the case, for instance relying on photographs or defence admissions. If property has to be kept the police will explain this to the victim.

The Home Office produces a leaflet called 'Witness in Court' which tells witnesses who may not have been to court before something about the procedure and what to expect. Witnesses should always receive this with the notice which tells them that they may be needed to give evidence and should attend.

Many magistrates' courts also distribute their own leaflets showing exactly where they are, how to get there, where there is parking, and so on. This is an excellent practice, to be encouraged.

At court

Many courts are in old and sometimes historic buildings where there is not much space. (In city centres there is hardly ever space near the building for public parking.) Because of this it is not always possible to find separate waiting rooms for witnesses and for people facing charges, and their families. Everyone concerned recognises that this can be intimidating to witnesses, and is not at all ideal. Similarly, not all courts can offer refreshment facilities or pay or card telephones which give reasonable privacy. Everything possible is being done to improve conditions, within the inevitable constraints of public expenditure.

Even where buildings present these problems, much can be done to improve matters for victims. Many magistrates' courts are now trying to list cases in separate blocks, rather than requiring everyone to attend for the start of the day's business. The aim is to give witnesses a better idea of when they will be required and cut down unnecessary waiting time. In the Crown Court, where it is known in advance that a trial in progress will finish during the day, listing officers will whenever possible list the following case with a time marking so that witnesses and others involved are not kept waiting unnecessarily.

These arrangements have the advantage that there will be fewer people waiting at court at any time, making conditions better for all of them. All magistrates' courts have been urged to adopt improved listing systems.

Newer buildings usually offer better conditions. The Home Office is revising the Design Guide it issues to Magistrates' Courts Committees to draw attention to witnesses' special needs for Committees to consider when planning new buildings. The latest design standards for new Crown Court buildings provide for an ample number of witness waiting rooms per courtroom. They also provide for a special witness suite which includes toilet facilities and most recently there have been introduced into the standards witness waiting rooms with separate doors leading directly to the witness box in the courtroom, so that victims and other witnesses can avoid contact with the public in the courtroom when going to the witness box.

Meanwhile, all magistrates' courts are urged to look at the facilities they do have to make the best use of them, bearing in mind witnesses' needs.

In a few courts Victim Support are running projects to identify more fully what special needs victims may have when attending court, and how they can best be met, either by new facilities or by adapting old ones. This is an ambitious project which will take two years to produce results.

The prosecutor must be careful not to discuss the case with the victim (or any other witness) in a way which makes it seem as if he is telling the witness what to say. The prosecutor may have other cases at court on the same day and for this or other reasons may not have the opportunity to speak to the victim before the case begins. So far as possible and proper a CPS representative will endeavour to make contact with the victim before court proceedings begin.

Giving evidence

Where appropriate, arrangements may be made for witnesses to refresh their memories before giving evidence in court from copies of statements that they have made to the police many months earlier. The lawyer who has conduct of the case at court decides whether it is appropriate for the witness to read this statement for this purpose.

The general principle is that court business should be conducted openly. The witness' name and address is usually given before he or she begins to give evidence. In exceptional cases it may be possible to ask the court for the address to be given in a note so that it is not announced openly. Section 11 of the Contempt of Court Act 1981 allows the court in limited circumstances to prohibit the publication of a name and address or other matter which it has allowed to be kept from the public in this way.

The Government has introduced special arrangements for children to give evidence. A new law allows live television links to be used in the Crown Court at centres which have the facility to take the child's evidence from outside the courtroom in cases involving offences of sex, violence or cruelty. This way the child need not see his alleged attacker in court.

A child's sworn statement no longer has to be corroborated by other evidence for the court to hear it.

The Government has also commissioned and received a report on whether video-recorded evidence should be admitted. This is being considered.

How the case is presented

It is up to the magistrates, or the judge in the Crown Court, to control how the case is conducted. In this country no one can be convicted unless the prosecution prove the case *beyond reasonable doubt*. This high standard of proof is designed to minimise the risk that an innocent person may be convicted. It can occasionally mean the acquittal of someone the victim or the police feel sure is guilty. This is never a judgement on the victim – it is a judgement of the strength of the prosecution case as a whole, and what evidence can be assembled.

When an offender is convicted, he or his lawyer may argue for a lighter sentence. This plea in mitigation may mean trying to persuade the court that the offence was not so serious as it might seem, or that the victim in some way provoked it. Victims often feel aggrieved in such cases that their version of events is not being put clearly at the same time.

Victims can be reassured that the court will not simply accept at face value defence claims in mitigation which try to push blame on to the victim. If the accused has pleaded not guilty and has been tried the court will have heard evidence of the facts. If he has pleaded guilty the court will not simply accept a story which would shift the blame onto the victim without asking the defence to produce evidence which the prosecution can then challenge. The court is not in the ordinary course obliged to comment on a defence plea in mitigation, so it can be difficult for the victim to know exactly which version of events has been accepted.

It would not be right to require the court or the prosecution to comment on everything the defence says, because sentencing depends on looking at cases in the round. But a prosecutor must be ready to intervene when necessary to correct any misleading speech in mitigation, particularly where attempts are made to denigrate the character of the victim.

Compensation

When an offender is convicted, the court must always consider ordering him to pay some compensation to his victim. Compensation for the victim must come ahead of a fine if the court is considering both. Compensation may have to be reduced to what the offender can reasonably afford, so it may not cover the injury or loss completely. Larger sums are generally payable in instalments. Despite these drawbacks, compensation is valuable as a token to the victim and as a means of bringing home to the offender the consequences of his action.

Since 1988 the courts have been *obliged* to consider compensation in suitable cases. This is why the prosecution must be ready to inform the court of the extent of the victim's losses. To help magistrates make compensation orders for personal injury, the Home Office sends all magistrates a table showing the amounts typically payable for injuries of different kinds. It is generally easier to assess the cost of damage to property.

This procedure is intended to give the victim the chance of receiving some compensation without being put to trouble himself or herself. The procedure is not suitable when losses are disputed or hard to assess. In such cases the victim may be better advised – if the offender has means to pay – to make a civil claim for damages. This is best done with a solicitor's advice.

If the offender fails to pay compensation as ordered, the court responsible for collecting payment will normally remind him of his obligations. If he still does not pay, it can enforce the order, if necessary sending him to prison instead. The recovery of amounts awarded in compensation to the victims must be put ahead of the recovery of fines.

The Criminal Injuries Compensation Board pays compensation for more serious personal injuries suffered as a result of crime. It is important that the crime should have been reported to the police without unreasonable delay, and the victim should have co-operated with their inquiries. The Board will ask the police for a report on the case.

Hearing the result of the case

After giving evidence any witness is allowed to sit in the court to hear the rest of the proceedings. But he may choose not to, or may leave before the final result is known.

The victim can expect to be told the result of the court case if he or she is not there to hear it. It may be practical for the police – who need the information for their own purposes – to pass it on to the victim. There have been difficulties over communicating the outcomes of court cases. Work is being done to tackle these problems.

Publicity

Some victims are concerned about coverage of their case in the mass media. Court hearings are public unless there are strong reasons why not – generally because it would be against the interests of justice for them to be public, at least at that stage. But there are safeguards.

By law, once a woman has complained of rape, no one can publish her name or address, or a photograph of her (still or moving). If it is necessary for the investigation a court may allow some other facts to be made known, for example a description of the victim or the location of the crime; but once a man has been charged nothing can be published which would be likely to lead to her being identified in this context. In both cases more can be published if she consents, but she cannot be harassed to give her agreement. This protection remains for the rest of her life, even if in the event no court proceedings are taken.

In addition to this anonymity, there are special rules on what a woman who complains of rape may be asked in court about her sexual history, except any with the man she accuses of rape.

Generally there is no legal bar to press reporting of other types of court case, because it is important that justice should be open. But sometimes newspapers publish material about victims' private lives which did not come out in open court; or pay criminals, their families or associates for stories. Neither is against the law; the question of what controls there should be over invasion of privacy is currently under review. But there are voluntary codes of practice. If victims are concerned about press treatment of private information, or payments made by the press, they can complain to the editor or to the Press Council at 1 Salisbury Square, London EC4 8AE.

Offenders in custody

If an offender is sentenced to a period in custody in a prison establishment, he will not be allowed to write to his victim and/or the victim's family, but can reply if the victim writes to him.

It is not generally practicable to tell the victim and/or the victim's family that an offender who has been sentenced to imprisonment is shortly to be released. It may be many years after the event. Victims may have moved away. The offender may not plan to return to where the crime or crimes were committed.

If the victim is afraid that the offender when released will be a threat, he or she should tell the police. If in their judgement special precautions are needed they will take them.

A murderer must be sentenced to imprisonment for life, and certain other serious offences may also be. If a life sentence prisoner is released at all, it is only when the Home Secretary, advised by the Parole Board, is satisfied that he no longer presents a serious risk. Even then, it is on licence from which he may be recalled if he behaves in a way which suggests he may present a risk, or if he breaches the conditions on which he is let out. When possible release of a life sentence prisoner is being considered, the Probation Service makes careful plans, including arrangements for supervision. The Probation Service will, whenever possible, get in touch with the victim or the victim's family to see if they do have anxieties about the offender's release (particularly when it may be appropriate to meet these anxieties by imposing restrictions on where the offender works, lives or goes).

Mentally disordered offenders are detained in mental hospitals because their primary requirement is for treatment. But this does not override the need to protect the public, and no patient will be given greater freedom or be discharged from hospital if this is thought likely to put others at risk. The treatment of patients will normally require their rehabilitation with the active help of the health and social services in their home areas. Everything will be done to avoid distress to victims or their relatives, but it will not normally be possible or desirable to move the patient away from his home area.

From: Home Office, *Victim's Charter*, London, Home Office, 1990.

BIBLIOGRAPHY

ACOP (1988) *More Demanding Than Prison*, Wakefield: ACOP.

ACOP (1994) *Finance and Resource Newsbrief*, Wakefield: ACOP, March.

Adam Smith Institute (1984) *The Omega Justice Report*, London: Adam Smith Institute.

Adler, Z. (1987) *Rape on Trial*, London: Routledge & Kegan Paul.

Adler, Z. (1988) Prosecuting child sexual abuse: A challenge to the status quo, in Maguire and Pointing (eds) *Victims of Crime: A New Deal?*, Milton Keynes: Open University Press.

Alderson, J. (1979) *Policing Freedom*, Plymouth: McDonald and Evans.

Allen, F. (1981) *The Decline of the Rehabilitative Ideal*, New Haven: Yale University Press.

Allen, R. (1991) Out of jail: The reduction in the use of penal custody for male juveniles 1981–88, *Howard Journal* 30(1).

Anna T. (1988) Feminist responses to sexual abuse: The work of the Birmingham Rape Crisis Centre, in Maguire, M. and Pointing, J. (eds) *Victims of Crime: A New Deal?*, Milton Keynes: Open University Press.

Aries, P. (1962) *Centuries of Childhood*, London: Jonathan Cape.

Ashworth, A. (1983) *Sentencing and Penal Policy*, London: Weidenfeld & Nicolson.

Ashworth, A. (1984) *Sentencing in the Crown Court*, Occasional Paper No.10, Centre for Criminological Research, University of Oxford.

Ashworth, A. (1990) The White Paper on Criminal Justice Policy and Sentencing, *Criminal Law Review*, April.

Ashworth, A. (1992) *Sentencing and Criminal Justice*, London: Weidenfeld & Nicholson.

Ashworth, A. (1994a) *The Criminal Process*, Oxford: Oxford University Press.

Ashworth, A. (1994b) Sentencing, in Maguire, M., Morgan, R. and Reiner, R. (eds) *The Oxford Handbook of Criminology*, Oxford: Oxford University Press.

Atkinson, R. and Cope, S. (1994) Changing styles of governance since 1979, in Savage, S., Atkinson, R. and Robins, L. (eds) *Public Policy in Britain*, Basingstoke: Macmillan.

Audit Commission (1989) *The Probation Service: Promoting Value for Money*, London: HMSO.

Audit Commission (1994) *Cheques and Balances: A Management Handbook on Police Planning and Financial Delegation*. London: Audit Commission.

Aries, P. (1962) *Centuries of Childhood*, London: Jonathan Cape.

Bailey, V. (1987) *Delinquency and Citizenship: Reclaiming the Young Offender 1914–48*, Oxford: Clarendon Press.

Beattie, J.M. (1986) *Crime and the Courts in England 1660–1800*, Oxford: Clarendon Press.

Bell, S. (1988) *When Salem Came to the Boro: The True Story of the Cleveland Child Abuse Crisis*, London: Pan.

Bellamy, J.G. (1973) *Crime and Public Order in the Later Middle Ages*, London: Routledge & Kegan Paul.

Belson, W. (1975) *Juvenile Theft: The Causal Factors*, London: Harper & Row.

Bennett, T. (1990) *Evaluating Neighbourhood Watch*, Aldershot: Gower.

Benyon, J. and Bourn, C. (eds) (1986) *The Police: Powers, Procedures and Proprieties*, Oxford, Pergamon.

Berger, V. (1977) Man's trial, women's tribulation: Rape cases in the court room, *Columbia Law Review*, 77:1 .

Binney, V., Harkell, G. and Nixon, J. (1981) *Leaving Violent Men: A Study of Refuges and Housing for Battered Women*, Leeds, Women's Aid Federation England.

Bochel, D. (1976) *Probation and After-Care. Its Development in England and Wales.* Edinburgh: Scottish Academic Press.

Bottomley, A.K. (1984) Dilemmas of parole in a penal crisis, *Howard Journal*, 25, 1, 24–40.

Bottomley, A.K. (1994) Long-term prisoners, in Player, E. and Jenkins, M. (eds) *Prisons After Woolf: Reform through Riot*, London: Routledge.

Bottomley, A.K. and Pease, K. (1986) *Crime and Punishment: Interpreting the Data*, Buckingham: Open University Press.

Bottoms, A.E. (1974) On the decriminalisation of English juvenile courts, in Hood, R. (ed.) *Crime, Criminology and Public Policy*, London: Heinemann.

Bottoms, A.E. (1977) Reflections on the renaissance of dangerousness, *Howard Journal*, 16, 70-96.

Bottoms, A.E. (1980) The suspended sentence after ten years: A review and assessment, University of Leeds: Centre for Social Work and Applied Social Studies, Occasional Paper No.2.

Bottoms, A.E. (1981) The suspended sentence in England 1967–78, *British Journal of Criminology*, 21:1.

Bottoms, A.E. (1983) Neglected topics in contemporary penal systems, in Garland, D. and Young, P. (eds) *The Power to Punish*, Aldershot: Gower.

Bottoms, A.E. (1987) Limiting prison use: Experience in England and Wales, *Howard Journal*, 26, 3, 177–202.

Bottoms, A.E. (1990a) Crime Prevention: Facing the 1990s, *Policing and Society*, 1:1, pp.3–22.

Bottoms, A.E. (1990b) The aims of imprisonment, in Garland, D. (ed.) *Justice, Guilt and Forgiveness in the Penal System*, Centre for Theology and Public Issues: University of Edinburgh.

Bottoms, A.E. and Light, R. (eds) (1987) *Problems of Long-Term Imprisonment*, Aldershot: Gower.

Bottoms, A.E. and McWilliams, W. (1979) A non-treatment paradigm for probation practice, *British Journal of Social Work*, 9, 2, 159–202.

Bottoms, A.E. and Stevenson. S. (1992) What went wrong? Criminal justice policy in England and Wales, 1945–70, in Downes, D. (ed.) *Unravelling Criminal Justice*, Basingstoke: Macmillan.

Brake, M. and Hale, C. (1992) *Public Order and Private Lives*, London: Routledge.

Brody, S.R. (1976) *The Effectiveness of Sentencing*, Home Office Research Study No.35, London: HMSO.

Brogden, M. (1982) *The Police: Autonomy and Consent*, London: Academic Press.

Brown, D. (1989) *Detention at the Police Station under the Police and Criminal Evidence Act 1984*, London: HMSO.

Brown, D., Ellis, T. and Larcombe, K. (1992) *Changing the Code: Police Detention under the Revised PACE Codes of Practice*, London: HMSO.

Brown, D. and Iles, S. (1985) *Community Constables: A Study of a Policing Initiative*, Research and Planning Unit Paper 30, London: Home Office.

Burrows, J. and Lewis, H. (1988) *Directing Patrolwork: A Study of Uniformed Policing*, Home Office Research Study No.99, London: HMSO.

Butler-Sloss, E. (1988) *Report of the Inquiry into Child Abuse in Cleveland, 1987*, Cmnd 412, London: HMSO.

Campbell, B. (1988) *Unofficial Secrets: Child Sexual Abuse – The Cleveland Case*, London: Virago.

Campbell, B. (1993) *Goliath: Britain's Dangerous Places*, London: Methuen.

Casale, S. (1984) *Minimum Standards for Prison Establishments*, London: NACRO.

Casale, S. (1994) Conditions and standards, in Player, E. and Jenkins, M. (eds) *Prisons After Woolf: Reform through Riot*, London: Routledge.

Cavadino, M. and Dignan, J (1992) *The Penal System: An Introduction*, London: Sage.

Cavadino, P. (1992) Reflections on the Criminal Justice Act 1991, *Criminal Justice Matters*, No.9, Autumn.

Chambers, G. and Millar, A. (1983) *Investigating Sexual Assault*, Scottish Office Central Research Unit, Edinburgh: HMSO.

Chatterton, M. and Rogers, M. (1989) Focused policing, in R. Morgan and D. Smith (eds) *Coming to Terms With Policing*, London: Routledge.

Chibnall, S. (1977) *Law and Order News*, London: Tavistock.

Clarke, J. (1980) Social democratic delinquents and Fabian families, in National Deviancy Conference (ed.), *Permissiveness and Control: The Fate of Sixties Legislation*, London: Macmillan.

Clarke, R.V.G. (1981) The prospects for controlling crime. *Research Bulletin* No.12 London: Home Office.

Clarke, R.V.G. (ed.) (1992) *Situational Crime Prevention*, New York: Harrow & Heston.

Clarke, R.V.G. and Mayhew, P. (eds) (1980) *Designing Out Crime*, London: HMSO.

Clarkson, C.M.V. and Morgan, R. (1994) Sentencing Reform: Lessons from abroad, *Journal of Crime, Criminal Law and Criminal Justice*, 2 (2), 105–119.

Coggan, G. and Walker, M. (1982) *Frightened for my Life*, London: Fontana.

Cohen, S. (1979) The punitive city: Notes on the dispersal of social control, *Contemporary Crises*, 3: 339–63.

Cohen, S. (1985) *Visions of Social Control*, Oxford: Polity Press.

Cohen, S. and Taylor, L. (1972) *Psychological Survival: The Experience of Long-term Imprisonment*, Harmondsworth: Penguin.

Conservative Political Centre (1962) *A Report on Compensation for Injuries through Crimes of Violence*, London: Conservative Political Centre.

Coote, A. and Campbell, B. (1987) *Sweet Freedom: The Struggle for Women's Liberation*, 2nd edition, Oxford: Blackwell.

Corbett, C. and Hobdell, K. (1988) Volunteer-based services to rape victims: Some recent developments, in Maguire, M. and Pointing, J. (eds) *Victims of Crime: A New Deal?*, Milton Keynes: Open University Press.

Cox, B., Shirley, J. and Short, M. (1977) *The Fall of Scotland Yard*, Harmondsworth: Penguin.

Criminal Law Revision Committee (1984) *Fifteenth Report: Sexual Offences*, Cmnd. 9213, London: HMSO.

Critchley, T.A. (1978) *A History of the Police in England and Wales*, London: Constable.

Davies, G. (1992) *Making Amends: Mediation and Reparation in Criminal Justice*, London: Routledge.

Dijk, J.J.M. van (1988) Ideological trends within the victims movement: an international perspective, in Maguire, M. and Pointing, J. (eds) *Victims of Crime: A New Deal?*, Milton Keynes: Open University Press.

Ditchfield, J. (1976) *Police Cautioning in England and Wales*, Home Office Research Study No.37, London: HMSO.

Dobash, R.E. and Dobash, R.P. (1992) *Women, Violence and Social Change*, London: Routledge.

Downes, D. and Morgan, R. (1994) Hostages to fortune? The politics of law and order in post-war Britain, in Maguire, M., Morgan, R. and Reiner, R. (eds) *The Oxford Handbook of Criminology*, Oxford: Oxford University Press.

Duff, P. (1988) The 'victim movement' and legal reform, in Maguire, M. and Pointing, J. (eds) *Victims of Crime: A New Deal?*, Milton Keynes: Open University Press.

Dunbar, I. (1985) *A Sense of Direction*, London: Home Office.

Dunlop, A. and McCabe, S. (1965) *Young Men in Detention Centres*, London: Routledge & Kegan Paul.

Edwards, S. (1989) *Policing 'Domestic' Violence: Women, Law and the State*, London: Sage.

Emsley, C. (1983) *Policing and its Context 1750–1870*, London: Macmillan.

Emsley, C. (1987) *Crime and Society in England, 1750–1900*, London: Longman.

Emsley, C. (1991) *The English Police: A Political and Social History*, Hemel Hempstead: Harvester Wheatsheaf.

Evans, R. and Wilkinson, C. (1990) Variations in police cautioning policy and practice in England and Wales, *Howard Journal of Criminal Justice* 29.

Farrington, D. (1984) England and Wales, in Klein, M. (ed.), *Western Systems of Juvenile Justice*, Beverly Hills: Sage.

Farrington, D. (1986) Age and crime, in Tonry, M. and Morris, N. (eds), *Crime and Justice*, vol. 7, Chicago: University of Chicago Press.

Farrington, D. (1990) Age, period, cohort and offending, in Gottfredson, D.M. and Clarke, R.V. (eds) *Policy and Theory in Criminal Justice*, Aldershot: Avebury.

Farrington, D. and Bennett, T. (1981) Police cautioning of juveniles in London, *British Journal of Criminology*, 21: 123–35.

Fattah, E.A. (1992) Victims and victimology: The facts and the rhetoric, in Fattah, E.A. (ed.), *Towards a Critical Victimology*, Basingstoke: Macmillan.

Faulkner, D.E.R. (1992) Magistrates in the Youth Court, *The Magistrate*, September.

Feldman, D. (1990) 'Regulating treatment of suspects in police stations: judicial interpretations of detention provisions in the Police and Criminal Evidence Act 1984', *Criminal Law Review*, 452–71.

Fitzgerald, M. and Sim, J. (1980) Legitimating the prison crisis: A critical review of the May Report, *Howard Journal*, vol.XIX, 73–84.

Fitzgerald, M. and Sim, J. (1982) *British Prisons*, Oxford: Blackwell.

Fitzmaurice, C. and Pease, K. (1982) Prison sentences and population: A comparison of some European countries, *Justice of the Peace*, 148: 575–9.

Fitzmaurice, C. and Pease, K. (1986) *The Psychology of Judicial Sentencing*, Manchester: Manchester University Press.

Folkard, M.S., Fowles, A.J., McWilliams, B.C., McWilliams, W., Smith, D.D., Smith, D.E. and Walmsley, G.R. (1974) *IMPACT vol. 1. The Design of the Probation Experiment and an Interim Evaluation*, Home Office Research Study No.24, London: HMSO.

Folkard, M.S., Smith, D.D., and Smith, D.E. (1976) *IMPACT vol. 2. The Results of the Experiment*, Home Office Research Study No.36, London: HMSO.

Fowles, A. (1990) Monitoring expenditure in the criminal justice system, *Howard Journal*, 29(2), 82–100.

Garland, D. (1985) *Punishment and Welfare: A History of Penal Strategies*, Aldershot: Gower.

Garland, D. (1990) *Punishment and Modern Society*, Oxford: Clarendon Press.

Gatrell, V.A.C. (1980) The decline of theft and violence in Victorian and Edwardian England, in Gatrell, V.A.C., Lenman, B. and Parker, G. (eds) *Crime and the Law: the Social History of Crime since 1500*, London: Europa.

Gelsthorpe, L. and Morris, A. (1990) *Feminist Perspectives in Criminology*, Milton Keynes: Open University Press.

Gelsthorpe, L. and Morris, A. (1994) Juvenile justice 1945–1992, in Maguire, M., Morgan, R. and Reiner, R. (eds) *The Oxford Handbook of Criminology*, Oxford: Oxford University Press.

Gibson, B., Cavadino, P., Rutherford, A., Ashworth, A. and Harding, J. (1994) *Criminal Justice in Transition*, Winchester: Waterside Press.

Gladstone, F.J. (1980) *Coordinating Crime Prevention Efforts*, Home Office Research Study No.62, London: HMSO.

Gottfredson, M.R. and Hirschi, T. (1990) *A General Theory of Crime*, Stanford: Stanford University Press.

Graef, R. (1989) *Talking Blues*, London: Collins.

Graham, J. and Moxon, D. (1986) Some trends in juvenile justice, *Home Office Research Bulletin*, 22: 10–13.

Gurr, T.R. (1976) *Rogues, Rebels and Reformers*, London: Sage.

Gusfield, J. (1963) *Symbolic Crusade: Status Politics and the American Temperance Movement*, Urbana: University of Illinois Press.

Hagell, A. and Newburn, T. (1994) *Persistent Young Offenders*, London: Policy Studies Institute.

Hall, S. (1979) The great moving-right show, *Marxism Today*, 23.

240 *Crime and Criminal Justice Policy*

Hall, S., Critcher, C., Jefferson, T., Clarke, J. and Roberts, B. (1978) *Policing the Crisis. Mugging, the State and Law and Order*, London: Macmillan.

Harding, C., Hines, B., Ireland, R. and Rawlings, P. (1985) *Imprisonment in England and Wales: A Concise History*, Beckenham: Croom Helm.

Harris, R. (1992) *Crime, Criminal Justice and the Probation Service*, London: Routledge.

Harris, R. (1994) Continuity and Change: probation and politics in contemporary Britain, *International Journal of Offenders Therapy and Comparative Criminology*, 31(1).

Harris, R. and Webb, D. (1987) *Welfare, Power and Juvenile Justice*, London: Tavistock.

Harvey, L., Grimshaw, P. and Pease, K. (1989) Crime prevention delivery: the work of crime prevention officers, in Morgan and Smith (eds) *Coming to Terms with Policing*. London: Routledge.

Harwin, J. (1982) The battle for the delinquent, in Jones, C. and Stevenson, J. (eds) *The Yearbook of Social Policy in Britain, 1980–81*, London: Routledge & Kegan Paul.

Haxby, D. (1978) *Probation: A Changing Service*, London: Constable.

Hirschi, T. and Gottfredson, M.R. (1983) Age and the explanation of crime, *American Journal of Sociology*, 89

Holdaway, S. (1983) *Inside the British Police*, Oxford: Basil Blackwell.

Holtom, C. and Raynor, P. (1988) Origins of victims support philosophy and practice, in Maguire, M. and Pointing, J. (eds) *Victims of Crime: A New Deal?*, Milton Keynes: Open University Press.

Home Affairs Committee (1993) *Juvenile Offenders*, Sixth Report, London: HMSO.

Home Office (1936) *Report of the Departmental Committee on the Social Services in the Courts of Summary Jurisdiction*, London: Home Office.

Home Office (1961a) *Compensation for Victims of Crimes of Violence*, Cmnd 1406, London: HMSO.

Home Office (1961b) *Report of the Interdepartmental Committee in the Business of the Criminal Courts* (The Streatfield Committee), Cmnd 1289, London: HMSO.

Home Office (1962) *Report of the Departmental Committee on the Probation Service* (The Morison Report), Cmnd 1650, London: HMSO.

Home Office (1964) *Compensation for Victims of Crimes of Violence*, Cm 2323, London: HMSO.

Home Office (1965a) *The Adult Offender*, Cmnd 2582, London: HMSO.

Home Office (1965b) *Report of the Committee on the Prevention and Detection of Crime*, London: HMSO.

Home Office (1969) *People in Prison*, London: HMSO.

Home Office (1970) *Reparation by the Offender: Report of the Advisory Council on the Penal System*, London: HMSO.

Home Office (1971) *Crime Prevention Panels*, Home Office Circular 48/1971.

Home Office (1979) *Committee of Inquiry into the United Kingdom Prison Services* (The May Inquiry), Cmnd 7673, London: HMSO.

Home Office (1984a) *Criminal Justice: A Working Paper*, London: HMSO.

Home Office (1984b) *Managing the Long-Term Prison System: The Report of the Control Review Committee*, London: HMSO.

Home Office (1984c) *Probation Service in England and Wales: Statement of National Objectives and Priorities*, London: Home Office.

Home Office (1984d) *Tougher Regimes in Detention Centres: Report of an Evaluation by the Young Offender Psychology Unit*, London: HMSO.

Home Office (1985) *New Directions in Prison Design, Report of a Home Office Study of New Generation Prisons in the USA*, London: HMSO.

Home Office (1986) *Reparation: A Discussion Document*, London: HMSO.

Home Office (1987) *Efficiency Scrutiny of Her Majesty's Probation Inspectorate*, London: Home Office.

Home Office (1988a) *National Standards for Community Service Orders*, London: Home Office.

Home Office (1988b) *Punishment, Custody and the Community*, Cm 424, London: HMSO.

Home Office (1988c) *Tackling Offending: An Action Plan*, London: HMSO.

Home Office (1989) *Report of the Advisory Group on Video Evidence*, London: HMSO.

Home Office (1990a) *Supervision and Punishment in the Community: A Framework for Action* London: Home Office.

Home Office (1990b) *Victims' Charter*, London: Home Office.

Home Office (1990c) *Crime, Justice and Protecting the Public*, Cmnd. 965, London: HMSO.

Home Office (1991) *Custody, Care and Justice: The Way Ahead for the Prison Service in England and Wales*, Cm 1647, London: HMSO.

Home Office (1992) Projection of long-term trends in the prison population to 2000, *Home Office Statistical Bulletin* 10/92, London: Home Office.

Home Office (1993a) *Compensating Victims of Violent Crime: Changes to the Criminal Injuries Compensation Scheme*, Cm 2434, London: HMSO.

Home Office (1993b) *Partnership in Dealing with Offenders in the Community*, London: Home Office.

Home Office (1994a) *Monitoring of the Criminal Justice Acts 1991 and 1993 – Results from a Special Data Collection Exercise*, Home Office Statistical Bulletin 20/94, London: Home Office.

Home Office (1994b) *Core and Ancillary Tasks Review: Interim Report*, London: Home Office.

Home Office and others (1976) *Children and Young Persons Act 1969: Observations on the Eleventh Report of the Expenditure Committee*, Cmnd 6494, London: HMSO.

Home Office and others (1984) *Crime Prevention*, Home Office circular 8/1984. London: Home Office.

Home Office Advisory Council on the Treatment of Offenders (1963) *The Organisation of After-Care*, London: Home Office.

Home Office Statistical Department (1985) *Criminal Careers of those born in 1953, 1958, 1963*, Statistical Bulletin No.5/85, London: Home Office Statistical Department.

Hope, T. (1985) *Implementing Crime Prevention Measures*, Home Office Research Study No.86, HMSO.

Hough, J.M. and Mayhew, P. (1985) *Taking Account of Crime: Key Findings from the 1984 British Crime Survey*, London: HMSO.

Hudson, B. (1993) *Penal Policy and Social Justice*, Basingstoke: Macmillan.

Humphries, S. (1981) *Hooligans or Rebels? An Oral History of Working Class Childhood and Youth 1889–1939*, Oxford: Basil Blackwell.

Husain, S. (1988) Neighbourhood Watch in England and Wales: a locational analysis, *Crime Prevention Unit Paper*, No.12 London: Home Office.

Ignatieff, M. (1978) *A Just Measure of Pain: The Penitentiary in the Industrial Revolution 1750–1850*, Harmondsworth: Penguin.

Irving, B., Bird, C., Hibberd, M. and Willmore, J. (1989) *Neighbourhood Policing: The Natural History of a Policing Experiment*, London: Police Foundation.

Jarvis, F.V. (1972) *Advise, Assist and Befriend. A History of the Probation and After-care Service*, London: National Association of Probation Officers.

Jefferson, T. (1990) *The Case Against Paramilitary Policing*, Milton Keynes: Open University Press.

Jefferson, T. and Grimshaw, R. (1984) *Controlling the Constable: Police Accountability in England and Wales*, London: Muller.

Jenkins, P. (1992) *Intimate Enemies: Moral Panics in Contemporary Great Britain*, New York: Walter de Gruyter.

Johnston, V., Shapland, J. and Wiles, P. (1993) *Developing Police Crime Prevention: Management and Organisational Change*, Police Research Group Crime Prevention Unit Series Paper No. 41, London: Home Office Police Department.

Jones, C. (1993) Auditing criminal justice, *British Journal of Criminology*, 33:3.

Jones, T. and Newburn, T. (1995) How big is the private security sector? *Policing and Society*, vol. 5.

Jones, T., Newburn, T. and Smith, D.J. (1994) *Democracy and Policing*, London: PSI.

Justice (1961) *Compensation for Victims of Crimes of Violence*, London: Stevens.

Katz, S. and Mazur, M. (1979) *Understanding the Rape Victim*, London: John Wiley and Sons.

Kelly, L. and Regan, L. (1990) 'Flawed protection', *Social Work Today*, 19 April.

Kemp, C. and Morgan, R. (1990) *Lay Visitors to Police Stations*, Bristol Centre for Criminal Justice. University of Bath.

King, H.E. and Webb, C. (1981) Rape crisis centres: Progress and problems. *Journal of Social Issues*, 37, 4, 93–104.

King, R.D. (1985) Control in prisons, in Maguire, M., Vagg, J. and Morgan, R. (eds) *Accountability in Prisons: Opening Up a Closed World*, London: Tavistock.

King, R.D. (1994) Order, disorder and the regimes in the prison services of Scotland, and England and Wales, in Player, E. and Jenkins, M. (eds) *Prisons After Woolf: Reform through Riot*, London: Routledge.

King, R.D. and McDermott, K. (1989) British prisons 1970–1987: The ever deepening crisis, *British Journal of Criminology*, 29 ,2, 107–28.

King, R.D. and McDermott, K. (1992) A fresh start: managing the prison service, in Reiner, R. and Cross, M. (eds) *Beyond Law and Order: Criminal Justice Policy and Politics into the 1990s*. London: Macmillan.

King, R.D. and Morgan, R. (1976) *A Taste of Prison: Custodial Conditions for Trial and Remand Prisoners*, London: Routledge & Kegan Paul.

King, R.D. and Morgan, R. with Martin, J.P. and Thomas, J.E. (1980) *The Future of the Prison System*, Farnborough: Gower.

Laycock, G. and Heal, K. (1989) Crime prevention: The British experience, in Evans, D.J. and Herbert, D.T. eds) *The Geography of Crime*, London: Routledge.

Laycock, G. and Tarling, R. (1985) Police force cautioning policy and practice in England and Wales, *Howard Journal of Criminal Justice*, 24.

Le Mesurier, L. (1935) *A Handbook of Probation and Social Work of the Courts*, London: NAPO.

Lipton, D., Martinson, R. and Wilks, J. (1975) *Effectiveness of Treatment Evaluation Studies*, New York: Praeger.

Livingstone, S (1994) The changing face of prison discipline, in Player, E. and Jenkins, M. (eds) *Prisons After Woolf: Reform through Riot*, London: Routledge.

Lloyd, C. (1986) *Response to SNOP*, Cambridge: Cambridge Institute of Criminology.

Loveday, B. (1987) Joint boards for police in Metropolitan areas – A preliminary assessment, *Local Government Studies*, 13:3, 85–101.

Loveday, B. (1991) The new police authorities, *Policing and Society* 1:3, 193–212.

Lustgarten, L. (1986) *The Governance of Police*, London: Sweet & Maxwell.

McConville, M., Sanders, A. and Leng, R. (1991) *The Case for the Prosecution*, London: Routledge.

McConville, M. and Shepherd, D. (1992) *Watching Police, Watching Communities*, London: Routledge.

McConville, S. and Hall Williams, J.E. (1985) *Crime and Punishment: A Radical Rethink*, London: Tawney Society.

McDermott, K. and King, R.D. (1989) A fresh start: The enhancement of prison regimes, *Howard Journal*, 28:3, 161–76.

McIvor, G. (1992) *Sentenced to Serve*, Aldershot: Avebury.

McLaughlin, E. and Muncie, J. (1993) The silent revolution: Market-based criminal justice in England, *Socio-Legal Bulletin*, Australia: La Trobe University.

McLaughlin, E. and Muncie, J. (1994) Managing the criminal justice system, in Clarke, J., Cochrane, A. and McLaughlin, E. (eds) *Managing Social Policy*, London: Sage.

McWilliams, W. (1981) The probation officer at court: From friend to acquaintance, *Howard Journal*, XX, 97–116.

McWilliams, W. (1983) The mission to the English Police Courts 1876–1936, *The Howard Journal*, XXII, 129–47.

McWilliams, W. (1985) The mission transformed: professionalisation of probation between the wars, *Howard Journal*, 24:4, 257–74.

McWilliams, W. (1986) The English probation system and the diagnostic ideal, *Howard Journal*, 25:4, 241–60.

McWilliams, W. (1987) Probation, pragmatism and policy, *Howard Journal*, 26: 2, 97–121.

Maguire, M. (1992) Parole, in Stockdale, E. and Casale, S. (eds) *Criminal Justice Under Stress*, London: Blackstone Press.

Maguire, M. (1994) Crime statistics, patterns, and trends, in Maguire, M., Morgan, R. and Reiner, R. (eds) *The Oxford Handbook of Criminology*, Oxford: Oxford University Press.

Maguire, M. and Corbett, C. (1987) *The Effects of Crime and the Work of Victims Support Schemes*, Aldershot: Gower.

Maguire, M. and Corbett, C. (1991) *A Study of the Police Complaints System*, London: HMSO.

Mair, G. (1989) Some developments in probation in the 1980s, *Home Office Research Bulletin*, No.27, London: Home Office.

Mair, G. (1991) *Part-Time Punishment: The Origins and Development of Senior Attendance Centres*, London: HMSO.

Mair, G. (1995) Developments in probation in England and Wales 1984–1993, in McIvor, G. (ed) Working with Offenders: Research Highlights in Social Work, London: Jessica Kingsley.

Mair, G. and Nee, C. (1990) *Electronic Monitoring: The Trials and their Results*, Home Office Research Study No.120, London: HMSO.

Mannheim, H. and Wilkins, L. (1955) *Prediction Methods in Relation to Borstal Training*, Home Office Study in Causes of Delinquency and the Treatment of Offenders, No.1, London: Home Office.

Marshall, G. (1973) The government of the police since 1963, in Alderson, J. and Stead, P. *The Police We Deserve*, London: Wolfe.

Marshall, G. (1978) Police accountability revisited, in, Butler, D. and Halsey, A. (eds) *Policy and Politics*, London: Macmillan.

Marshall, T.F. (1985) *Alternatives to Criminal Courts*, Aldershot: Gower.

Marshall, T.F. and Merry, S. (1990) *Crime and Accountability: Victim/Offender Mediation in Practice*, London: HMSO.

Marshall, T.F. and Walpole, M. (1985) *Bringing People Together: Mediation and Reparation Projects in Great Britain*, Research and Planning Unit Paper, No.33, London: Home Office.

Mathieson, D. (1992) The Probation Service, in Stockdale, E. and Casale, S. (eds) *Criminal Justice Under Stress*, London: Blackstone Press.

Mawby, R.I. (1988) Victims' needs or victims' rights?, in Maguire, M. and Pointing, J. (eds) *Victims of Crime: A New Deal?*, Milton Keynes: Open University Press.

Mawby, R.I. and Gill, M. (1987) *Crime Victims: Needs, Services and the Voluntary Sector*, London: Tavistock.

Mawby, R.I. and Walklate, S. (1994) *Critical Victimology*, London: Sage.

May, M. (1973) Innocence and experience: the evolution of the concept of juvenile delinquency in the mid-nineteenth century, *Victorian Studies* 17:1.

May, T. (1991) *Probation: Politics, Policy and Practice*, Milton Keynes: Open University Press.

May, T. (1994) Probation and community sanctions, in Maguire, M., Morgan, R. and Reiner, R. (eds) *The Oxford Handbook of Criminology*, Oxford: Oxford University Press.

Mayhew, P., Elliott, D. and Dowds, E.A. (1989) *The 1988 British Crime Survey*, Home Office Research Study No.111, London: HMSO.

Melossi, D. and Pavarini, M. (1981) *The Prison and the Factory*, London: Macmillan.

Metropolitan Police and the London Borough of Bexley (1987) *Child Sexual Abuse Joint Investigative Project: Final Report*, London: HMSO.

Miers, D. (1990) *Compensation for Criminal Injuries*, London: Butterworths.

Morgan, J. and Zedner, L. (1991) *Child Victims*, Oxford: Oxford University Press.

Morgan, N. (1983) The shaping of parole in England and Wales, *Criminal Law Review*, 137.

Morgan, R. (1987) The local determinants of policing policy, in Willmott, P. (ed.) *Policing and the Community*, London: Policy Studies Institute.

Morgan, R. (1989) Policing by consent: legitimating the doctrine in Morgan, R. and Smith, D. (eds) *Coming To Terms With Policing*, London: Routledge.

Morgan, R. (1991) Woolf: In retrospect and prospect, *Modern Law Review*, 54:5, 713–25.

Morgan, R. (1992a) Following Woolf: The prospects for prisons policy, *Journal of Law and Society*, 19: 2, 231–50.

Morgan, R. (1992b) Not just prisons: Reflections on prison disturbances, *Policy Studies*, 13:2.

Morgan, R. (1992c) Talking about policing, in Downes, D. (ed.) *Unravelling Criminal Justice*, London: Macmillan.

Morgan, R. (1994a) An awkward anomaly: Remand prisoners, in Player, E. and Jenkins, M. (eds) *Prisons After Woolf: Reform through Riot*, London: Routledge.

Morgan, R. (1994b) Imprisonment, in Maguire, M., Morgan, R. and Reiner, R. (eds) *The Oxford Handbook of Criminology*, Oxford: Oxford University Press.

Morgan, R. (1994c) Justice and responsibility in prisons, in Gwynedd Jones, I. and Williams, G. (eds) *Social Policy, Crime and Punishment: Essays in Memory of Jane Morgan*, Cardiff: University of Wales Press.

Morgan, R. and Jones, S. (1991) Prison discipline: The case for implementing Woolf, *British Journal of Criminology*, 31:280–91.

Morgan, R. and Jones, S. (1992) Bail or jail? in Stockdale, E. and Casale, S. (eds) *Criminal Justice Under Stress*, London: Blackstone.

Morgan, R. and Maggs, C. (1985) Police community dialogues: consultative groups in action, in Brown, J. (ed) *Models of Public/Police Consultation in Europe*, Cranfield-Wolfson Colloquium Papers.

Morgan, R. and Smith, D.J. (1989) Opening the debate, in Morgan, R. and Smith, D. (eds) *Coming To Terms With Policing*. London: Routledge.

Morris, A. and Giller, H. (1987) *Understanding Juvenile Justice*, Beckenham: Croom Helm.

Morris, A. and McIsaac, M. (1978) *Juvenile Justice?*, London: Heinemann.

Morris, T. (1989) *Crime and Criminal Justice since 1945*, Oxford: Blackwell.

Moxon, D. (1993) *Use of Compensation Orders in Magistrates' Courts*, Home Office Research and Statistics Department Research Bulletin, No.33.

Moxon, D., Sutton, M. and Hedderman, C. (1990) *Unit Fines: Experiments in Four Courts*, Research and Planning Unit Paper; No. 59, London: Home Office.

Muncie, J. (1984) *The Trouble With Kids Today*, London: Hutchinson.

Nash, M. and Savage, S. (1994) A criminal record? Law, order and Conservative policy, in Savage, S., Atkinson, R. and Robins, L. (eds) *Public Policy in Britain*, Basingstoke: Macmillan.

NACRO (1987) *Diverting Juveniles from Custody: Findings from the Fourth Census of the Projects Funded under the DHSS Intermediate Treatment Initiative*, London: NACRO Juvenile Crime Section.

NACRO (1989) *Progress Through Partnership*, London: NACRO.

NACRO (1992) Expenditure on the criminal justice system, *Criminal Justice Digest*, 73, 21.

NACRO (1993) *Evidence to the Home Affairs Committee*, London: NACRO.

NACRO (1994) *The Criminal Justice and Public Order Bill and Young Offenders*, London: NACRO, May.

National Association of Victim Support Schemes (1988) *The Victim in Court: Report of a Working Party*, London: NAVSS.

National Audit Office (1989) *Home Office: Control and Management of Probation Services in England and Wales*, London: HMSO.

NCH (1993) *Setting the Record Straight: Juvenile Crime in Perspective* London: NCH.

Newburn, T. (1988) *The Use and Enforcement of Compensation Orders in Magistrates' Courts*, Home Office Research Study No.102, London: HMSO.

Newburn, T. (1989) *The Settlement of Claims at the Criminal Injuries Compensation Board*, Home Office Research Study No.112, London: HMSO.

Newburn, T. (1990) Compensation by the offender and the state, in Viano, E. (ed.) *The Victimology Research Handbook*, New York: Garland.

Newburn, T. (1991) *Permission and Regulation: Law and Morals in Post-war Britain*, London/New York: Routledge.

Newburn, T. and Merry, S. (1990) *Keeping in Touch: Police-Victim Communication in Two Areas*, Home Office Research Study No.116, London: HMSO.

Newburn, T. and Stanko, E.A. (eds) (1994) *Just Boys Doing Business? Men, Masculinities and Crime*, London: Routledge.

Northam, G. (1989) *Shooting in the Dark*, London: Faber and Faber.

Pahl, J. (1982) Police response to battered women *Journal of Social Welfare Law*, November.

Parnas, R.I. (1972) The police response to domestic disturbance, in L. Radnowitz and M.E. Wolfgang (eds) *The Criminal in the Arms of the Law*, New York: Basic Books.

Parton, N. (1985) *The Politics of Child Abuse*, London: Macmillan.

Pearson, G. (1975) *The Deviant Imagination*, London: Macmillan.

Pearson, G. (1983) *Hooligan: A History of Respectable Fears*, London: Macmillan.

Pease, K. (1980) Community service and prison: Are they alternatives?, in Pease, K. and McWilliams, W. (eds) *Community Service by Order*, Edinburgh: Scottish Academic Press.

Pease, K. (1985) Community Service Orders, in M. Tonry and N. Morris (eds) *Crime and Justice: An Annual Review of Research*, Chicago: University of Chicago Press.

Phipps, A. (1988) Ideologies, political parties, and victims of crime, in Maguire, M. and Pointing, J. (eds) *Victims of Crime: A New Deal?*, Milton Keynes: Open University Press.

Pitts, J. (1992) Juvenile justice policy in England and Wales, in Coleman, J.C. and Warren-Adamson, C. (eds) *Youth Policy in the 1990s*, London: Routledge.

Pizzey, E. (1974) *Scream Quietly or the Neighbours will Hear*, Harmondsworth: Penguin.

Platt, A. (1969) *The Child Savers*, Chicago: University of Chicago Press.

Player, E. and Jenkins, M. (1994) *Prisons After Woolf: Reform through riot*, London: Routledge.

Pointing, J. and Maguire, M. (1988) The rediscovery of the crime victim, in Maguire and Pointing (eds) *Victims of Crime: A New Deal?*, Milton Keynes, Open University Press.

Radzinowicz, L. (1948) *A History of English Criminal Law and its Administration, vol.1, The Movement for Reform*, London: Stevens & Stevens.

Radzinowicz, L. and Hood, R. (1990) *The Emergence of Penal Policy in Victorian and Edwardian England*, Oxford: Clarendon.

Raine, J.W. and Walker, B. (1990) *Quality of Service in the Magistrates' Courts*, Home Office Research Bulletin, 28.

Raine, J.W. and Willson, M.J. (1993) *Managing Criminal Justice*, Hemel Hempstead: Harvester Wheatsheaf.

Raine, J.W. and Willson, M.J. (1995) New public management and criminal justice, *Public Money and Management*, January-March.

Rawlings, P. (1992) Creeping privatisation? The police, the Conservative government and policing in the late 1980s in Reiner, R. and Cross, M. (eds) *Beyond Law and Order: Criminal Justice Policy and Politics into the 1990s* London: Macmillan.

Reeves, H. (1989) The victim support perspective, in Wright, M. and Galaway, B. (eds) *Mediation and Criminal Justice*, London: Sage.

Reiner, R. (1985) *The Politics of the Police* Brighton: Harvester.

Reiner, R. (1991) *Chief Constables* Oxford: Oxford University Press.

Reiner, R. (1992) *The Politics of the Police* (Second edition) Brighton: Harvester.

Reiner, R. (1993) Police accountability: Principles, patterns and practices, in Reiner, R. and Spencer, S. (eds) *Accountable Policing: Effectiveness, Empowerment and Equity*, London: Institute for Public Policy Research.

Reith, C. (1938) *The Police Idea*, Oxford: Oxford University Press.

Roberts, J. (1994) The relationship between the community and the prison, in Player, E. and Jenkins, M. (eds) *Prisons After Woolf: Reform through Riot*, London: Routledge.

Rock, P. (1990) *Helping Victims of Crime*, Oxford: Clarendon Press.

Rock, P. (1993) *The Social World of an English Crown Court*, Oxford: Clarendon Press.

Rosenbaum, D.P. (ed) (1994) *The Challenge of Community Policing*, London: Sage.

Royal Commission on the Police (1962) *Final Report*, Cmnd 1728, London: HMSO.

Royal Commission on Criminal Justice (1993) *Report*, London: HMSO.

Rutherford, A. (1986a) *Growing Out of Crime: Society and Young People in Trouble*, Harmondsworth: Penguin.

Rutherford, A. (1986b) *Prisons and the Process of Justice*, Oxford: Oxford University Press.

Rutherford, A. (1990) British penal policy and the idea of prison privatization, in McDonald, D.C. (ed.) *Private Prisons and the Public Interest*, New Brunswick, Rutgers University Press.

Rutherford, A. (1993) Penal policy and prison management, *Prison Service Journal*, Issue 90.

Rutter, M. and Giller, H. (1983) *Juvenile Delinquency: Trends and Perspectives*, Harmondsworth: Penguin.

Ryan, M. (1983) *The Politics of Penal Reform*, Harlow: Longman.

Ryan, M. (1992) The Woolf Report: on the treadmill of prison reform?, *Political Quarterly*, 63: 1, Jan.-Mar., 50–6.

Ryan, M. and Ward, T. (1989) Privatisation and penal politics, in Matthews, R. (ed) *Privatising Criminal Justice*, London: Sage.

Sanders, A. and Young, R. (1994) *Criminal Justice*, London: Butterworths.

Scarman, Lord (1982) *The Scarman Report*, Harmondsworth: Penguin.

Scottish Law Commission (1990) *Report on the Evidence of Children and Other Potentially Vulnerable Witnesses*, Scottish Law Commission Study No.125, Edinburgh.

Scraton, P., Sim, J. and Skidmore, P. (1991) *Prisons Under Protest*, Milton Keynes: Open University Press.

Shapland, J. (1988) Fiefs and peasants: accomplishing change for victims in the criminal justice system, in Maguire, M. and Pointing, J. (eds) *Victims of Crime: A New Deal?*, Milton Keynes: Open University Press.

Shapland, J. and Cohen, D. (1987) Facilities for victims: the role of the police and the courts, *Criminal Law Review*, January.

Shapland, J., Willmore, J. and Duff, P. (1985) *Victims in the Criminal Justice System*, Aldershot: Gower.

Sharpe, J.A. (1988) A history of crime in England c. 1300–1924, in Rock, P. (ed.) *A History of British Criminology*, special edition of the *British Journal of Criminology*, vol.28, no.2, Spring.

Sharpe, J.A. (1990) *Judicial Punishment in England*, London: Faber and Faber.

Shaw, S. (1992) Prisons, in Stockdale, E. and Casale, S. (eds) *Criminal Justice Under Stress*, London: Blackstone Press.

Sheerman, B. (1991) 'What Labour wants' *Policing*, vol.7 no.3.

Sherman *et al.* (1992) The variable effects of arrest on criminal careers: the Milwaukee Domestic Violence Experiment, *Journal of Criminal Law and Criminology* 83:1 Spring.

Silver, A. (1967) The demand for order in a civil society, in Bordua, D. (ed.) *The Police*, New York: Wiley.

Sim, J. (1987) Working for the clampdown: Prisons and politics in England and Wales, in Scraton, P. (ed.) *Law, Order and the Authoritarian State*, Milton Keynes: Open University Press.

Sim, J. (1991) 'We are not animals, we are human beings': Prisons, protest and politics in England and Wales, 1969–90, *Social Justice*, vol.18, no.3.

Sim, J. (1994) Reforming the penal wasteland? A critical review of the Woolf Report, in Player, E. and Jenkins, M. (eds) *Prisons After Woolf: Reform through Riot*, London: Routledge.

Skogan, W.G. (1990) *The Police and Public in England and Wales: A British Crime Survey Report*, Home Office Research Study No. 117, London: HMSO.

Smith, D.J. (1987) Research, the community and the police, in Willmott, P. (ed.) *Policing and the Community*, London: PSI.

Smith, L.J.F. (1989a) *Concerns About Rape*, Home Office Research Study No.106, London: HMSO.

Smith L.J.F. (1989b) *Domestic Violence: An Overview of the Literature*, London: HMSO.

Softley, P. (1978) *Compensation Orders in Magistrates' Courts*, Home Office Research Study No.43, London: HMSO.

Spencer, S. (1985) *Called to Account: The Case for Police Accountability in England and Wales*, London: NCCL. .

Stanko, E.A. (1988) Hidden violence against women, in Maguire, M. and Pointing, J. (eds) *Victims of Crime: A New Deal?*, Milton Keynes: Open University Press.

Stern, V. (1989) *Bricks of Shame: Britain's Prisons*, second edition, Harmondsworth: Penguin.

Stevenson, S. (1989) Some social and political tides affecting the development of juvenile justice 1938–64, in Gorst, A. Johnman, L. and Lucas, W.S. (eds) *Post-War Britain: Themes and Perspectives, 1945–64*, London: Pinter Press and the Institute of Contemporary British History.

Stevenson, S. and Bottoms, A.E. (1989) The politics of the police 1955–1964: A Royal Commission in a decade of transition, in Morgan, R. (ed.) *Policing Organised Crime and Crime Prevention*, British Criminology Conference volume 4.

Taylor, I., Walton, P. and Young, J. (1973) *The New Criminology: For a Social Theory of Deviance*, London: Routledge & Kegan Paul.

Thane, P. (1981) Childhood in history, in King, M. (ed.) *Childhood, Welfare and Justice*, London: Bedford.

Thomas, J.E. (1972) *The English Prison Officer since 1850: A Study in Conflict*, London: Routledge & Kegan Paul.

Thomas, J.E. (1994) Woolf and prison staff: Still looking for 'good gaolers', in Player, E. and Jenkins, M. (eds) *Prisons After Woolf: Reform through Riot*, London: Routledge.

Thomas, J.E. and Pooley, R. (1980) *The Exploding Prison: Prison Riots and the Case of Hull*, London: Junction Books.

Thorpe, D., Smith, D., Green, C. and Paley, J. (1980) *Out of Care*, London: Allen & Unwin.

Tobias, J.J. (1972) *Crime and Industrial Society in the Nineteenth Century*, Harmondsworth: Penguin.

Tuck, M. (1989) *Drinking and Disorder: A Study of Non-Metropolitan Violence*, Home Office Research Study No.108, London: HMSO.

Tutt, N. (1981) A decade of policy, *British Journal of Criminology*, 21:4.

Tutt, N. and Giller, H. (1983) Manifesto for management – the elimination of custody, *Justice of the Peace*, 151, 200–2.

Waddington, D. (1992) *Contemporary Issues in Public Disorder*, London: Routledge.

Waddington, D., Jones, K and Critcher, C. (1989) *Flashpoints: Studies in Public Disorder*, London: Routledge.

Waddington, P.A.J. (1991) *The Strong Arm of the Law*, Oxford: Oxford University Press.

Waddington, P.A.J. (1993) The case of the hidden agenda, *Independent*. 1 July.

Walklate, S. (1989) *Victimology: The Victim and the Criminal Justice Process*, London: Unwin Hyman.

Wasik, M. (1978) The place of compensation in the penal system, *Criminal Law Review*, 599–611.

Wasik, M. (1992) Sentencing: A fresh look at aims and objectives, in Stockdale, E. and Casale, S. (eds) *Criminal Justice Under Stress*, London: Blackstone Press.

Wasik, M. and von Hirsch, A. (1990) Statutory sentencing principles: The 1990 White Paper, *Modern Law Review*, 53:4.

Weatheritt, M. (1986) *Innovations in Policing*. London: Croom Helm.

West, D. (1982) *Delinquency: Its Roots, Careers and Prospects*, London: Heinemann Educational.

Willmott, P. (ed) (1987) *Policing and the Community*, London: PSI.

Windlesham, Lord (1987) *Responses to Crime*, Oxford: Oxford University Press.

Windlesham, Lord (1993) *Responses to Crime (vol. 2): Penal Policy in the Making*, Oxford: Oxford University Press. .

Women's National Commission (1985) *Violence Against Women*, London: Cabinet Office.

Woolf, Lord Justice (1991) *Prison Disturbances April 1990: Report of an Inquiry by the Rt Hon Lord Justice Woolf (Parts I and II) and His Honour Judge Stephen Tumim (Part II)*, Cm 1456, London: HMSO.

Wright, M. (1982) *Making Good: Prisons, Punishment and Beyond*, London: Unwin Hyman.

Wright, M. (1991) *Justice for Victims and Offenders*, Milton Keynes: Open University Press.

Young, W. (1979) *Community Service Orders: The Development and Use of a New Penal Measure*, London: Heinemann.

Zedner, L. (1994) Victims, in Maguire, M., Morgan, R. and Reiner, R. (eds) *The Oxford Handbook of Criminology*, Oxford: Oxford University Press.